Orson Welles and the Unfinished RKO Projects

Congratulations & Best Wishes!

Orson Welles and the Unfinished RKO Projects

A Postmodern Perspective

Marguerite H. Rippy

Southern Illinois University Press / Carbondale

Printed in the United States of America

12 11 10 09 4 3 2 1

Library of Congress Cataloging-in-Publication Data
Rippy, Marguerite H., 1967–
Orson Welles and the unfinished RKO projects : a postmodern perspective / Marguerite H. Rippy.
p. cm.
Includes bibliographical references and index.
ISBN-13: 978-0-8093-2912-0 (pbk. : alk. paper)
ISBN-10: 0-8093-2912-3 (pbk. : alk. paper)
1. Welles, Orson, 1915–1985—Criticism and interpretation. 2. RKO Radio Pictures, inc. I. Title.
PN1998.3.W45R57 2009
791.4302'33092—dc22 2008038163

Printed on recycled paper. ♻
The paper used in this publication meets the minimum requirements of American National Standard for Information Sciences—Permanence of Paper for Printed Library Materials, ANSI Z39.48-1992. ∞

To Merrill, for creating both a beginning and an end

Contents

Figures

Acknowledgments

I first saw *Citizen Kane* in the now-defunct Key Theatre in Washington, D.C., and I am happy to say I skipped out of work early to go see it. It made a strong impression on me, enough so that when I visited the Lilly Library in Bloomington, Indiana, on a fishing expedition for another project, I made sure to take a look at the Welles Manuscripts. I could not believe the richness of materials related to Welles's RKO years, particularly all the projects that never made it into theaters. When I mentioned the amount of information on Welles's unfinished projects to my mother, she blithely said, "That's a book waiting to happen." That made it sound like this project was inevitable, a gift my mother had for duping me into serious work. I also believe that as old theaters like the Key disappear, the next generation of film scholars is far more likely to see Welles's work in fragmentary form, on DVDs, on the Internet, and in media forms that I can only imagine. This book reflects that belief, and I hope the next generation of film scholars will be able to love the old forms of cinema even as they discover new modes of media entertainment.

Projects like this simply cannot happen without financial support, and this book was generously supported by two Lilly Library Helm Fellowships, several grants from the Marymount University Faculty Development Committee, a Maurice Mednick Fellowship from the Virginia Foundation for Independent Colleges, and a "We the People" Grant from the National Endowment for the Humanities. I am deeply indebted to the gracious hospitality and formidable knowledge of the librarians at the Lilly Library and the Special Collections of the University of Michigan at Ann Arbor. In particular, Kathleen Dow, Peggy Daub, Sarah Rentz, and Breon Mitchell were very helpful in granting permission to publish excerpts and helping prepare images from the archives. Karl Kageff, Wayne Larsen, Kristine Priddy, and Barb Martin of Southern Illinois University Press provided valued support and comments that greatly improved the final product as well.

At every stage of the writing process, I was given excellent feedback from a variety of colleagues and friends. The conversations I had with Sherri Smith, Doug Mao, Daniel Bernardi, Courtney Lehmann, and Frank Chorba about the project were as illuminating and rewarding as the research itself. My deepest thanks to Scott Newstok and Dudley Andrew for inviting me to join the "Transnational Welles" conference at Yale University in 2006, where my conversations with Michael Anderegg, Catherine Benamou, Leslie Weisman, and James Naremore—who had already deepened my love of cinema studies as a graduate student—and others helped refine my ideas and expand my knowledge of Welles. My writing group of Janine DeWitt, Carolyn Oxenford, Jacquelyn Porter, Barbara Kinney, and Marcia Dursi helped me rephrase my argument at several junctures to reach a broader audience, and Ulrich Knoepflmacher and John Glavin offered timely feedback on chapter 2 in particular. I greatly miss the astute comments of the late Mary Lane on both writing and teaching, and one could not have asked for a better mentor in all things than Stephen Watt.

I feel fortunate to work as part of a department that cares deeply for each other and offers the collegiality that helps one in every aspect of life. Sean Hoare, well known in my department as the best editor around, read over several chapters with patience and insight. Lillian Bisson, George McLoone, Susan Fay, Susan Heumann, Nyla Carney, Rosemary Hubbard, Tonya Howe, Laura Valdez-Pagliaro, and Karen Waters were always ready with supportive comments and a glass of wine when needed. In addition, the manuscript benefited at every phase from the assistance of graduate students, including Andrea Rutan, Galina Palyvian, Emily Dewey, Katharine Torrey, A. Michelle Bolger, Megan Devers, Jennifer Elena, Rebecca Gibbs Jones, Snezana Pavlovic, and Mary Nyingi. Many other colleagues and friends offered support and ideas as well along the way, including Teresa Reed, Brian Doyle, Meg Mulrooney, Chris Snyder, Hazel Sirett, and Norah Falcon.

Of course family pays the greatest price for a project like this, and I am blessed to be part of an unerringly supportive, if eccentric, clan. All the Rippys, including both Conrads, Felix, and my parents, Merrill and Frances, are woven deeply into the pages of this book. Conrad Mayhew even helped with final edits and copyright permissions, as well as finding Café Rosso when I needed it most. I cannot believe the patience of Rick, Hobie, K.K., and Merrill during my years of research. They acted like it's perfectly normal to spend weekends curled up around the computer, and they knew just when to insist I pull away and go on a walk as well. For both walks and patience, I am grateful.

Orson Welles and the Unfinished RKO Projects

Introduction

A Postmodern Auteur? Approaches to the Unfinished Wellesian Works

In 1999 a group of scholars gathered in Málaga, Spain, for the centenary Shakespeare on Screen conference. The shadow of Orson Welles loomed large over the meeting, since no other American director has experimented with adapting the Bard as often or as interestingly as Welles. As scholars, we dissected the work of Welles with typical rational distance and discernment. Then we boarded a bus for Ronda, where Welles is buried, and proceeded to unravel into a hoard of camera-clicking tourists, jockeying for position around Welles's grave on a private estate, agog at our own disheveled, sweaty proximity to an American Bard.

Our behavior points out a countermovement, or perhaps really a crosscurrent, to the recent antiauteurist vein of cinema and media studies, articulated by Krin Gabbard as "a centrifugal force away from canonical directors and the old Hollywood."[1] For although academe can proclaim the decline of the auteur, star directors like Steven Spielberg still dominate commercial cinema, as well as generating course enrollment and textbook sales. The capitalist structure of commercial film demands a "star" to be recognized as author or key performer within what are undeniably collective works in order for the mechanisms of commercial promotion and payment to function smoothly. As cinema and media studies scholars, we must continue to consider the role of the star persona even while we look through poststructural lenses. *Star director* has a slightly different nuance than *auteur* in that the former term emphasizes the financial importance of the director over the artistic power, and thinking in terms of moviemaking as an industry as well as an art acknowledges the role of directors without overly privileging their roles in production.

Part of the goal of this book is to reconcile what have traditionally been labeled opposing strands of cinema and media studies: auteur theory on the one hand and the "post" theory approaches like feminism, identity theory, critical race theory, and narrative deconstruction on the other. As cinema and media studies matures, we need to integrate the study of canonical auteurs like Welles into the posttheory world, and when we do, we are likely to find that they are not as autocratic as we once thought; that it was, in fact, our way of studying their bodies of work and modes of production that were restrictive. This is particularly true of Welles, who seduces us into studying of the cult of personality—and while this danger exists to an extent in the study of any artist, there are few artists who engage so actively, charmingly, and effectively in the production (and deconstruction) of their own public personas. Welles is often regarded as a quintessential modernist auteur, but his working process fits just as comfortably within what are often labeled postmodern modes of production—pastiche, collage, incompletion, self-referentiality, and multimedia experimentation. In fact, as new media forms such as YouTube and the DVD "extra" emerge, Welles's "unfinished" works and media ephemera become increasingly accessible to mainstream viewers, who can get to know him both from his YouTube outtakes and from films like *Citizen Kane.*

As these media forms evolve, we are better able to see Welles in his full complexity, to integrate his commercial personality and his art with their contexts, and to see his work as a process, rather than as the fragmentary bits and pieces of commercially released products. Welles produced more "unfinished" than finished works, and these works are equal in complexity to his commercially marketed products in film and radio; in fact, they call into question the very category of "finished" performances. There are so many of these "unfinished" works that I found it necessary to limit my field of study to only the first phase of Welles's cinema career, his years with RKO. Looking at Welles's "unfinished" RKO projects rather than just at the distributed films helps to contextualize not only Welles's work but also the evolution of mass media performance within mid-twentieth-century American culture. Ultimately, this book aims to establish that these projects were neither "failed" nor "unfinished" other than in the eyes of commercial expectations of their era.

The RKO projects that were shelved by the studio or by Welles himself demand an approach that embraces rather than resists textual ambiguity, an alternative to the two dominant approaches to the study of American film directors, auteurism and genre studies. When faced with the incomplete texts, critics have tended traditionally to focus on questions of intentionality—what did Welles *intend* for these films to look like? How could we piece them together to best reflect his authorial intentions? Instead, I emphasize the postmodern aspects of Welles's unfinished work as a rich field for cultural analysis in and of themselves. His use of multiple performance modes and self-critique within these works makes them ripe for rediscovery through new media forms such as the interactive format of the DVD or the spontaneous, fragmented, viewing environment of Internet sites. As outtakes, variant scripts, trailers, promotional materials, and clips of his unfinished works become available to viewers, we develop new relationships with these previously unvisualized works. Welles's resistance to linear narrative makes him increasingly pertinent to postmodern readers, and his enduring influence on performance narrative is indebted every bit as much to his incomplete projects as to his completed texts. The approach this book takes, therefore, emphasizes the study of Welles's creative process, as well as his commercial products in an effort to deepen and enrich our understanding of his artistry.

To create a critical wedge between authorial intention and a body of works associated with Welles-as-director, I have found it helpful to think of Welles's unfinished projects as representative of a Wellesian brand of entertainment that Welles, RKO, and the Mercury Theatre built together in the late 1930s and early 1940s. The evolution of his unique narrative style, ironically, became a stumbling block for the commercial objectives of the studio, for the Mercury Theatre, and for Welles himself. The symbiotic relationship of these three entities created entertainment products that looked commercially promising but were limited by the constraints of technology and mass marketing of their era. Welles's RKO projects represent a discrete body of work associated with an individual, but they were also collaborative projects focused on commercial goals—after all, it was not Welles's ambition at this point in his career to be a Hollywood outsider. He went to Hollywood with every intention of expanding his own commercial success, as well as that of RKO and the Mercury Theatre. His particular form of art, however, was dictated by commercial demands as much as by aesthetic demands, and the studies of his film projects in this book seek to analyze how these competing demands intersected to create uniquely Wellesian products.

Another central goal of this work is to open the Wellesian brand to a larger audience—to reposition auteurism in order to analyze the radical potential within its fissures and to emphasize its creation as a commercial construct. In examining Welles, I find the term *star director* more useful than *auteur* to emphasize the director's commercial connection to a work while avoiding the tendency to assign the director sole artistic authority. Performance texts are by nature deeply collaborative and flexible, and the star director, like a star actor, is a vehicle to market the work more than he or she is a representation of sole authorship. The directorial brand name is a powerful marketing tool, and as Gabbard admits, even "most American film scholars are still likely to say, 'Have you seen the new Cronenberg film?' rather than 'Have you seen *A History of Violence*?'"[2] This tendency reflects the establishment of a shorthand brand name more than an art form, and suggests that the works of star directors are just as subject to radical critique as more marginalized films and visual products. By their existence, Welles's unfinished films deconstruct the ideal of organic unity within an artistic product, thus making an argument for a countertradition within the work of one of the most canonical of the auteurs. This approach suggests that alternate readings of auteurs are possible, combining elements of postmodern cultural critique with an acknowledgment that these works are associated with a constellation of themes, images, and techniques that are marketed around specific individuals. The author in cinema is not dead; she is just better thought of as a commercially available spokesperson than as the sole origin of creative genius.

Each chapter probes at least one film project that was *not* fully realized by Welles, exposing his narrative strategies, cultural contexts, aesthetic goals, and ultimate economic failures. The films failed in that they were not commercially released, making them tangible representations of Welles's fractured relationship with RKO. But economic failure, particularly in Welles's case, does not necessarily equal artistic failure. All of Welles's unfinished RKO projects have complex narrative genealogies, richly conceived and deeply indebted to Welles's radio career, which cannot be separated from his film career aesthetically, financially, or chronologically. This book highlights the interwoven nature of these two creative venues, suggesting that Welles's radio projects shaped his concept of narrative entertainment and influenced his open-ended, improvisational style of filmmaking.

Radio in 1938 occupied a rhetorical space similar to that of television today in the American imagination. Radio then, like television now, acted as a media source that Americans turned to for reliable, real-time information about the world outside their homes. But yesterday's radio, like today's television, also negotiated with the American public regarding the line between news and entertainment. Misleading the American public by means of media manipulation was regarded as dangerous and transgressive in the 1930s and 1940s, as evidenced by the fallout over Welles's *War of the Worlds* broadcast. But over time it has become a common entertainment strategy that Stephen Colbert recently, with a wink and a nudge, designated as "truthiness." The last two chapters of this study explicitly analyze Welles's early experiments with the line between fact and fiction—a theme often explored in his later cinema work—and suggest that he helped originate stylistic erosions of the "real" in mass media broadcast.

Welles's unfinished projects predict recurrent patterns in his career, particularly in terms of four features: experimentation with narrative that focused on the exploration of a first-person narrator; desire to adapt classic texts for mass media audiences; recurrent use of expressionist images from modernist primitivism for the purposes of collective politics; and finally exploration of the line between reality and fiction, tangibly linked to the line between commercially marketable wartime propaganda and marginalized cinematic art. Through these four modes, a Wellesian rhetoric develops that reflects pleasure in language, performance, and power and invites interpretations that focus on interplay and ambivalence rather than linear explication.

For example, Welles's characters often verbally challenge or contradict the visual images that surround them.[3] Central characters are often figures of authority on reluctant quests for truth that involve engaging multiple perspectives: reporters and detectives permeate the Wellesian landscape. The most famous of these inquiries, driven by the reporter Thompson in *Citizen Kane*, remains unresolved—Kane's "Rosebud" eludes understanding within the film and remains only partially known to the viewer.[4] As critics like Frank Tomasulo point out, the visual rhetoric of the film also positions Thompson as only one of a variety of narrators. Using techniques he learned from the radio, Welles nested tales within tales and qualified the power of the designated narrator.[5]

Welles's first radio series, *First Person Singular: Mercury Theatre on the Air*, is key to understanding his emerging performance rhetoric. The series reflects his desire to explore the possibilities of storytelling through a mass medium and creates an aesthetic bridge between the collaborative performance concepts he had been integrating into the theater and his increasing interest in exploring the parameters of identity, a theme that would infuse his later cinema work. In *First Person Singular*, Welles wanted both to revitalize literary classics for a mass audience and to establish himself as the first-person-singular auteur of these cross-media performance studies. Thus Wellesian entertainment, even prior to his RKO contract, simultaneously embraces two very different storytelling traditions: the cultural griot and the star director.[6]

Chapter 1: *First Person Singular* and Narrative Strategy

Although "stars" are products of western capitalism and griots derive from African communal tradition, aspects of both traditions are present in

Wellesian storytelling. The first chapter traces these two storytelling traditions in the sphere of modern filmmaking and attempts to place Welles within the swirling eddies of these techniques. Today Hollywood "star" directors consolidate financial and aesthetic power in a way that Welles's RKO contract suggested might be possible but that he was unable to sustain over the course of his career.[7] The first chapter suggests that Welles established himself as one of the first star directors by exploring themes and structures of the first-person singular in his early work, particularly in his proposed projects for *Heart of Darkness* and a *Life of Christ*, as well as his most famous project, *Citizen Kane*.

The first chapter culminates in the application of his first-person-singular philosophy to the ultimate first person, Christ, and juxtaposes Welles's brief interest in a film version of the life of Christ with his fully realized vision of Charles Foster Kane. Research suggests that Welles rejected his initial interest in Christ because of a cultural resistance to updating and Americanizing Christ's story. He planned to present Jesus Christ in an American pastoral setting as a type of folk passion play and focus on Christ as a community storyteller, the type of cultural artist and magician that Welles himself aspired to be—a type of griot. The Kane/Christ paradigm ties back to Welles's vision of himself as a first-person storyteller, a combination actor-director-writer who forges an artistic persona as both star and genius. Although this artistic persona led him to be categorized as an auteur, he is not really the "author" in any conventional sense of these highly collaborative performances. Each work is wildly unstable, a living example of the ambiguity of any text performed before a mass audience, particularly those derived in large part from collaborations with multiple authors in the process of adapting literary works for performance. As an artist, Welles mimics the very conditions of modernity: he hides the mechanisms of his own textual production while proliferating his products among the masses in a highly flexible, adaptive, and powerful way.

Chapter 2: Classics for the Masses—Dickens and Welles

Welles employed his weekly radio series not only to experiment with first-person narrative but also to forge a connection between classic literature and popular entertainment. This interest in classic literary adaptation defines another aspect of Wellesian rhetoric. Dickens became Welles's most-adapted author during 1938 and seemed a natural choice for his first RKO film. The second chapter culminates in a study of a version of *Pickwick Papers* that never happened.

Welles was willing to share his first-person status with an author of stature, and an integral part of his practice of self-creation included associating himself with master authors through adaptation of literary "classics." The Columbia Broadcasting System (CBS) hoped to capitalize on the success of Mercury Theatre adaptations like *Macbeth* and *Native Son* by translating theater into radio, promising in a publicity release on June 8, 1938, prior to the debut of *First Person Singular,* that Welles would "explore fields of literature heretofore untouched by radio and bring to that medium the same spirit of adventure which he brought to the theatre last season."[8] CBS hoped to mine the commercial promise of merging weekly broadcasts of "classic" literature for mass entertainment and Welles's increasingly intertextual and experimental performances. The merger led to several successful adaptations of one of the prime figures of literary serialization, Charles Dickens, who perhaps more than any other author influenced Welles in his first year on the radio. The relationship between these two authors-entertainers reflects their similar abilities to generate serial narratives that encourage audiences to identify with and depend on the storyteller for regular, commercial entertainment.

Welles adapted a Dickens text almost monthly in 1938, staging productions of *A Tale of Two Cities, Oliver Twist, Pickwick Papers,* and *A Christmas Carol.* Dickens's form suited Welles's needs in that his serial narratives compressed easily for radio, offering opportunities for station breaks as well as chances to interweave character development, lively and suspenseful plots, and social critique. Welles's first Dickens adaptation, *A Tale of Two Cities,* compresses time and history into a double narrative told by Dr. Manette and Sidney Carton. This broadcast employs several techniques that reappear in later Welles films, including the aural equivalent of long takes and dissolves. *Oliver Twist* attempted several of these strategies as well, but with less success. By alternating Oliver's narration with Brownlow's, Welles divides the listener's attention without offering a motivation for this distraction. He retains long passages of sociopolitical critique instead of focusing on character or plot development, and the story ultimately fails to build a relationship between the listener and Oliver. In contrast, *A Christmas Carol* succeeded dramatically and commercially, in part because it avoided the trap that befell *Oliver Twist*—an overemphasis on the didactic political message rather than the drama itself. Welles's most successful adaptations strike a balance between cultural immediacy and dramatic effect, a balance that made Dickens a perfect source.

Adapting these classics worked beautifully for Welles on the radio, since it afforded him a fast method of script development, while still allowing him to put his artistic imprint on each production. His knowledge of classic literature, coupled with narrative and technological experimentation, enhanced his reputation as a genius who had mastered both classic and modern dramatic techniques. This talent at adaptation led directly to his film contract with RKO, which hired Welles with the hope that he would produce a picture a year, based on his success at adapting classic literature for the masses. His stay at RKO did not fulfill this goal, and between 1940 and 1942 the RKO lot was strewn with the bodies of Welles's ideas. In fact, until his 1948 *Macbeth*, Welles did not really bring a classic to film as a director. Instead, Welles's creative interest shifted to current topics of politics and identity, always themes of his adaptations. Specifically, his interests shifted toward primitivist expressionism and south-of-the-border politics.

Chapter 3: Expressionist Primitivism and Welles

Welles's third rhetorical mode centered on an interest in multiethnic performance and took two distinct and yet related forms. The first approach merged romantic racialism of the nineteenth century and the expressionist primitivism often associated with "high" modernism into a Wellesian version of psychological primitivism. The second approach, indebted to his interest in the first trope, was a more overtly political, documentary impulse. In some ways these two strains of Wellesian primitivism are simply a matter of emphasis—the former putting the accent on the "artistic" modes of the primitive via masks, drums, and metaphors of light and dark within the mind of a white protagonist; the latter accenting a concept of political reality that attempts to record the quotidian details of "primitive" cultures for political purposes and that positions itself as "journalism" rather than "art."

To understand Welles's simultaneous interest in primitivism and European classic literature, one need look no farther than modernism and its fascination with African masks and Latin American art. To classify Welles as a direct inheritor of modernist primitivism would be, however, an oversimplification, since his political interests associated primitivism with collective, socialist politics at least as early as his 1936 "Voodoo" *Macbeth*. The third chapter looks back to Welles's stage career to understand his later radio and film uses of primitivism. Starting with the 1936 "Voodoo" *Macbeth*, this chapter traces the legacy of modernist primitivism into later radio plays like "Algiers" and *The Shadow*, and finally into the structure of the film script for yet another proposed first film project for RKO, *Heart of Darkness*.

Welles strongly identified with the *Heart of Darkness* script, and drafts suggest that the film would have drawn heavily on Welles's previous stage and radio adaptations of primitivism and directly on his radio performance of this novel. In addition, the cast was largely composed of actors Welles had worked with before on stage or radio, including Jack Carter from his "Voodoo" *Macbeth* stage production. But in contrast to *Macbeth*, the *Heart of Darkness* project blended an attempt at ethnography with its expressionistic elements. Welles saw the project as educational, as well as entertaining, and attempted to conduct anthropological research into the representation of "primitive" cultures to present an accurate and yet aesthetically pleasing image of primitive culture.

The saving grace of this film might have been Welles's self-critical eye, which is alluded to in his vision of Marlow's journey as articulated in the plot treatment for *Heart of Darkness.* Welles promises his film will be a story of "Exploiters in Surroundings Not Healthy for a White Man." Aligning himself with the Company and Marlow, Welles acknowledges implicitly that he is himself an exploiter and that his pursuit of exotic fantasies is not healthy for himself or others. Nevertheless, it is impossible to say how much this film would have critiqued its own use of the primitive, since it was never finished. While the script itself is revealing, it is no closer to an actual distributed film than the original script "American" is to *Citizen Kane.* What is clear is that at this early point in his career, Welles had a deep interest in the intersection of racial and national identity, and this interest remained a constant in his performances from stage to radio to film. His work reflected increasingly self-referential ideas about racial and American identities, often specifically formulated in terms of desire and denial in a central white male protagonist, often played by Welles himself.

Chapter 4: Reality and Fiction—The Documentary Narrative

A second strain of Wellesian primitivism attempts to distance itself from the "aesthetic" in favor of the "real" and thus links the third and fourth modes of Wellesian rhetoric: uses of primitivism and explorations of reality and fiction. The conjunction of a primitivist aesthetic with political reality is finally and tragically manifest in the Brazilian film *It's All True.* This is the only unfinished film project of this study to come after the release of *Citizen Kane.* As a result, the fourth chapter explores this unfinished film as the culmination of Welles's RKO experience. *It's All True* exhibits Welles's interest in mingling political aspirations with creative vision and suggests that this mix became increasingly problematic in terms of his relationship with RKO. Studio restraints on Welles's artistic vision were missing in his production of *It's All True,* since he was shooting on location in a prewar environment that made travel increasingly difficult. Far away from the studio, working without any powerful collaborator like the Mercury Theatre's John Houseman, Welles was given a great deal of creative latitude on this project in its early stages. The result was a total departure from the narrative style of his earlier feature-film projects and an overt attempt to explore a desire for "authenticity" (also manifest in his increasing appearances on wartime news radio). His concept for the film rejected the traditional binaries of primitivism that had haunted his *Heart of Darkness*—white/black, true/false, good/evil. Instead, it sought a polyglot, multiracial narrative form that could represent the diversity of Brazilian culture. In short, *It's All True* rejected the conventions of "classic" Hollywood cinema.[9]

This ambitious attempt at a "truth narrative" told by a white, North American visitor to South American culture, however, was positioned within a cultural and historical matrix of conditions that ensured its failure. Freed—and isolated—by political support and wartime travel restrictions, Welles operated beyond studio parameters in Brazil, exploring his philosophical and political aspirations on film. Although his new attempts at narrative construction were revolutionary (and disturbing to the studio), Welles was unable to dislodge himself from a position of privileged observation, and his narrative attempt at unstructured, polyglot truth was relegated first to RKO's film vault and then largely to the open sea.[10]

The critical debate over this unfinished film, like the debate surrounding much of Welles's work, tends to focus on defending or rejecting its value in terms of Welles as artist-auteur. But as Catherine Benamou has usefully pointed out, Welles's suggestion that this picture would act as a type of magazine feature rejected the very concept of "author" in its conventional sense.[11] The project challenged cultural values of the time, including RKO's desire for quick commercial success in the face of war and the mainstream concept of entertainment narrative. The very mechanisms of production—studio staffing practices, camera equipment, marketing strategies, audience expectations—were set against a project that simultaneously experimented with the concept of visual narrative, pushed the envelope of contemporary politics and race relations, and reworked traditional production concepts of casting, scripting, and editing.

It's All True represented the farthest step in a concept Welles had been exploring for some time—the documentary fiction. To make the classics compelling to a modern audience, Welles repeatedly infused his adaptations with cultural politics.[12] The potential power of this conjunction between narrative experimentation and contemporary political meaning fully emerged in his *War of the Worlds* broadcast, which successfully exploited an American culture of prewar fear and created "truth" out of "fiction" for many listeners. This interest in juxtaposing reality and fiction culminated in *It's All True*, the last of his RKO film projects.

Afterword: Wellesian Legacies—Star Directors and Truthiness

The afterword returns to two traditions that the emergent Wellesian brand helped establish and that have particular resonance in contemporary American culture: the Christ narrative and its correlation with the star director, and explorations of media truthiness. The Christ narrative represents the ultimate first-person-singular narrative in its cultural power and controversy, whereas the concept of truthiness directly reflects the aftermath of Wellesian experimentation with fake documentary expression and the elusive nature of cinematic authenticity. This final section fast-forwards to the legacies of Welles's narrative experiments and suggests why his early projects are of such importance to understanding contemporary media entertainment.

The Christ project has become a type of test for budding star directors to establish themselves or, in the case of Mel Gibson, for the crossover star actor to establish credibility and prestige as a director. The Christ narrative takes on a cultural topic of historic and spiritual importance and seeks to assert masculinist control over an übernarrative. It can be seen as the ultimate challenge in terms of textual adaptation and is accordingly fraught with peril in terms of potential public censure. The assumption is that if the (male) director can assert creative control over this master narrative, then he has achieved technical, commercial, and cultural proficiency. Specifically examining the spectacle of male suffering and Gibson's *The Passion of the Christ*, the first section of this chapter traces the contemporary relevance of an idea Welles played with a generation earlier and suggests both its continuing power and its limitations.

While Gibson is interesting in terms of offering a case study of an actor attempting to build a directorial brand, Steven Spielberg offers us a glimpse of the commercial aftermath of the Wellesian brand at its most extreme. Through Amblin Entertainment and DreamWorks, Spielberg has created a commercial umbrella that extends over not only his own projects but also those of other filmmakers whom he sponsors. In addition, Spielberg produced his own version of Welles's most famous adaptation, *War of the Worlds.* One might at first expect that Spielberg's 2005 adaptation of *War of the Worlds* would more directly link to Welles's entertainment legacy than Gibson's Christ project, but there is little Wellesian influence in the Spielberg adaptation. Although Spielberg attempts to adapt a classic text into a post-9/11 context, his adaptation fails to achieve the immediacy of Welles's 1938 radio broadcast. Looking at Gibson and Spielberg, we see a tenuous connection to Welles's directorial products, even though they mimic some of his early professional projects. Overall, there is less Wellesian residue in the figure of the star director than in the other strand of Wellesian entertainment legacy—the exploration of truthiness.

The second part of the afterword analyzes a Wellesian tradition that resonates broadly within contemporary culture: the erosion of truth in mass media entertainment. The success of *The Daily Show* and its spin-off *The Colbert Report* is frequently traced back to *Saturday Night Live*'s Weekend Update, but actually the "fake news" format owes its success to much earlier experiments by Orson Welles. I suggest that Welles provoked awareness of the potential of truthiness in his 1938 *War of the Worlds* broadcast, and that the logical conclusion of his career-long exploration of the line between fact and fiction has been the reduction of the panic provoked by his initial 1938 broadcast to the laughter provoked by contemporary fake news shows. The devolution of American trust in the news format reflects the transition from modern to postmodern subjectivity, not just an emerging distrust of truth in the media but a pleasure taken from the interplay between truth and fiction. The quest for Truth, for Rosebud, is replaced instead by pleasure in the excavation of its multiple meanings (and panic over elusive truth is replaced by laughter at the slippery nature of such a concept). Similarly, Welles's unfinished works reflect a pleasure in their lack of closure. They defied RKO's filmmaking structure, instead remaining in multiple potential imaginary forms. Increasingly, this sense of interplay would capture Welles's style, and later projects like *Mr. Arkadin* and *F for Fake* fully embrace narrative ambiguity.

Conclusion

The four Wellesian narrative modes of first-person singular, classic adaptation, expressionist primitivism, and truthiness developed early in Welles's career and result directly from his simultaneous work on radio and film. Each style served specific cultural and commercial purposes. First-person narrative allowed Welles to be closely associated with his work, which in turn allowed him to appear as the conduit for the stories themselves and to build the myth of individual authorship and its accompanying star status. Contemporary political associations lent his projects a cultural immediacy that studio executives hoped would bring money into the theater, and his innovative infusion of politics into classic texts helped give his views cultural legitimacy. Welles's interest in the primitive often led him to represent his political consciousness through a connection to dark, exotic bodies, both shocking and mesmerizing studio executives. These narrative styles converged in his final unmade project, *It's All True*, which challenged patterns of classic narrative cinema and marked a decided shift in his career toward the margins and away from the center of cultural and commercial production. His exploration of first-person narration, classic adaptation, expressionist primitivism, and pseudodocumentary forms had been glimpsed in his earlier theater and radio careers, but they fully emerged during his early and abbreviated relationship with RKO.

Ironically, we see the Wellesian performance genealogy most clearly in his unreleased RKO films: *The Life of Christ, Pickwick Papers, Heart of Darkness* and *It's All True.* Each owed great debts to his radio interests in narrative experimentation, adaptation and primitivism,[13] and each of these works reveals much about Welles's working process, remaining highly suggestive in their multiple meanings and cultural implications while refusing definition by industrial commerce. Their lack of final distribution suggests both that traditional Hollywood was not ready for Welles and that Welles was ill-fitted to the commercial, logistical, and cultural constraints of Hollywood. RKO wanted Welles to reproduce his radio success on film, but the more Welles tried to create a cinematic version of the balance of commerce, art, and entertainment present in his radio programs, the more he failed. The films that were able to survive the RKO system of generation strongly emphasize a single aspect of his four rhetorical modes: *Citizen Kane* embodied first-person, retrospective inquiry; *The Magnificent Ambersons* offered the adaptation of a comparatively straightforward author in Booth Tarkington; *Journey into Fear* emphasized Welles as "star" but not narrator-director. Delving into his incomplete texts illuminates the problems and the rewards of textual production that transcend commerce. The very notion of an "incomplete" text is oxymoronic in a performance medium; although such texts have not gone through the commercial editing and marketing process, they are often highly developed conceptually. They reflect personal expression, collaborative give-and-take, and a unifying vision.

Welles was equal parts communal storyteller and capitalist star; his work has clear relevance to several media entertainment traditions that dominate the digital universe today. These early and unfinished works evoke his late and unfinished *Don Quixote,* and we are left with images of him tilting at windmills in one of the most tantalizingly unfinished projects of his career, skirting along the periphery of Spain, exploring the territories of Cervantes with his own rhetorical flourish, establishing himself firmly within the canon of cinema studies, and conjuring sweaty hoards of admirers, even among the cool and distant circles of academe.

Chapter 1

Origins of the First-Person Singular: Mercurial Theatre on the Air

In 1938, Orson Welles moved Mercury Theatre from stage to radio, beginning his dramatic series *First Person Singular: Mercury Theatre on the Air*. By the end of this year, Welles would be beckoned to Hollywood to begin his film career with RKO. During this time Welles established a creative process that interwove narrative strategies from stage, radio, and screen. He created a unique artistic persona and a trademark brand of narrative that invited publicity and allowed him to move to Hollywood not just as an actor but as an actor-director-writer with a record-breaking contract in terms of the money and power that it promised.

Welles often adapted social-realist narratives through a psychoanalytic lens, using interpretations conveyed by a first-person narrator. His narrative strategies developed unconventional notions of "text," "author," and "audience," which became easily recognizable to his audience—a Wellesian brand attractive to customers. This chapter examines the commercial "failure" of the Wellesian brand and argues that it was only a temporary promotional failure, for the Wellesian brand wields perhaps more influence now than ever, and the very proliferation of Wellesian "texts" begs postmodern examination. Thus the image of Welles as famed modernist auteur gives way to that of a Wellesian commercial and cultural brand—a multifaceted success that flourishes even at the expense of the traditional concept of individual authorship.

The Wellesian Brand: A Classic for the Masses

It is helpful to think of Welles's work as a brand rather than a text—a constellation of materials that results in various "texts," whether these are performed, photographed, or merely generated through surrounding letters, photographs, and newspaper clippings. The term "brand" also captures the commercial pressures and goals surrounding the Wellesian productions for RKO, as well as the results of his artistic and commercial partnerships with entities as diverse as the Mercury Theatre, Campbell Soup, and the U.S. government. Welles's RKO era coincides with the consolidation of brand marketing strategies in larger American culture. As Simon Anholt and Jeremy Hildreth note in their history of American branding, "The walls between marketing, entertainment, politics and the military, always somewhat permeable in the American culture, had truly been dismantled" by the mid 1940s,[1] in part because of World War II.[2] In Welles's case, pro-Ally, anti-Axis propaganda funds directly supported his final RKO project, *It's All True*, as well as his Pan-American broadcasts of the era.

First-Person Narrative and the Wellesian Voice

Brands have personalities that, like people, "consist of a whole range of moods and attitudes."[3] Any brand establishes its personality by matching its strengths to the needs of the marketplace, making an emotional connection with the consumer, and being broad enough in scope to encompass a variety of products. One of the most effective strategies for connecting with the consumer is "sensory branding," or the use of stimuli to help the consumer associate positive experiences and images with the brand. As Martin Lindstrom describes, "The purpose of a sensory branding strategy is emotional engagement."[4] The rise of the Wellesian brand was enormously aided by his distinctive voice and thus by Welles's work on the radio, which offered built-in sensory marketing.

Welles's resonant voice became his primary semiotic identifier, or "logo." The sound of his voice became a distinctive sign of the Wellesian brand, much like the label of his radio sponsor, Campbell's Soup. Welles was tremendously successful at using his voice as an icon of his brand, which offered "quick concentrations of meaning" and "sensory imprints that instantly summon the brand essence."[5] Welles's voice summoned associations with entertainment, narrative experimentation, and classical quality. It was so integral to his work that when in October 1942 he asked for format ideas regarding a new show sponsored by Lockheed Vega,[6] Arthur Miller responded,

> Your voice is a format. The only two things that must be heard at the beginning of the show every week are your voice and Lockheed-Vega. Those are the two things that must be the same every week[. . . .] Your voice, if I may say so, portends much. It and Lockheed-Vega identify the show, along with the title. That's all a format can do, portend and identify.[7]

Apropos of Welles's film work, Dudley Andrew suggests that Welles's voice allowed him to "break decisively with Hollywood sound practice and to give his films a new tone bearing an unaccustomed feeling."[8] His voice came to represent narrative innovation and the promise of a certain level of intellectual quality.

Welles's voice was a clear and emphatic icon of a particular point of view, a dominant persona, which in its narrative form will be referred to here as the "first-person singular." Wellesian productions are characterized by an ambiguity or oscillation at the heart of the narrative, often manifest in attitudes toward a grand, complex, central figure—the "first person singular" of the performance. Michael Denning sees these as "gigantic figures which combine a political demonology with overtones of Shakespearean tragedy."[9] The concept of a narrative driven by the first-person perspective, often delivered by direct address and representing an immense personage at the center of the film, drives his three earliest film projects: the unfinished *Heart of Darkness*, *Citizen Kane*, and his proposal for a life of Christ, to star himself. Each of these three central characters (Kurtz, Kane, Christ) would have offered viewers a complex point of identification in that they are enormously compelling and yet tragic figures. In addition, the Wellesian larger-than-life character is both human and deeply flawed, a requirement that raised serious difficulties in the *Life of Christ* project.[10]

These gigantic central figures dominate the screen both visually and aurally, and their rhetorical power embodies strategies of storytelling that Welles had developed on the radio. Welles's storytelling process constructed imaginative worlds for listeners and viewers alike, fully engaging both aural and visual fields of representation. Welles consciously used tricks from each performance medium to whet the appetite for another, translating his skills in the theater into marketable qualities for radio, and translating his radio successes into collateral for film success. In return, many ideas he used on radio moved back into theater, and actors he couldn't afford to pay for work on stalled film projects appeared on his radio shows instead.

On radio, personal connection to the aural narrative is key, since as Robert Spadoni observes, radio connects to the audience not through the picture plane but through a "shared space of imagination."[11] Welles's voice became a familiar guide within this shared imaginative space. Not coincidentally, his first-person approach foregrounded Welles as the storyteller, positioning him as the filter for the audience's experience and promoting him as the central figure of deeply collaborative productions.

Welles decided to give most of the stories in his 1938 radio series the immediacy of a first-person narrator. *Dracula*, *A Tale of Two Cities*, and *Oliver*

Twist, for example, are powerfully told in this manner. Use of the first-person narrator gave him the ability to collapse past memory into present commentary and offered the radio listener a sense of "intimacy." Welles described the effectiveness of this form of narration: "when a person comes on the air and says, 'This happened to me!,' you've got to listen."[12] Welles's personal connection with the audience facilitated the misinterpretation of his famous *War of the Worlds* broadcast, because the authoritative tones of Professor Pierson (played by Welles) eroded into panic, taking the audience with him. The performance played with aural expectations in several ways, misleading the audience in part, Titus Ensink suggests, because it manipulated familiar audio codes of the era. Ensink points to radio's status as "a major and trustworthy source of information," the frequent use of on-the-spot reporting during major events, and the ability of listeners to join the play in progress, as features that undermined the opening statement that the work was fictional.[13] In sum, Welles "exploited expectations as to the conventions of the [radio play] genre."[14]

The aural techniques that Welles borrowed from radio and used in his RKO cinema productions often had a postmodern deconstructive effect. For example, his faux documentary *It's All True* blurred the line between propaganda and fiction. Similarly, aural techniques such as the "interrelating of voice-over commentary, diegetic chorus, and dramatic dialog" created dissonance within the visual world of cinema.[15] Innovations like overlapping dialogue and a spatial soundtrack gave listeners a sense of depth of field and the feeling of listening to a storytelling "voice" rather than reading a "text."[16] But these techniques also disoriented viewers. The Wellesian voice thus comprises much more than Welles's actual voice. It is a collage of images, sounds, and stylistic innovations that form a Wellesian rhetoric evocative of "Welles" as author, narrator, and performer.

Welles was able to translate his unusual storytelling "voice" into cinema, offering the sense of a Wellesian narrator who guides the textual experience. In his proposed opening for *Heart of Darkness,* for example, he establishes himself as the dominant owner-creator of audience experience, caging them as canaries, shooting them and electrocuting them. This dominating Wellesian voice is often associated with either "excess" or "fascism." It is also explicitly first-person singular, a symptom of the larger-than-life character that Slavoj Žižek associates with both the fascist and Quixotic in Wellesian cinema.[17] Frank Tomasulo argues that figurations of sound, angle, focus, and blocking create a "very specific authorial presence: the motion picture director" in Welles's work.[18] Yet Welles had already developed this sense of an authorial voice, an intermediary between audience and actor, on radio. As a result,

Welles was a star director even before he made his first film, and his presence conveys the sense of a first-person singular narrator behind the camera even when a character performing first-person narration is absent.

Modernist Rhetoric: Erosions of Truth and Fiction

The emerging Wellesian performance rhetoric is marked by four features: experimentation with a first-person narrator, adaptation of classic texts for mass media, recurrent use of images from modernist primitivism, and finally exploration of the line between reality and fiction. Each of these four rhetorical modes has its origin in the movement of modernism, and the tension inherent in Welles's efforts to fuse literary adaptation and narrative experimentation often positions him as a modernist.[19] In particular, there is a very close relationship between Welles's use of the first-person narrator and his exploration of subjective "truths." *Citizen Kane*, his most respected and studied work, has been critically described as a modernist exploration of subjectivity. It is also frequently interpreted as a novelistic work of social realism. André Bazin, for example, sees both *Citizen Kane* and *The Magnificent Ambersons* as "the cinematic equivalents of realistic novels."[20] Welles himself described his radio plays, which he developed concurrently with *Citizen Kane*, as "more akin to the form of the novel, to story telling, than to anything else."[21] And when Welles paradoxically asserted, "I do not want to resemble the majority of Americans who are demagogues and rhetoricians. This is one of America's great weaknesses, and rhetoric is one of the greatest weaknesses of American artists,"[22] he positioned himself as a spokesman for modernist dependence on and yet suspicion of rhetoric, a practitioner of "an anti-rhetorical rhetoric that almost defined the modernist ethos."[23]

Ambiguity and irresolution lie at the heart of the modernist text, and the Wellesian narrative embraces modernist discomfort with closure.[24] Welles even extends his playfulness with authenticity and truth into the realm of self-performance. Despite the fact that Welles treated public address in *Citizen Kane* "as a hollow deception," he was also a public orator who used such speech to manipulate audiences (consumers) to buy his own specific brand of entertainment.[25] Ambivalence, then, lies not just at the heart of his finished performance texts but also at the heart of his performance *process*. The instability of performance-as-text, coupled with Wellesian senses of irony, self-referentiality, and dissolution of structure, combine to make even his "finished" texts deeply unstable in their meanings, much less his unfinished texts, which continue to resonate with possibilities and questions rather than achieving closure. In this way, the "unfinished" texts are more Wellesian than are the commercially released RKO projects. The unmarketed works offer an imaginative richness that is more powerful specifically because they remain within the field of the audience's imagination. Traditionally, the lack of commercial finality of Wellesian texts has been regarded as a problem, a symptom of his status as an "outcast" modernist, rather than a sign of an emerging postmodern aesthetic. But this lack of resolution is a hallmark of his performance brand, and the pleasures of irresolution and ambiguity are quintessentially Wellesian.

Welles's exploration of the disjuncture between public and private self-representations, for example, resonates in *Citizen Kane*. Disparate images of the "truth" of Kane emerge from the juxtaposition of public speech—words published by Kane's empire and other news sources—against images of Kane's private life. The film chronicles a failed quest to establish the personal meaning of even a single word, "Rosebud."[26] *Citizen Kane* reflects a theme and style consistent within Welles's oeuvre. Throughout his career Welles was interested in interrogations of truth and fiction so probing as to erode the meaning of narrative subjectivity.[27] This theme is most overtly present in the "unfinished" *It's All True*, but it is also central to later films such as *Mr. Arkadin* and *F for Fake*. Stylistically, Welles embodied this erosion of truth telling by using new broadcast tactics within fictitious performances.[28]

Treading the line between truth and fiction—in fact, exploiting the audience's interest in this line—became a primary signifier of the Wellesian brand.[29] Ultimately, this part of the Wellesian aesthetic was detrimental to the mass-market appeal of his products, proving a hard sell to average consumers. Nevertheless, in the first stage of his career both Welles and Hollywood saw potential for the sale of his brand to the masses rather than to a niche market by positioning Welles as an innovative young artist struggling "against crusty conventions of style and narration."[30] Welles was at times deeply concerned with the mass marketing of his works, and the stated goal of the Mercury Theatre, after all, was to bring the classics *to the masses*. To make Welles's experimentalism more palatable, the *First Person Singular* series attached his voice and innovative narrative methods to familiar "classic" works.[31] This early version of the Wellesian brand was based on mass marketing, not niche marketing.

To meet his goal of revitalizing literary classics for a radio audience, Welles had to figure out how to retell canonical narratives in a one-hour, sound-only format. Adapting such classics as *Dracula*, *A Tale of Two Cities*, and *Heart of Darkness* for radio broadcast served twin needs for Welles, since they reinforced his association with elite literature and yet contained enough melodrama and violence that he could pitch them as mass entertainment. He funneled the novels through his own narrative persona, and thus emerged Welles the American griot—a storyteller able to take established narratives and convey them within a new cultural and technological context, to act not just as a truth teller but also as a witness to archetypal sequences of events. Via this system, Welles emerged as the first-person-singular author of highly collaborative works.

"Problem" Texts: Postmodernity and the Irresolution of Performance

Stylistically a modernist filmmaker, Welles nevertheless became adept at representing the state of modern consciousness as it evolved toward postmodern disorientation, and his characters often represent an inability to construct any single "truth" when it comes to personal or public history. His embrace of disorientating nonlinear texts actually enhances the contemporary relevance of his unfinished works in particular, since these works tend to erode the line between the designations of modernism and postmodernism, positioning Welles as easily within the latter category as the former.

Completion of any Wellesian cinematic text is, first and foremost, imaginary. Welles shot footage that wasn't used, was notoriously undermined or disengaged during the editing process of his released works, and struggled with a sense of authorial ownership of his finished films ranging from the scriptwriting controversy of *Citizen Kane* to the multiple versions of his 1950s project *Mr. Arkadin/Confidential Report*. The problem Welles poses for scholars of his work is primarily a postmodern one: how does one attempt to discuss his work as a stable piece of art when its very form is unstable? And how does one attribute his work to a solo artist named Welles when his working style was always highly collaborative, spontaneous, and subject to revision over the course of decades? As Jonathan Rosenbaum points out, Welles's intentions were rarely stable or clear.[32]

The unfulfilled promise of an imaginary completion, however, makes his incomplete projects all the more resonant. If one can put aside the quest for authorial intentionality and let the "incomplete" texts reside in the same field of inquiry as the "complete" texts, then a fertile set of images emerges, revealing the plurality of the Wellesian text, the creation of shifting and suggestive narrative voices that alternately embrace and reject the demands of commercial finality without capitulating to them. Even if we were to search for authorial intentionality, it seems as if Welles's partial intent was incompletion, since in a 1939 speech he rejected the "assembly-line method of manufacturing entertainment" that he attributed to Hollywood and positioned himself as an artist interested in the craft of moviemaking rather than "the business of selling it."[33]

The correspondence surrounding Welles's RKO productions suggests not only that he was ambivalent about the relationship between craft and commerce but also that his ambivalence was imbedded within the mechanics of performance. This insured that the production process would preserve ambivalence rather than resolve it and that a final commercially viable product might be wanting. RKO, the Mercury Theatre publicity machine, Welles's own lawyer, and the actors and writers with whom he worked were all implicated in his construction of "texts" and their commercial distribution (or lack thereof). Precisely by remaining unfinished, these Wellesian texts became an enduring brand that supersedes association with a single "author," a sort of urtext that mimics the central problem posed by his finished films: how to transcend the first-person singular as a personal event and tie it instead to its multiple cultural and social contexts. The process of constructing and deconstructing the concept of "I" is a central theme in both his finished and unfinished works, but the unfinished works pose this problem in structure as well as in theme.

Psychology, Doubleness, and the First-Person Narrator

> We are born into stories. Everything we remember is remembered through narratives, verbal constructions, images which individual history imbues with the luster of myth[. . . .] Telling, writing, interpreting these stories is the stuff of psychoanalysis as well as literature[.][34]

Welles's narrative style has often been tied to just the sort of personal yet mythic storytelling described above by Linda Williams, particularly obvious in his *First Person Singular* radio series and in the figure of Charles Foster Kane. *Citizen Kane* is often regarded as posing the problem of coherent identity both for Kane and for Welles,[35] but the larger-than-life Wellesian "I" existed in two other RKO projects, both unrealized: the proposed *Heart of Darkness* and *The Life of Christ.*

Welles's "larger-than-life" characters pose problems of personal, cultural, and national identity for the viewer. These questions, while innovative for mid-twentieth-century media performance, were not new to narrative in general. Part of the storyteller's traditional function has been to pose fundamental problems of subjectivity, authenticity, and knowledge—epistemological problems heightened in modernity.[36] Welles developed a brand of narration that posed these complex questions but marketed them to mass consumers. What was *War of the Worlds* if not a demonstration of the difficulty of perceiving reality in a mass media world? Welles's narrative brand established a preoccupation with duality, ambiguity, and the threat of a lack of meaning at the heart of even his finished texts. His unfinished texts pose these difficulties more fluently than the finished ones in that they show little effort to reconcile thematic and structural contradictions, embracing a lack of resolution and eschewing the sense of a coherent narrative "I."

Since Welles himself is integrated into his first-person performance texts as both author and performer, the deconstruction of his modern subjects often operates on two registers, one of which questions the trustworthiness of the author and another of which erodes the coherence of the character or narrator. Dudley Andrew regards this duality as a Wellesian hallmark: "the doubleness and distance that so define the world of Orson Welles."[37] Similarly, Tomasulo interprets *Citizen Kane* as evoking the duality between not only Kane himself as man/boy and narrator/character but also "Orson Welles as actor/author."[38] Thus sense of a quest for first-person meaning expands narrative beyond the diegetic space of film and transforms questions about the meaning of Kane's Rosebud into questions about meaning in modern existence. Performance becomes a metonym for the location of the self within modernity.[39] The Wellesian narrative deconstructs selfhood both within and outside the text.

The problem of locating a discrete Wellesian text emerges partly from the conditions of performance. Performances mix art and commerce and exist only ephemerally in the audience's imagination.[40] These conditions are especially pronounced in radio performance, which projects itself into as many situational contexts as there are listeners. Each home has its own performance environment that affects the listener's way of listening; it is impossible to locate a single "text" of these radio plays. The scripts themselves represent only intentions, not the actual experiences of the performances.

"Primal Branding" and Welles

Notably, the Wellesian narrative brand emerged first on radio, most powerfully through the infamous *War of the Worlds* broadcast and the subsequent coupling of Welles with the iconic brand Campbell Soup. By partnering with Campbell Soup, Welles established a brand alliance, or a co-brand, such as often forms "between businesses with similar philosophies."[41] Campbell Soup was well on its way to becoming an iconic brand even in the late 1930s.[42] At first glance the Wellesian brand shared few values with the "soup people," as John Houseman referred to them.[43] There were, however, certain cross-associations: quality, wholesomeness, and a sense that classic literature, like soup, is "good food." But there were also inherent conflicts, since the Wellesian brand was associated with experimentation, deconstruction of subjectivity, and socially progressive politics—all decidedly not goals of Campbell Soup.

CBS originally hoped to capitalize on the stage success of the Mercury Theatre by translating their classics-for-the-masses format into radio. A publicity release on June 8, 1938, promoting *First Person Singular*, promised that Welles would "explore fields of literature heretofore untouched by radio and bring to that medium the same spirit of adventure which he brought to the theatre last season."[44] But as CBS would soon discover, there are both strengths and weaknesses in a marketing brand based on the cult of personality. The Mercury Theatre brand depended on the mercurial temper of its brand personality, Orson Welles.

Brand personalities comprise a distinct subset of marketing brands overall. They are powerful in their emotional hold over consumers but are also notoriously volatile and often short-lived in market draw. The Wellesian brand fits the paradigm of a brand personality in many ways, except that Welles exceeded the role of a mere spokesperson. Any brand personality automatically covers two of seven categories in what Patrick Hanlon describes as "primal branding"—the development of icons and leaders—in a paradigm that invokes a decidedly Freudian structure to capture the psychological power of certain brand personalities. All seven of Hanlon's brand components exist within the Wellesian brand: icons, leaders, creation stories, creeds, rituals, pagans, and sacred words.[45]

Welles's voice provided the icon, and he additionally fulfilled the role of brand leader, the "person who is the catalyst, the risk taker, the visionary, the iconoclast who set out against all odds (and often against the world at large) to re-create the world according to their own sense of self, community, and opportunity."[46] In this way, Welles functions as his own larger-than-life character, much like Kane.

Welles was the type of brand personality who became a commodity himself rather than just allying himself with a particular product. Like most iconic figures, he was surrounded by personal anecdotes of his success and his exceptionality, "creation stories" in Hanlon's terms. Simon Anholt and Jeremy Hildreth indicate that the purpose of these anecdotes is to make key attributes of the personal brand "striking and memorable."[47] Welles's publicity team often tailored the stories of his origins to specific project needs. When Welles was planning his Rio project, they highlighted his connection to Brazil, even going so far as to suggest that he was either conceived in Brazil or almost born there, and thus considered himself "Cariocan."[48] In the fall of 1939 Welles's publicist Herb Drake wrote to inquire of Maurice Bernstein about the "prehistoric days of the Christ Child" (meaning Welles's childhood), and Bernstein replied that Welles "arrived in Kenosha on the 6th of May 1915. On the 7th of May, 1915, he spoke his first words [. . .] he said 'I am a genius' [. . .] on May 15th he seduced his first woman."[49] The essence of the Welles creation tale is that he is a cosmopolitan genius. The specifics of the tale vary according to the audience (or potential consumer). Since the creation story is the cornerstone for the other pieces of the primal branding structure, the telling of it is a sensitive operation: "like telling a good tale, the opportunity is how to make it interesting. Then you must decide where to communicate it. Do you include it in public relation efforts, on the Internet, in advertising, on packaging?"[50] Welles, always a fabulous storyteller with a penchant for the press, made an ideal icon for the Wellesian brand, since he could reiterate the creation story for various audiences in diverse media, while always remaining recognizable by his resonant voice and sardonic wit.

The "creed" is an equally important part of Hanlon's primal branding code because it clarifies the brand's mission. The early Wellesian brand depended heavily on the Mercury Theatre, a sign of credibility and continuity that bridged Welles's transitions from stage to radio to screen. Through his work with the Mercury Theatre, he was able to articulate a series of concrete aims regarding performance style, target audience, and political allegiance. Houseman and Welles stipulated the goals for their Mercury Theatre productions in speeches, newspaper articles, and press releases. A June 8, 1938, CBS press release quoted Welles:

> I think it is time [. . .] that radio came to realize the fact that no matter how wonderful a play may be for the stage it cannot be as wonderful for the air. The Mercury Theater has no intention of producing its stage repertoire in these broadcasts. Instead we plan to bring to radio the experimental techniques which have proved so successful in another medium and to treat radio itself with the intelligence and respect such a beautiful and powerful medium deserves.[51]

Welles wanted to create intimacy through a mass medium, to convey individual experience in a collective broadcast. In a *Newsweek* article published July 11, 1938, he promised to use the resources of radio to move beyond the "cut-and-dried dramatic technique" of theater. To do so, he would focus on his own power as narrator in the radio series, cultivating his ability to draw "his listeners into the charmed circle" of his storytelling.[52] Recognizing the intimate nature of radio as a performance medium that entered individual homes, he believed, as James Naremore surmises, that the 'invisible audience should never be considered collectively, but individually."[53] The Wellesian brand of storytelling offered personal, emotional, and individual connections by positioning Welles himself at the center of his narratives as a touchstone for the listener, a facilitator of personal experience amid a mass event. Ordinarily, this type of connection is a positive thing, helping to build the emotional bond of the brand. In cases like the *War of the Worlds* broadcast, however, it proved more problematic, spurring individual feelings of anxiety as Welles's character, Professor Pierson, dissolved into panic. Nevertheless, Campbell Soup saw marketing potential in any performer who could elicit such a strong emotional response from an audience, and soon after the *War of the Worlds* broadcast, *Mercury Theatre on the Air* became *Campbell Playhouse.*

The original title capitalized on the association with quality experimentation by invoking Welles's prior work with the Mercury Theatre. Welles transferred not only the Mercury production name to his radio program but also his creative partners and actors. The main goal of the Mercury Theatre, articulated by John Houseman in his letter to Burns Mantle of the *Daily News* on October 13, 1937, was to form a theater "at which the public may see exciting productions of great plays at prices easily within their reach."[54] Houseman and Welles intended to "bring back into the theatre some of the violence and immediacy" of the Elizabethan theater while also looking for new playwrights and material.[55] As indicated by press releases from CBS during 1938, the goal was to adapt the Mercury Theatre performance model of narrative experimentation with classic texts into the medium of radio, bringing the public memory of the Mercury's manifesto to the new productions.

By 1938 the Wellesian brand had also established rituals of performance, or what Hanlon terms "sacred words." The serial format allowed for the predictable weekly availability of the Wellesian brand, increasing the chances for positive interactions with consumers that create brand "vitality."[56] Within the world of his performances, Welles employed audio cues and catch phrases to initiate listeners and viewers. His later radio broadcasts in particular made clear efforts to open with tag lines such as "Hello, Americans," which he used in his Pan-American broadcasts and which became the series title. Even the 1938 broadcasts included consistent audio cues: for instance, Ernest Chappell's voice distinguished the Campbell Soup commercials from the passages of drama, and an excerpt from Tchaikovsky's Piano Concerto no. 1 in B-flat minor opened the show.

Sacred Wellesian words emerge as well in the reactions to his work, words repeated not by Welles but by his admirers. As Hanlon says, "all belief systems come with a set of specialized words that must be learned before people can belong," and in primal branding the goal is to create an emotional need for people to "belong" by purchasing the brand. Thus sacred words in branding become "not simply professional jargon but crucial to understanding a technical process."[57] In the case of Welles, the sacred words of cinema can convert audience members into fans—emotionally bonded consumers. Terms like "deep focus" or "Rosebud" initiate the Wellesian consumer into the club of critics and the niche market of the cinephile or auteur, demonstrating both knowledge of and relationship to the product and reiterating the traditional associations of Welles's work with prestige and innovation.[58] Consumers who speak these sacred words often purchase Wellesian products (DVDs, books, CDs), propagating the Wellesian brand. Since it meets all the requirements for primal branding then, why did the Wellesian entertainment brand fail to flourish under the RKO studio system?

Failure of the Wellesian Brand?

If one thinks of Welles's shift from radio into film as a brand extension, then it failed in the short term because it didn't link strongly enough to the Mercury Theatre "creed" of populism but became instead a singular vehicle for Welles's personal stardom. Paradoxically, his brand name grew as his bankroll languished. He experienced what is known as "blowback": "when the disconnect between the brand message and corporate behaviour becomes too great, the marketing too hypocritical, the end justifying the means a little too often, then public protest tends to be intense in proportion to the strength of the brand."[59] Thus his popularity and status following *War of the Worlds* and *Citizen Kane* invited proportionate levels of scrutiny and criticism of his subsequent projects. He ran afoul of RKO with *Heart of Darkness, The Magnificent Ambersons,* and *It's All True,* and simultaneously consumers were deprived of his regular radio broadcasts and theater performances, both of which became less routinely available as he devoted more time to cinema.

Nevertheless, the Wellesian brand can be seen at worst as a temporary failure. It failed only in the sense that it did not flourish within the closed circuit of the Hollywood studio system. As Paul Arthur points out, "Fifteen years after his death, we are suddenly awash in Wellesiana, inundated by Orson."[60] The Wellesian brand today is a viable commercial product, albeit within a niche market. Welles failed, however, to live up to the commercial expectations of RKO when he produced fewer complete than incomplete projects. One way to regard the waning appeal of the Wellesian brand in the mid-1940s is in terms of a fracture in Welles's "temperamental affinity" with American politics in post–World War II culture, all too neatly symbolized by his role shift from propagandist to expatriate.[61] His last RKO project was funded as part of the U. S. Government's "Good Neighbor" policy, but his post-RKO work was done largely in Europe. This fracture was exacerbated by Welles's abiding interest in deconstructing the first-person-singular figure of excess, which was increasingly out of synch with American culture.

By 1954 Welles had become a comic reference in Hollywood, spoofed by commercial successes like Bob Hope.[62] Whereas the threat of fascism had encouraged Welles's critique of the power of the iconic first person, the threat of communism shifted national rhetoric toward a fear of lost individuality. In the context of the Cold War, Kane looked like a heroic figure, championing American capitalism and the free press. Welles himself was increasingly situated as an outsider, not a member of the nationalist (anticommunist) "team" of Hollywood insiders, and his personality-driven brand moved to the margins of American culture, eventually becoming an expatriate product with European associations.

Ironically, considering his thematic preoccupation with the critique of individual power, Welles's short-term marketing strategy in the 1940s suffered from an embrace of individual artistic production at the expense of collaboration. Publicly, Welles began to disavow creative partnerships. He broke with Houseman and became embroiled in a controversy with Herman Mankiewicz over script credit for *Citizen Kane*. Welles's rising stardom inhibited the Mercury, which "went from an experiment in people's theater to a trademark for a star."[63] In his incisive analysis of the Mercury aesthetic, Michael Denning notes that the Mercury Theatre was caught between the politics of the popular front and the corporate elitism of RKO and Henry Luce.[64] The result was "a people's theater without the people,"[65] even though Welles himself remained "an instinctive populist and ardent antiracist who despite a storied arrogance reveled in collaborative exchanges with almost anyone in his path."[66]

The long-term benefits of Welles's isolationist marketing strategy, however, ensured the durable legend of Welles the auteur that continues to hold great sway with critics and fans—yet it also ensures critical neglect of some of his most interesting work. Projects deemed less authentically "Wellesian" than others because they are collaborative or incomplete tend to be given less attention. As Lorna Fitzsimmons argues in her analysis of *The Magnificent Ambersons*, "for years Welles's loss of control functioned as both a catch-all explanation for the film's 'imperfections' and a rationale for engaging in commentaries limited by their auteurist assumptions."[67] In this way, the Wellesian brand was at odds with Welles-the-man, and his brand took on the connotation of "Outcast Genius," an association that ensured its position at the periphery of the studio system.

Welles's working style never really matched his billing as individual genius. He took the collaborative Mercury Theatre ideology to Hollywood, and a CBS press release dated November 30, 1939, announced that Welles as a film director "wishes to continue the rehearsal system he has always adhered to in his Campbell Playhouse broadcasts."[68] He anticipated keeping the actors wholly involved in the production, retaining Bernard Herrmann's musical accompaniment and following "the Group Theater method of working over a play" so that actors could "if necessary, 'ad lib' their scenes." He also articulated his concept for an emerging visual rhetoric, which would show, "from the standpoint of the camera, how the story is to unfold and what the camera will see, since a movie script is more a record of what is seen rather than what is heard." A direct challenge to classic cinema techniques was clearly announced as well: "This unusual blend of broadcasting and recording technique with established motion picture practice is a radical departure in Hollywood procedure and already the 'Orson Welles Plan' has aroused wide-spread discussion."[69] Welles's collaborative rehearsals, nontraditional scripting, and visual experimentation resulted in markers of his brand that would be at odds with its commercial viability.

Commercially, the Orson Welles Plan reflects the desire for co-branding between radio and cinema. At first, the Mercury Theatre tried to reassure radio sponsors like Campbell Soup that the move to cinema would be mutually beneficial. Houseman wrote sponsor Ward Wheelock on July 27, 1939: "Many radio stars have made appearances in pictures but no recognizable and complete radio show with its formula intact has ever before been made into a motion picture."[70] CBS integrated Houseman's language in their own marketing plan, incorporating the idea of a radio show translated into cinema in a press release four months later, "Welles Uses Radio and Recording Techniques in Readying First Film."[71] The press release's emphasis on improvisational rehearsal techniques and actor-driven productions undermines the myth of Welles as a solo scriptwriter while highlighting the arrival of the Mercury Theatre in movies.

The tension between marketing a first-person "star" and a collaborative creative enterprise created a short-term crisis that compromised Welles's standing with RKO. Over the long term, however, the iconography of the Wellesian brand depended not just on the first-person singular as incarnate in Welles himself but on a general fascination with the American first person, with an exploration and erosion of a national "I." Welles's own contradictory positions as an American expatriate and a star who worked collaboratively make his body of work increasingly relevant to viewers interested in the contradictions (and failures) of postmodern subjectivity. Over the course of Welles's career, his work came to evoke the difficulty of constructing the concept of "I," and his brand returned to cultural relevance.

I/Eye on America: Welles's RKO Projects

Although this chapter is primarily concerned with the first-person-singular component of the Wellesian brand, this narrative style is interwoven with three other styles discussed in later chapters: the adaptation of classics, use of modernist primitivism, and the exploration of the truth-fiction binary. In any Wellesian production one of these components might be highlighted, but usually several are present. When we look at three of his RKO projects, two unfinished and one finished, the interplay of the first-person singular with the other styles readily emerges. In addition, it becomes clear that the Wellesian first person in these early projects is explicitly positioned from an American perspective. These projects evoke conflicts within and between personal and American identity, often as challenged by increasingly global contexts. Each project engaged American identity, even though *Heart of Darkness* and the Christ project needed significant adaptation to address these issues. Moving from Kurtz to Kane to Christ, the latter half of this chapter studies Welles's earliest proposed RKO projects specifically in terms of their use of the first-person singular and a national context.

The Imperial "I": *Heart of Darkness*

The difficulty of translating Welles's first-person narrative strategy from radio to film is illustrated by his first RKO film project, *Heart of Darkness*.[72] Welles had already adapted *Heart of Darkness* for radio in 1938 as part of the *First Person Singular* series, and he was eager to reproduce on film the theoretical dimensions of the first-person narrator he had established in that radio broadcast. *First Person Singular* often adapted novels that had a strong oral/aural component, and as Spadoni notes, Conrad's *Heart of Darkness* already contains three levels of performance: reading, listening, and seeing. The reader reads the novel itself but shifts into the position of listener on the *Nellie* and then "sees" Kurtz and the river through visual imagination.[73] Radio broadcast could explore the listening/seeing tactics of the novel more thoroughly than film because radio could mimic the narrative frame of the novel, aurally positioning the listeners as though they were on the *Nellie*, and then requiring them to visualize Kurtz and Marlow's story through imagination rather than direct visual representation.

Aural narrative can not only transmit an authorial "I" directly to the listener but also extend this first-person perspective to more than one central character. In fact it was common for radio actors to play more than one character and for more than one character to narrate. This strategy is echoed in Welles's approach to the radio adaptations of Charles Dickens, which employed more than one central narrator. In Welles's *Tale of Two Cities*, for example, three characters speak directly to the audience: Manette, Carton, and Lorry; his later *Oliver Twist* splits the narration between Oliver and Mr. Brownlow.[74] In contrast, classic Hollywood films sparingly used even a single voiceover narrator. Welles's proposal for a cinematic *Heart of Darkness* reflects his previous radio experimentation, even in his original plan to play both Marlow and Kurtz (apparently a short-lived idea). If he had played both roles, he would have awkwardly split Marlow's narrative voice—disguise only goes so far, particularly when it comes to Welles's distinctive vocal tones, and an audience was sure to be confused by Welles's voiceover as Marlow meditating on his body playing Kurtz.

A second problem posed for Welles's translation of this text from radio to film was that the use of the camera to evoke the aural added a layer of complexity to the act of filming, as well as to the narrative structure. Welles wanted to experiment with using the camera to express two narrative perspectives engaging each other and the audience. Even if he had been able to extend the traditions of classic cinema in this way, it was almost impossible to achieve the effects Welles desired without breaking RKO's budget and extending shooting for an unacceptable amount of time. So, despite the fact that roles had already been cast and actors were on salary, the project was shelved by RKO at a substantial cost. Welles was finding his ideas difficult to translate into the medium of film, which offered more tantalizing technical possibilities than either stage or radio but imposed limitations as well.

Conflicts of national identity were central to Welles's vision of *Heart of Darkness*, and his opening relocates the frame story from the Thames to the Hudson. Aurally, it also situates the exotic within the United States, as "snatches of jazz music" are heard from the "radios in the moving taxicabs."[75] *Heart of Darkness* is thus set in the context of a distinctly American first-person singular, framed within the discourses of nationality and selfhood.

In his study of this unmade film, Naremore suggests that by substituting "the eye of the camera for the 'I' of Conrad's narrator, the camera would become Marlow, whose voice, that of Welles himself, would be heard off-screen."[76] This dichotomy of *I vs. eye* appears clearly and explicitly in the introduction to *Heart of Darkness* in which Welles actually offers it as a graphic equation (see Figure 1, in the gallery).[77] Critics have analyzed this opening in depth, and Spadoni, Naremore, and Guerric DeBona all offer persuasive readings of it as a potentially powerful piece of cinema. The correlation between its visual manipulation and the aural strategies Welles employed on the radio series *First Person Singular* are clear: "Welles was seeking a filmic equivalent of the kind of identification that novels can effect in readers, and that his own Mercury radio show—subtitled *First Person Singular*—routinely evoked in listeners." But the world of the camera is very different from that of the microphone, and the heavy-handed self-referential approach that Welles proposed would have been at odds with classical cinematic techniques, which are designed to make the viewer identify seamlessly with the inhabitants of the visual world of the cinema. Didacticism does not lead to identification in cinema, and Welles's powerful, iconic voice did not hold the same sway in the visual world that it had in the aural world. As Spadoni succinctly summarizes, "the more Welles insists on his formula's "i," the more the *yous* proliferate."[78]

During the introductory sequence, Welles guides the audience into a personal interaction with the film by means of visual tricks. First he cages them; then he takes them into the death chamber, all the while using the camera as a surrogate for the viewers' eyes and using direct address to personalize the experience. Welles maintained this process of creating an individual sensory and psychic experience via performance as a central value throughout his cinematic career. DeBona aptly assesses the promise of this innovative opening sequence, saying it "would have been a remarkable piece of cinema" in part because of its innovative use of a visual rather than aural first person.[79] Perhaps the best way to envision the possibilities and limitations of his opening is to review the "canary sequence":

> Introduction: This has no direct connection with the motion picture itself. It is intended to instruct and acquaint the audience as amusingly as possible with the special technique used in "The Heart of Darkness."
>
> Dark Screen. WELLES' VOICE
>
> Ladies and Gentlemen, this is Orson Welles. Don't worry. There's nothing to look at for a while. You can close your eyes, if you want to, but—please open them when I tell you to . . . First of all, I am going to divide this audience into two parts—you and everybody else in the theatre. Now, then, open your eyes. IRIS INTO Int. Bird Cage—(Process)
>
> SHOOTING FROM inside the bird cage, as it would appear to a bird inside the cage, looking out. The cage fills the entire screen. Beyond the bars can be seen chin and mouth of Welles, tremendously magnified.
>
> WELLES' VOICE The big hole in the middle there is my mouth. You play the part of a canary. I'm asking you to sing and you refuse. That's the plot. I offer you an olive.
>
> A couple of Gargantuan fingers appear from below cage and thrust an enormous olive toward CAMERA, through bars of the cage.
>
> WELLES' VOICE (cont'd) You don't want an olive. This enrages me.
>
> Welles' chin moves down and his nose and eyes are revealed. He is scowling fiercely.

WELLES' VOICE (cont'd) Here is a bird's-eye view of me being enraged. I threaten you with a gun.

Now the muzzle of a pistol is stuck between the bars of the cage. It looks like a Big Bertha.

WELLES' VOICE (cont.) That's the way a gun looks to a canary. I give you to the count of three to sing.

Welles' head moves up, showing his mouth on the words, 'One, two, three.' His voice is heard over echo chambers and the narration is synchronized on the count with the movement of his lips.

WELLES (cont'd)

One . . . Two . . . (on normal level, cheerfully) You still don't want to sing so I shoot you.

The gun goes off with a cloud of smoke and a shower of brightly colored sparks. As this fades out,

WELLES' VOICE (cont'd) That's the end of this picture. FADE OUT

FADE IN

CREDIT TITLE [. . .]

BLACK SCREEN

WELLES' VOICE Now, of course, this movie isn't about a canary and I am not going to threaten you with firearms [. . .] but I do want you to understand that you're part of the story. In fact, you are the star. Of course, you're not going to see yourself on the screen but everything you see on the screen is going to be seen through your eyes and you're somebody else. Understand? (1–3)

This introduction contains all the hallmarks of the Wellesian first-person singular but articulates them through distinctly visual rhetoric. It includes reflexivity that shatters classic cinema techniques, direct confrontation between the narrator and the audience, a preoccupation with overlapping realms of fantasy and reality, and even disavowal of portions of the text itself. If this text has "no direct connection" with *Heart of Darkness*, why is it literally part of the script? This urge to disavow the complexity of textual production is a hallmark of the Wellesian brand. Disavowal is also a hallmark of the brand's endurance, since these are precisely the contradictions that establish the continuing relevance of his brand for critics and scholars and that make his process as relevant to postmodernity as his products were to modernity.

First-Person Plural: Controversy and *Citizen Kane*

Welles was able to realize parts of the visual first-person singular in his first complete project for RKO, *Citizen Kane*, which is undoubtedly the

Wellesian product most discussed in terms of his use of this concept. The Wellesian point of view in *Citizen Kane* oscillates between the objective and subjective, driving the unattainable quest for the "truth" of Kane's Rosebud. Tomasulo explores this division between subjective narration and objective description in *Citizen Kane,* labeling implied authorial voice as "monophonic" and ironic narrational agency as "more polyphonic." *Citizen Kane* establishes a style of "authorial agency" that "*narrates* from the points of view of the participating characters and *describes* from the viewpoint of a more impersonal author."[80] The ironic, or polyphonic, visual narration of the film is associated with diegetic rupture or self-reflection. Tomasulo sees this most clearly in the Thatcher sequence, which shows "many marks of direct address between filmmaker and spectator by rupturing the seamless transparency of the diegetic world."[81]

There are at least three perspectives at work in the Thatcher sequence: that of the reporter Thompson reading Thatcher's report, Thatcher's own version on the page, and the audience's interpretation of certain events that are shown on screen but cannot be known to either Thompson or Thatcher. As we read Thatcher's story over Thompson's shoulder, we see it transformed into a visual drama. Within this drama are images clearly not generated by either Thatcher's words or Thompson's imagination as he reads those words. Thatcher does not see Rosebud's importance, for example, and therefore would not put it at the center of the visual field as the young Kane plays or once the sled is relegated to storage within Kane's subconscious. These images are from the polyphonic discourse. They are the images of the audience, of Kane himself, of the filmmaker, or of Truth. The "unstable economy of discourse" that results from the conjunction of the camera's voice (objective Truth) and the characters' voices (subjective experience) has kept critics and consumers interested for many years.[82]

The visual rhetoric of *Kane* exposes the subjective construction of reality at several points, perhaps most notably by juxtaposing the *March of Time* sequence regarding the life and death of Kane with the beginning of the audience's and Thompson's quest for alternate visions of the inner life of Kane. This sequence creates a schism between the public and private concepts of "I," especially when contrasted with the subsequent personal perspectives of characters who knew Kane. As William Simon summarizes, the "truth value" of the *March of Time* sequence "is challenged by the competing versions of Kane's life"[83] In the prewar context of *Citizen Kane*'s theatrical release, to question the scenario of a newsreel was a radical act, foreshadowing Welles's future (conflicted) role as national propagandist during his final RKO project, *It's All True.*

By creating in Kane a national icon[84] who is yet unknowable, whose ultimate Truth remains inaccessible,[85] Welles again merged his camera's first-person singular with nationalist rhetoric. Although Kane is an undeniably strong image of an American protagonist, the form of the film contests the coherence of a national "I." The visual "I" of *Citizen Kane* invokes the untrustworthy public rhetoric of Kane himself, and he becomes a model of modern American subjectivity under interrogation. In addition, by linking *Citizen Kane* to "real" events beyond the realm of cinematic fantasy, the *March of Time* sequence in particular displays the ability of the Wellesian brand to merge truth and fiction and to integrate political relevance into the product. In *Citizen Kane*, as Stephanie Dennison and Lisa Shaw note, "populism and propaganda are the form and content of the film."[86]

Controversy was already part of the Wellesian brand by 1940, since he had transformed performance into public spectacle with *The Cradle Will Rock* and *War of the Worlds*, ensuring that he "would come to Hollywood on a wave of publicity."[87] If anything, the sensation created by his radio controversy increased his public worth in the eyes of studio executives—in effect *War of the Worlds* had established his brand name. Before he had released a single film, RKO was more than happy to exploit Welles's public personality as a key to his box-office success. Press releases and interviews disseminated the image of Welles as the talented sole creator of his high-profile productions. Richard O'Brien raved over Welles's "courage to produce, write, cast, direct and play a leading part in a picture."[88] *Citizen Kane* effected a new opportunity for controversy, however, in that it created a schism between the collaborative working process on which Welles had relied and the growing first-person mythology of his brand name. The very success of Welles's attempt to merge his directorial/authorial presence with the first-person visual rhetoric of *Citizen Kane* created the need to suppress the recognition of Herman Mankiewicz as coauthor of the script, and the additional obstacle of William Randolph Hearst's campaign against the film could not have come at a worse time for either RKO or Welles.

The Wellesian brand was part of a larger cultural shift toward commercialism in the 1930s that was particularly pronounced in radio: as Michael Anderegg points out, the proportion of commercially sponsored programs on NBC grew from 23.6% to 49.9% between 1933 and 1944, and commercial sponsorship of shows on CBS increased from 22.7% to 47.8% during the same period.[89] By early 1941 Welles relied heavily on radio sponsorships for his living. His attorney, Arnold Weissberger, expressed his own pleasure with these sponsorships: "I am all a-glow at the prospect of commitments for the International Silver Theater, Cavalcade of America, and Campbell soup."[90]

Welles's popularity was thus essential to his financial survival. A single farcical appearance on the Rudy Vallee show with John Barrymore on December 19 earned him $1,700 during his midwinter fiscal crisis of 1940–41.[91] RKO regarded his personality and the public perception of him as the author of his works as central to his box-office prospects; therefore, both Welles and the studio needed to maintain his lone-genius image at all costs, a desire clearly shown in the controversy over the writing credit for *Citizen Kane.*

Welles's contract with RKO stipulated that he should be the sole creator, director, and star of his works. Wellesian drama was associated with both quality and experimentation, a combination that RKO president George Schaefer specifically brought Welles to RKO to reproduce. A "prestige producer," Schaefer was part of the RCA-Rockefeller group "who wanted a 'quality' image."[92] Yet the quality image had to turn a profit as well. Welles, already known as an "Innovator on Stage, [who] Experiments on the Air"[93] and who had turned radio "to a New Art Form,"[94] fit Schaefer's ideal. At a time when the average weekly salary for a radio employee was reported to be $45.12,[95] Welles was thought to earn between $1,000 and $1,700 a week from radio alone.[96] Schaefer hoped that he would bring the same high-profile entertainment to film and generate similar financial returns. If he could do that, he was welcome to sole credit.

The controversy over *Citizen Kane* emerged from two sources simultaneously: William Randolph Hearst and his adherents resented Kane's resemblance to Hearst, and Herman Mankiewicz wanted to be acknowledged for his role in writing the screenplay. Mankiewicz had originally signed an agreement to sell his rights as author of the screenplay but began reasserting his right to screen credit in the fall of 1940.[97] The authorship controversy seems to have erupted when Mankiewicz read a Louella Parsons column that quoted Welles as saying he wrote *Citizen Kane.* A letter from Herb Drake to Welles on August 26, 1940, described Mankiewicz as "in the biggest fever yet" over the column, and reported him to have called Welles a "juvenile delinquent credit stealer beginning with the Mars broadcast and carrying on with tremendous consistency." According to Drake, Mankiewicz threatened to take out a full-page advertisement in trade papers, send out wire stories, and let Ben Hecht write a story for the *Saturday Evening Post* refuting Welles's sole authorship of the film.[98]

Weissberger began advising Welles on how to handle this volatile situation, consistently recommending a combination of tact and threat. In a letter on September 23, 1940,[99] Weissberger counseled Welles: "the fact that you have the power to exclude him from credit under his agreement can be used by you tactfully to indicate that your allowing him to have credit is a matter of good will on your part." But the situation was complicated by a recent Screen Writers Guild policy that demanded more recognition for writers, and Mankiewicz threatened to take the matter before the guild. Such publicity would defeat the purpose of omitting Mankiewicz's name from the credits in the first place. Weissberger acknowledged this when he wrote to Welles on October 1, 1940:

> it would be most imprudent to allow a dispute of this sort to be aired before the Screen Writers Guild. To do so would defeat the very object that we have in mind with respect to credit on the picture. It would be unwise to deny Mankiewicz credit on the screen and have him get credit therefor[e] through the press by publicizing his complaint.

Since Welles had been promoted as the new resident genius of Hollywood, it would have been awkward to admit that his productions—whether on stage, radio, or film—were collaborations. As the first major cinematic effort of the all-round genius, *Citizen Kane* needed to have his name on it as director, star, and writer.

Welles helped diffuse the threat of the solo authorship controversy by returning to collaboration, this time in the form of the theatrical adaptation of *Native Son*. Welles's assistant Richard Baer replied to Weissberger that they owed Mankiewicz money for the theatrical script for *Native Son*, soon to open on Broadway under Welles's direction, in collaboration with Houseman. *Native Son* stoked the fires of public controversy with its interracial relationships and Communist themes, and it gave Welles another chance at successful collaboration.[100] Baer suggested, "For reasons which are obvious, I think it might be well to pay one or both of these debts at this time."[101] The successful collaboration on *Native Son* fulfilled two of Welles's immediate needs: to have a bargaining chip in his negotiations with Mankiewicz and to provide an influx of cash. Mankiewicz's ire seems to have subsided by January 1941, and he maintained his collaborative relationship with Welles.

The Mankiewicz problem preoccupied Welles's attorney from September 1940 until January 1941. Baer reported to Weissberger that Mankiewicz had "conceded to Orson's wishes in the question of credits in the picture" on January 3, but the Screen Writers Guild got involved anyway, alerting Weissberger that even a shared screen credit would violate the Producer–Screen Writers Guild Agreement, which stated that a producer could not claim screenplay credit unless he had in fact written the screenplay "without the collaboration of any other writer."[102] However, as Weissberger was quick to point out to Welles, the agreement was made in October 1940, after Mankiewicz had waived his screenplay rights, and it was "therefore inapplicable." Weissberger emphasized that Welles would be further in violation of his RKO contract if he conceded to Mankiewicz; he was already violating it with his slow production pace.[103] A screen credit contract between Welles and Mankiewicz, dated January 22, 1941, resolves the conflict in a screen credit that would read:

Original Screenplay
by
Herman J. Mankiewicz
Orson Welles[104]

Add the Hearst controversy to the screenwriting controversy, and the diversification of the Wellesian brand into cinema was in serious jeopardy. At the January 1941 preview, Hedda Hopper immediately identified the protagonist with her media mogul boss, causing Hearst's attempt to squelch the film even before its release. On January 8, 1941, Welles wrote directly to Louella Parsons to explain that *Citizen Kane* was not about Hearst and that any such rumors were "a good deal of nonsense."[105] His effort failed miserably, and Hearst was soon publicly at odds with RKO. A *Newsweek* article in January 1941 emphasizes both the public's expectations for Welles and the reasons for his growing tension with RKO and its president, George Schaefer. The article points out that Welles, the "No. 1 *enfant terrible* of the theater and radio," had been known to flourish amid controversy. But the article also reveals that Welles was losing the feeling of support that he sought from Schaefer, reputedly the only studio executive allowed to read the full script of *Kane* during production. Hearst was putting financial pressure on RKO by refusing to publish a word about the studio or its productions in any of his numerous papers.[106] This, in turn, put pressure on Schaefer as the changing management of RKO continued to demand that he make the boy wonder show profits rather than losses.[107]

The stress of losing Schaefer's sympathy is obvious in a four-page, tortuous letter from Welles to Schaefer on March 6, 1941, begging RKO to release *Citizen Kane* over Hearst's objections. The letter marks the dark midpoint of an anxious phase for Welles that lasted from the January preview of *Citizen Kane* until its eventual New York premiere on May 1. The letter is alternately petulant, adoring, hostile, and depressed. Welles writes,

> When all this trouble first descended upon us, we spoke almost twice daily by phone. Now I have to sit up until four o'clock in the morning trying to get in touch with you and failing to do so[. . . .] I cannot think you are deliberately avoiding me. I can only suppose that you are pursuing some policy the nature of which must be kept secret[. . . .] Always

> remember that I well know you're the best man I'll ever work for, but do try to realize that you owe both of us something better than what I now receive[. . . .] I must know if I overrate our friendship. Maybe all I owe you in my turn is the two moving pictures called for in our contract[. . . .] Maybe that's all you want since you know that's what you'll get.[108]

Finally, Welles voices his fear that his audience is turning on him: "My mail is one long accusation from the American public which truly believes I have sold out. . . . My nights are sleepless and my days are a torture." Worthy of a key place in an epistolary novel, this outburst from Welles symbolizes not only a personal dark night of the soul but a desperate turn in his overall aesthetic and recognizes an emerging threat to the popularity of his brand name. It appeared that even when a film project was completed, there were to be inherent marketing problems with Welles's use of a larger-than-life, first-person singular in film, particularly when it was combined with the exploration of the line between fact and fiction.

One remarkable sequence in *Citizen Kane* portends his next RKO proposal for a *Life of Christ*. Between the retrospective snow scene in the Thatcher sequence and Kane's emergence as an adult icon, Kane matures by twenty years. At the same time, the scenes themselves move from Christmas to New Year's Eve. As Tomasulo notes, the symbolism evokes the eight-day "Biblical passage from birth to circumcision, from infancy to the ritual of coming into manhood."[109] The larger-than-life treatment of Kane as an American icon left Welles with a logical trajectory: to pursue the ascendancy of the first-person from Kurtz to Kane and on to Christ.

Deification of the First-Person Singular: *Life of Christ*

We know much less about Welles's *Life of Christ* than about either of the other RKO projects discussed here, but it remains a suggestive culminating example of his cinematic exploration of the first-person singular. Following Kurtz and Kane, Welles played with the idea of doing a version of the life of Jesus Christ, who would be relocated to the United States.[110] Welles, of course, would have been the omnipotent director and star. In part, the opportunity to handle a controversial subject "correctly" drew Welles to the project. The Christ project would show off several hallmarks of his brand—an ultimate first-person singular, a politically relevant topic, and an experimental interpretation of a (or *the*) classic piece of literature.

Welles had already used his iconic voice to play the supernatural role of the Shadow on radio. He had often used voice-over to create the sense of a "voice of God, confident because omniscient, demanding that we hearken to it and interpret our situation in relation to its message."[111] Certainly this omnipotent persona pervades the introductory sequence of *Heart of Darkness* as well. *The Life of Christ* promised to embody characteristics of two other roughly contemporary projects as well: the religious controversy that had resulted from his radio production of *Liliom* in August 1939 and the emerging idea for *It's All True*, which was originally conceived as a medley of various stories of North American identity.

In the *Liliom* controversy, which lasted from August to November of 1939, Welles had to defend his creative freedom against attempts at censorship by religious organizations. *Liliom*, best known as the basis for the later musical *Carousel*, represents scenes of heaven and the afterlife that were deemed controversial, and Welles felt frustrated and yet intrigued by the challenge of bringing it to broadcast. The greatest problem identified by Catholic organizations was the representation of heaven in an entertainment medium, and as a result Welles agreed to drop a scene in heaven.[112] The Wheelock agency for Campbell Soup negotiated script approval with the Catholic Charities and Publicities Bureau to minimize controversy, a process that Welles and Houseman grudgingly accepted. On November 4, 1939, Welles wrote to Ward Wheelock, explaining an article in the *Philadelphia Record* by Leonard Lyons that quoted Welles as lamenting the burden of censorship. Welles explained,

> The basis of the Lyons crack was a remark I made in Liederkranz Hall to two or three Columbia [Broadcast System] people who were bedeviling me with censorship on "Liliom." I said [. . .] I thought the best thing to do would be to just go on the air and read the Bible, which would all be censorable but uncensored.[113]

Liliom aired on October 22, 1939, with Helen Hayes as guest star. Highlighting the controversial nature of Molnár's original tale, Welles introduces the story as one that was first suppressed. But he calls the tale an "incredibly beautiful and beautifully incredible little fantasy," positioning it in the realm of magic.[114] He describes fantasy as "the highest reach of the mind. It is our first conclusion and our last. A tall story was told after the first fire that was ever built. And we haven't outgrown magic even if we know better."[115] Welles frames the violent story as a fable, emphasizing the unreal qualities of the work, a contrast to the infusion of contemporary politics into works like his theatrical *Julius Caesar* and cinematic *Citizen Kane*, although he does relocate *Liliom* to an American setting. Demonstrating a fluid move between commerce and fantasy, Welles uses the fabulous to hawk the mundane, saying,

> Liliom [*sic*] like all fables, is dedicated to the proposition that the unlikely is not unnecessary. That you and I are interested in the impossible, that even in these times there is time for . . . once upon a time . . . (MUSIC UP . . . THEN DOWN) But before our play begins, Ernest Chappell I know, has a comment to make on a food preference of most people. Mr. Chappell—"[116]

Chappell then connects the magic of entertainment to sponsor Campbell Soup, extolling "the magic, matchless flavor of tomato soup."[117] This transition from storytelling to salesmanship was a hallmark of Welles's radio series, embodying the intersection of entertainment and commerce that Schaefer hoped Welles would bring to RKO. Having successfully negotiated the religious controversy of *Liliom,* Welles proposed *Life of Christ* less than a year later and set out to get prior approval for his project from various religious factions.

In August 1940, Welles sent letters to the heads of several religious congregations to see how they might feel about a film depicting an American Christ.[118] Several respondents articulated a vision of Welles as an American icon, one of the few men worthy of assuming the Christ role. One major worry that echoed the concern regarding *Liliom* had to do with the humanization of Christ, but additional problems surfaced as well, including the potential erasure of Christ's rejection by the Jewish community, and the inability of Hollywood to adopt a sacred tone for a sacred text. The reactions of clergy to Welles's proposal were mixed, but even rejections of the idea tended to praise the potential pairing of Welles and Christ.[119] The president of the American Unitarian Association expressed concern that an American Christ would fail to reflect the proper Christian spirit as exemplified by the Corpus Christi cycle:

> the inherent difficulties, from both the artistic and the religious points of view, seem to me so appallingly great that your courage leaves me breathless with admiration but pretty thoroughly skeptical as to the outcome. Your suggestion that the story might be "told simply in the spirit of a folk passion play" makes me wonder whether you have hold of the right end of the stick[.][120]

The Rev. William Barrow Pugh of the Presbyterian Church, Office of the General Assembly, took a more optimistic view:

> Frankly, I think your idea of a motion picture of the life of Christ is a most commendable one. I have often wondered why more was not done in motion pictures so far as portraying the Bible and its real message is

> concerned. Certainly the life of Christ, developed as I know you would do it, would be of inestimable value in these days.[121]

He indicates that he is aware of Welles's work from reading magazines and suggests "if any one could do what you set forth in your letter, that man would be yourself." Viewing the project with a more detached interest, George Tucker of the Protestant Episcopal Church indicates that he is "extremely interested" in the project and that its general lines seem "proper and wise."[122] L. R. Scarborough, president of the Southwestern Baptist Theological Seminary, agrees in a short, professional note that "there are possibilities for great good, if it can be done in the proper way."[123]

The willingness of clergy to accept this project specifically because Welles would be at the helm indicates the emerging power of his cinematic brand. If one regards these religious organizations as "investors" in the Christian religion, they can be heard weighing whether or not an alliance with Welles might lead to an increase in the popularity of their own product. Christian leaders were already interested in using Hollywood to spread their message, and Pugh mentions that his own meeting with a representative of the Hays office had given him "very real ideas as to the power of the motion picture industry to portray the finer aspects of life."[124] Once again, Welles would function as a type of spokesperson, but this time he would be "selling" audience identification with Christ.

The two most interesting and detailed responses, however, were from F. H. Knubel and Msgr. Fulton Sheen. The suggestions of these two men (and Welles's responses to them) reveal a great deal about the reasons for the absence of a culminating first-person singular project for RKO. Both men are generally supportive but offer very specific warnings based on prior cinematic representations of Christ and on Welles's own proposed reinterpretations of the story. Knubel, of the United Lutheran Church, approaches Welles's work as one of artistic devotion, instructing Welles, "this effort of yours must be devout."[125] Knubel also stresses that Welles should adhere closely to the gospels, being sure that "no important omission or addition so far as the Gospel of the life of Christ is concerned." He demands that the resurrection must be shown, not just the death. Furthermore, he offers a cautionary critique of Cecil B. DeMille's 1927 film, *The King of Kings*, in which "the high priest uttered a startling statement that he alone of his people was responsible for the death of Jesus. This was naturally introduced so that there would be no objections from Jewish sources of the present day." Knubel argues, "I am very far away from any anti-Semitic thoughts in my own heart but this introduction [. . .] destroyed for me the value of that picture when I saw it a number of years ago." The political question of how to portray Pontius Pilate and the Jewish community remains central to current commercial adaptations of the Christ story, a legacy of tension that is further discussed relative to Mel Gibson's *The Passion of the Christ* (2004) in the final chapter of this study.

Msgr. Sheen's letter gives a bit more insight into details of Welles's proposed project, replying specifically to several propositions by Welles and stressing Sheen's own position as a savvy Hollywood insider and a well-read humanist. Sheen argues that Welles is "quite right in assuming that the Church never denies the artist the right to point. You are also to be most heartily complimented in your resolve to handle this tremendous theme without incurring the displeasure of the Church."[126] His main points of concern are that Welles should preserve the divine nature of Christ and retain the theme of Christ's rejection by the Jews. He suggests that Welles present Christ as "what He is, namely, the Son of God. The exclusion of the miraculous and the ignoring particularly of the Resurrection would be to a Christian the same mutilation as to leave the Prince of Denmark out of Hamlet." By positioning the Bible as a "great book" akin to *Hamlet*, Sheen takes a secular approach to the project, treating Christ as a protagonist but also implying that Christ, like Hamlet, would engage the audience in his own contemplations and choices. Like Kurtz, Kane, and Hamlet, Christ could provide a powerful point of audience identification within the performance narrative.

Sheen worries, however, that Welles's attempt to move the story to an American pastoral setting will erase "the Jewish background of Christ" and his rejection "by His own people," as well as create the "artistic difficulty of presenting the Divine only through the human." Ultimately, however, Sheen is supportive of the project, and even flatters Welles: "An extraordinary genius of the Theatre such as yourself could probably do it in a way that would do credit to the Theme and to the Theatre." He even offers to meet with Welles while in Los Angeles for a lecture.[127]

Welles's response to Sheen less than a month later on October 3, 1940, clarifies that the film will be a miraculous tale, bringing the supernatural into a familiar contemporary setting. Welles promises to present Christ as "true God and true Man" and promises that his adaptation would not modernize the theme to the extent of eliminating the miraculous. He reassures Sheen,

> Nor is my choice of an un-Asiatic setting a choice intended to deny, even by intimation, that Christ is God[. . . .] A miracle was no less miraculous in Galilee than it is in Texas but the centuries, (at least for many, many of us who contemplate His story,) have invested the world in which Christ lived with the gauzy unreality of a fable.[128]

Invoking the original mission of the Mercury Theatre to bring the classics to the masses, Welles argues, "I want to make a motion picture of the Story of Christ for everybody—not just those who know it to be true. I believe I can impress everybody with the truth of the story."[129] Welles seems eager both to please institutional power—in this case, the church—and to edify the masses, two recurrent aspirations of the Wellesian brand. He asserts,

> I am terribly anxious to offend no orthodox sensibility. In all candor, however, I must admit that I am more anxious still to impress the unconcerned[. . . .] Please believe that I would never dream of giving my effort to such an undertaking if I were convinced that in any particular such a picture ran contrary to the wishes of the Church.[130]

In this letter Welles sounds distant from the "maverick" genius reputation that he would later embrace, quite willing to appease influential persons and their constituencies in order to get his work completed. However, he stresses the centrality of his experimental interpretations of classic works, in this case his desire to explore an American vision of Christ:

> I speak of my projected setting as "American." By this, I mean that the picture's esthetic will be, as much as possible for an American audience a negation of any *period sense.* Accept my assurance that I do not contemplate any attempted subtraction from the Divinity of Christ, but rather, in a special *theatre* sense, a fresh affirmation of that Divinity.[131]

Even at this early point of his career, Welles recognizes the anticommercial nature of his interests, or rather expresses a desire to extend the boundaries of what was regarded as commercially acceptable. Defending the potential divinity of his American Christ, Welles writes, "Were [the portrayal of a Divine Christ] not my sincerest intention, I should, of course, have chosen merely some God-like man rather than God Himself. And the commercial success of such a picture, as I am sure you will understand, would have been somewhat more assured."[132] Here, Welles alludes to *Citizen Kane* and his preoccupation with the first-person singular, the godlike man who dominates his most successful commercial project. In his long response to Msgr. Sheen, Welles defends his ability to create an America abstracted from history and an American figure of divinity, even at the potential risk of commercial viability. Of course, paradoxically, Welles's desire to risk commerce for art would eventually become yet another aspect of his cinematic brand and part of its long-term appeal.

The Christ project would have proved an interesting study in the development of the Wellesian first-person singular. By taking on Christ after Kurtz and Kane, Welles envisioned a trilogy that would have traced the development of subjectivity, of the "I" through three incredibly important modes of conquest: imperialism, capitalism, and religion.[133] And while it is a loss that this final film does not exist in commercial form, the clear residue of the Wellesian "I" remains in his commercial brand. In some ways this unfinished project reveals more about his evolving cinematic style than do the polished surfaces of *Citizen Kane* and *The Magnificent Ambersons*. The Christ project and *Heart of Darkness* are Wellesian in conception rather than execution, but they also open possibilities for readership and interpretation that are closed or finite in the finished films. Somewhere in a barren Texan plain, Welles's Christ figure saunters toward the horizon (does he wear spurs? carry a gun?), unfinished on film but fully realizable in the Theatre of Imagination, which was after all, Welles's first theater.

These first RKO projects reveal that even at its earliest stages, the Wellesian brand depended on the larger-than-life first-person, which ultimately is not embodied in any single character but in Welles himself. Although Welles missed his chance at box-office popularity, he won the contest of image and prestige. In notes for a speech during 1940–41, Welles clearly articulates a vision of his first-person singular role in relationship to the development of a cinematic name brand:

> There has never been a picture of consequence that has not been the product for the most part of one man—the man who dominates the making of the picture. This man can be the producer, the director, the writer, the star or even the cameraman. Pictures invariably achieve the level of this dominant personality.[134]

Ultimately, this vision was realized, and Welles—independent of RKO, George Schaefer, or any Hollywood studio—became a symbol of American prestige in film, an American auteur and an iconic American brand.

Over the course of his career, the Wellesian brand subsumed Welles himself, and many came to know him as a consummate spokesperson rather than a consummate director. As Anderegg puts it, "In the 1930s Welles was selling soup by creating a product—radio drama—that involved him in aesthetic activity[. . . .] When, however, Welles sold Paul Masson's wine [in the 1980s], he was not creating a product: he *was* the product."[135] During the RKO years, Welles himself was not yet a household name. His brand of entertainment was respected, but he was not a box-office lure.

His inability to move from promoting a product as a spokesperson toward being the product itself became a crucial obstacle to Welles's success within the Hollywood studio system. The general public would not pack a theater to consume Welles-as-director. As an actor, Welles lacked star quality. He was impressive but not seductive,[136] and he was often placed in narratives that challenged the expectations of mainstream audiences. The cult of stardom demands a visible product, a body to draw the consumer into the spectacle; therefore, directorial stardom proved useless to sell Welles's films, even as it succeeded in selling Welles as a public personality. His products became famous but not popular. The audience wanted to see movie stars, not the products of their directors, and Welles was becoming first and foremost a star director rather than a star actor.[137]

Chapter 2

Classics for the Masses: Dickens and Welles

> The star director will go out as quickly as the old time star before him. He has begun to decline already.
>
> —Orson Welles, 1939

> It is impossible to doubt, of course, that Welles is an auteur in the fullest sense.
>
> —Grahame Smith, 2003

As developed in his radio series, Welles's first-person-singular approach to adaptation depended on the insertion of a contemporary, critical eye/I into a classic text. No author interested Welles more consistently than Charles Dickens during the era of Welles's shift from radio to Hollywood,[1] in part because of Dickens's cultivation of a performative style of literature that explores the fissures between personal and public identity. Dickens's interest in narrative experimentation evoked a complex, socially constructed, first-person singular that fascinated Welles. Adapting Dickens as a classic author also heightened the Wellesian brand by association. Finally, Dickensian style translated well into Wellesian performance with its brief, serial form, which included vivid visual scenes and populist themes. Welles's adaptations of Dickens from 1938–40, which range from popular radio projects to a proposed screen version of *Pickwick Papers*, reflect the zenith of his use of the serial form and the classic literary narrative. Classic adaptation, always to remain part of the Wellesian brand, was essential to the initiation of his relationship with RKO.

The association between Welles and fellow populist showman Charles Dickens helped Welles's career move from radio into film, and established his entertainment brand as both geared to the masses and culturally respectable. Welles's relationship to master authors enhanced (and continues to enhance) his reputation as artist and was key to establishing the Wellesian brand. The story of Welles's evolving relationship with Dickens captures the process of diversifying the Wellesian entertainment brand as it moved from radio into film. This diversification of his commercial potential suggests a key difference between an auteur and a star director: the auteur, over time, establishes a market presence based on elite credibility rather than mass popularity. A "classic" rather than a "star," the auteur often finds a niche market based on perceived artistry rather than a mass market based on box-office sales.

Whereas the next chapter will discuss the connection between Joseph Conrad's style of modernist expressionism and Welles, this chapter looks at the aspects of authorship that he shared with Dickens's very different literary personality. Dickens, associated with popular culture and often credited with creating mass literary circulation, blends the concepts of "author" and "entertainer," and provides an interesting counter example of Welles's use of literary adaptation when juxtaposed against Conrad's "high" modernist style. Critics have suggested that Dickens's writing style lends itself to visual adaptation, arguing that his precinematic sensibility frames him almost as prophet, and several critics link his narrative style directly to that of Welles. For example, Grahame Smith suggests that "Welles's major stylistic tool, his reliance on long takes made possible by deep focus, would have been the perfect filmic embodiment of Dickens' vision."[2]

Welles and Dickens are linked by their efforts to circulate their work among the mass populace, to spread their art beyond elite associations. In this way, Dickens and Welles share a certain "vulgarity" that flouts the very notion of "classic" by courting mass appeal.[3] Welles is similar to Dickens in that he created a serialized form of literature-based popular entertainment and that he was able to parlay his popularity into a lucrative career that paid him as much to be a public personality as to be an "author" of "texts" (to the great chagrin of the RKO studio executives).

From 1938 to 1941, Orson Welles underwent tremendous transitions in his life, moving from theater to radio and then to film, divorcing his wife, breaking with long-time collaborator John Houseman, and encountering a roller-coaster ride between public appreciation and derision. In July 1938, he debuted his *First Person Singular* CBS radio series—also known as *Mercury Theatre on the Air* and, later, as *Campbell Playhouse*—intending to wed the performance experimentation that he had brought to the Federal Theatre Project with the income and commercial appeal that radio had consistently afforded him since his 1935 appearances in *March of Time*.[4] Over the course of 1938, Welles produced four radio plays based on the work of Charles Dickens: *A Tale of Two Cities* (July 25), *Oliver Twist* (October 2), *The Pickwick*

Papers (November 20), and *A Christmas Carol* (December 23).[5] Dickens thus became Welles's most frequently adapted author in 1938. When he was lured to Hollywood with an RKO contract in 1939, it was widely expected that he would continue his practice of adapting the "classics" for the "masses," and in 1940 rumors circulated about a pending production of *The Pickwick Papers* to star W. C. Fields. This chapter explores why that film never materialized, and why after 1938, Welles became less reliant on classic adaptation, focusing equally on experiments with the manipulative possibilities of subjectivity, narration, and mass technology.

The *First Person Singular* Radio Series

Welles's concept for the radio series *First Person Singular* represents an aesthetic bridge between the visual performance concepts he had been integrating into the theater, including multimedia experiments, and an increasing interest in bending the parameters of narrative identity that would later infuse his cinema work. Welles's work has frequently been associated with bricolage or pastiche,[6] and he freely borrowed from the aesthetic and performative traditions of one entertainment medium to enrich another. In the case of *First Person Singular,* Welles's motive was twofold: to revitalize literary classics for a mass audience and to establish himself as the first-person-singular author of these cross-media performance studies.

Welles used one performance medium to whet the appetite for adaptations in other performance modes, and he often translated texts among theater, radio, and film. CBS hoped to capitalize on the success of the Mercury Theatre in the preceding year by translating theater into radio and explicitly promoted this concept in their June 8, 1938, publicity release for the debut of *First Person Singular.*[7] Following *Dracula* and *Treasure Island, A Tale of Two Cities* was Welles's third broadcast in this series, and its June 19 press release promised Welles as the auteur of the production—responsible for narration, script preparation, and direction. Welles fed the public perception that he was the sole creator of his theatrical, radio, and cinema productions, to the detriment of his relationship with collaborators like Houseman and often at the behest of commercial sponsors like Campbell Soup.

Dickens was an ideal choice for radio adaptation precisely because of the similarities between his own serial form of writing and serial broadcast. His works collapse into small scenes that are easily cut or rearranged and can be separated in anticipation of a commercial break. In a way, the radio series itself sought to emulate the type of mass literary popularity that Dickens attained. Upon Dickens's death the *Illustrated London News* observed that his form of serial publication had given readers "a sense of habitual dependence on their contemporary, the man Charles Dickens, for a continued supply of entertainment which he alone could furnish."[8] This is precisely the kind of mass dependence on narrative that Welles sought to achieve with his weekly radio series, offering himself as the voice of literary entertainment that could glue America to the radio. The success of his strategy would be demonstrated with his ability to create mass panic in *The War of the Worlds* broadcast, during which the public clearly gave Welles an authority as entertainer that nobody—including Welles—had previously anticipated.

In 1938 radio was proving to be the primary forum for narrative experimentation, and Welles articulated his goals for radio performance in *First Person Singular* in an article for *Radio Annual*:

> Looking ahead I see radio as a great field for the presentation of literary and poetic images; as the coming great field for fantasy[. . . .] Radio can do things which the realistic theater cannot and which, because of the multiplicity of images, would be impractical in the films. A few words can conjure up a scene beyond the furthest extension of the powers of the boldest and most resourceful technicians.[9]

Welles's first Dickens radio adaptation, *A Tale of Two Cities*, embodies the narrative strategy he outlines in the above quote, particularly in terms of using dual narrators to play with the listeners' perceptions of time.

A Tale of Two Cities

Dickens's *Tale of Two Cities* fit the needs of *First Person Singular* because it both fulfilled Welles's interest in the collapse of narrated time and offered a variety of possibilities for experimentation with the retelling of the story in first-person singular. Welles made the banker Lorry the principal storyteller, giving him the ability to collapse memory into present commentary, and offering the radio listener the sense of intimacy that he had set out to achieve over the airwaves via first-person narration. The performance actually split the narration among Manette, Lorry, and Carton, thereby fragmenting the listener's identification and creating a sense of three competing authors of this tale—two of whom, Manette and Carton, were played by Welles. These experiments with the collapse of time and perspective also mark his infamous *War of the Worlds* broadcast, as well as much of his cinema work. The dual narration strategy foreshadows his initial proposal to play both Kurtz and Marlow in his unfinished RKO *Heart of Darkness*. *A Tale of Two Cities* offered Welles the chance to explore his lifelong personal and professional interest in doubling. Michael Anderegg locates this theme once more in *Citizen Kane*: "Just as there are two Charles Foster Kanes . . . so there are two Orson

Welleses, one an eccentric, difficult genius, the other a huckster and eternal television personality."[10] These Wellesian doubles are mirrored in Dickens's huckster Carton and eccentric aristocrat Darnay, and Welles was no doubt drawn to Carton's theatrical courtroom rescue of the restrained Darnay.

The doubling patterns of *A Tale of Two Cities* run from the most superficial level of analysis through to the implicit structure of the narrative itself: it is literally a tale of divided selves and cities. Often seen as a novel indicative of its time, the Carton/Darnay split can be read as a Victorian expression of anxiety, a reaction to "the emotionally disturbed period which produced it."[11] The 1930's were an unsteady era as well, plagued by post-Depression and prewar anxieties. Welles's radio experimentation depended on merging public and private narratives, taking public performance into the home, and Welles wanted to create a sense of intimacy by capturing individual experience through collective broadcast. He wanted his own power as narrator to be the connection with the mass of listeners, giving the feeling that he was speaking to them each individually within the privacy of their homes.[12]

At the same time, however, he was profoundly aware of the breadth of his new audience. In fact, he became a master of manipulating individual experience within a mass performance, while remaining ambivalent about the tension between his own reputation as a solo genius and his collaborative working process.[13] What better source for the expression of this ambivalence than Dickens's narrative, which Catherine Gallagher describes "as a nightmare of transparency, of publicly displaying what is hidden, intimate, secret"?[14] Gallagher sees the revelations of the author as parallel to the courtroom exposures performed in *A Tale of Two Cities* and points out that this complicated novel contains metalevel[15] narrative doubling as well, producing constant images of the public voice at odds with a private author.

Dickens's sense of theatricality makes him a natural choice for performance adaptation, and *A Tale of Two Cities* is often regarded as one of his most theatrical works. Leonard Manheim describes the novel as "impregnated with the spirit of the theatre" in no small part because Dickens conceived the work while he was acting in Wilkie Collins's *The Frozen Deep* with his future wife Ellen Ternan.[16] The theatrical quality of the novel may have helped result in its popularity: Harold Bloom describes it as "the most popular of Dickens's books," with the exception of *The Pickwick Papers* and the "annual phenomenon of *A Christmas Carol*."[17] Welles adapted each of these novels as well during 1938, putting on a one-man revival of Dickens's works as radio drama.

Dickens's work lent itself easily to Wellesian adaptation since, as Sergei Eisenstein argues, Dickens achieves an "optical quality" that makes the visual image "inseparable from the aural."[18] Although Eisenstein is addressing cinematic technique, the oral/visual narrative quality is perhaps even more essential to radio, where the performer must establish a relationship with the listener through narrative alone, suggesting and evoking optical scenes through aural experience. As Eisenstein observes, Dickens used cinematic technique before the age of cinema, providing a clear example of intertextual performance long before theories emerged to accommodate an understanding of the complexity of his form. Before the technical equipment to create cinema existed, Dickens employed film techniques such as frame composition and close-up. He even used a rhetorical dissolve in the final chapter of *A Tale of Two Cities*.[19] Therefore, this text in particular begged adaptation into an emerging performance media that could fully showcase Dickens's narrative devices, and Welles could hardly have been unaware of its highly successful film adaptation starring Ronald Colman in 1935. In fact, his awareness of this film and the appearance of W. C. Fields's *David Copperfield* the same year probably prevented his consideration of them as RKO adaptations in 1939, although their success for MGM may have sparked RKO's interest in a Fields-Welles collaboration on *Pickwick* once the studio had contracted Welles.

Both the text of *A Tale of Two Cities* and the radio play depict a constant fear of exposure, particularly as it relates to narrative. Manette fears, and the reader fears for him, the discovery of his hidden jailhouse narrative, a narrative that ultimately threatens the security of his daughter's happiness and, in fact, her very life. Similarly, Darnay fears the exposure of the same story, but from a different narrative origin. Manette and Darnay share circumstances of past plot, but each conceals his perspective on the St. Evrémonde plot within very different narrative forms. Darnay's narrative exists as lived past, whereas Manette's exists as recorded memory. Darnay's past is therefore always mutable, open to reinterpretation, whether by a jury or by the reader. When Carton intervenes in Darnay's story at his first trial, he alters "reality" by adding a layer of narrative—he transforms the story from treason to twins. But when Manette's story is discovered by Defarge, it is revealed as static "truth," clear evidence against Darnay. The two French trials are conflated in Welles's version, but in both the novel and the radio play, the courtroom provides a forum for reinterpretation of Darnay's past; an audible struggle even ensues over who can control textual meaning for the listener in Welles's production. The Defarges turn the public tide against Darnay by trumping Manette's spoken word with his written word, thus ultimately controlling meaning and destiny.[20] Carton alone remains as the master-author, controlling the outcome of both trials, scripting his own death, and ensuring the legacy of its interpretation with his final vision of "a beautiful city and a brilliant people rising from this abyss[. . . .] the lives for which I lay down my life, peaceful, useful, prosperous and happy [. . .] Her with a child upon her bosom, who bears my name."[21]

Welles's production focuses on these anxieties of storytelling and interpretation, juxtaposing Manette's narrative with Madame Defarge's knitting, which Bloom calls "a metaphor for the storytelling of the novel itself."[22] The opening scene of Welles's broadcast reveals Manette in prison, writing with charcoal dipped in blood, the tale that he will hide but that will resurface. This opening marks a shift from the draft manuscript for the broadcast, which opened with Welles, as Jarvis Lorry, stating, "This is a history of events that took place in London and across the Channel in France in the years immediately preceding and during the great French Revolution. My name is Jarvis Lorry." In the actual broadcast, Lorry's speech is moved to the end of scene 2, therefore shifting the focus onto Manette's narrative within Lorry's. The change in narrative progression effected a change in Welles's own roles: he was to play Lorry in the rehearsal script, but in the broadcast he plays Manette and Carton. He thereby shifts the listener's point of identification from the exterior observer to the writer-within-the-narrative, particularly exploring the struggle to control meaning and the individual fear of being "misread" by the masses, fears mirrored by the radio series itself.[23] Welles's notorious *War of the Worlds* broadcast only three months later would tangibly illustrate the danger of mass narrative misinterpretation.

The changes between script and performance are interesting in several ways. First, they once again show the improvisational and collaborative method of Wellesian production, a method very much at odds with the requirements of RKO studio structures of script production, marketing, and editing. Welles's style of radio adaptation was ill-suited to cinematic modes of production, despite the studio's expectation that he would be able to translate his method into their structures. Thematically, however, the last-minute changes in the production emphasized explorations of identity as a negotiation between public and private selves—a hallmark of Wellesian performance texts.

Oliver Twist

The script for the October 2, 1938, broadcast of *Oliver Twist* shows Welles employing many of the same narrative conventions that he used in the earlier *Tale of Two Cities*, including beginning in medias res, narrating the story directly to the viewer via an interested observer (Brownlow in this case), and splitting the aural identification of the listener. However, the effect of these conventions in the *Oliver Twist* broadcast are much less sophisticated in their approach and therefore less powerful in their effect than that of *Tale of Two Cities*. The performance emphasizes the progressive political aspect of the Wellesian brand, subordinating first-person constructions of meaning to first-person moralizing speeches. In addition, the pattern of narration does not hold together well. Welles's *Oliver Twist* often shifts between Brownlow as a primary narrator and Oliver, who narrates sections of his life himself, to the confusion of the script typist as well as the potential listener.[24]

The social critique present in the original novel remains a central focus, and Welles echoes Dickens's criticisms of capital punishment, bureaucratic waste, and government poverty policies, showing that a shift between generations and continents had not made these issues less relevant. Through the character of the beadle, Mr. Bumble, the incompetence of Judge Fang, and the meditations of Fagin on capital punishment, Welles matches Dickens's balance between social reformer and showman.

The script makes extreme cuts in Dickens's text, particularly in the very early and very late parts of the novel pertaining to Oliver's life before London, his evil half brother, and the mystery of his parentage. The broadcast opens by dropping the listener directly into the scene of Oliver's arrest for picking Brownlow's pocket. Using Brownlow to narrate the event allows the listener to focus on Brownlow's relationship with Oliver, but the confusing and melodramatic mystery of Oliver's identity in the novel is omitted from the radio broadcast. In Welles's broadcast, he is simply a stranger to Brownlow, no more related to his interests or his family than any other street urchin. Rose and her family are cut from the text as well, and thus the question of Oliver's parentage is omitted from this version entirely, with even the veiled reference to his illegitimate birth crossed out in the rehearsal script.[25]

In line with this adaptation's emphasis of social reform, the script keeps a description of the parish board's decision to limit the diet of those in the poorhouse to "three meals of thin gruel a day, an onion twice a week, and half a roll on Sundays."[26] Oliver's own direct request for more gruel (famously present in the musical adaptation *Oliver!*) is kept only as a secondhand report from an outraged Bumble to the Chairman of the Board for the Parish. The script privileges Brownlow's retrospective, rational, social critique over direct action, speech, or dialogue in many cases, making it a less immediate narrative than *Tale of Two Cities*. Since very little of the actual action of the narrative happens to our first-person narrator, the show suffers from a didacticism not present in the earlier adaptation of *Tale of Two Cities*.

The social message focuses in particular on capital punishment and child welfare, and the Chairman's reaction to Bumble's story of Oliver's request for more gruel is delivered directly to the audience and followed by a musical flourish:

> BUMBLE: Oliver Twist has asked for more.
> VOICES: (GENERAL AMAZEMENT) What! For What! . . .
> CHAIRMAN: That boy will be hung. I know that boy will be hung!
> MUSIC . . .

Since the actual audio of the boys eating and Oliver asking for "more" is cut from the draft script, the performance narrative favors the secondhand account by Bumble, followed by Brownlow's assessment of the ensuing action of the board: "On the workhouse gate next morning a bill was posted offering a reward for five pounds to anybody who would take Oliver off the hands of the parish."[27] Thus the audience is directed to focus not on Oliver's action but on the government's perspective and role in his fate. In contrast to *A Tale of Two Cities*, the first part of *Oliver Twist* sounds more like an editorial commentary on social policy than the immediate drama often associated with Welles's radio productions.

Welles even decided to take on a social issue that Dickens failed to confront, by softening the anti-Semitic rhetoric surrounding Fagin—not referring to him as "the Jew" of Dickens's original text, for example. Instead, Welles depicts him as an example of the failure of bureaucracy and capital punishment in the justice system rather than as Satan himself, the embodiment of Christian fantasies of Jewish evil. Thus Welles keeps social critique while reducing the pervasive anti-Semitism of the era, which is no small feat. Welles may well have traded one ethnic stereotype for another, however, since the draft script suggests Fagin speaks in Irish brogue and refers to his dangling red hair as he faces the irate mob. In addition, the anti-Semitic connotations of greed and cannibalism do remain from the original text.

One example of Fagin's social critique occurs as he directly addresses the role of capital punishment in increasing, rather than decreasing, crime, as Oliver wakes and overhears him meditating on the topic while counting his hidden treasure:

> FAGIN: What a find [*sic*] thing capital punishment is! Dead men never repent. Dead men never bring awkward stories to light. Ah, it's a fine thing for the trade. Five of 'em strung up in a row, and none left to play booty or turn white-livered.

In the radio version, the listener is left to ponder what Fagin means, since we lack the background to contextualize his thoughts. At this point, Oliver steps in to narrate his own story, and of course, Oliver cannot explain Fagin's thoughts—those of a criminal adult—to us. This is a major problem in this adaptation: the narrator is either Brownlow, who is largely uninvolved in the events of the story, or Oliver, who is a child and therefore unable to explain events fully. With Fagin playing a much larger role in this narrative than Sikes or Dodger, the criminal mind becomes embodied in his voice, which speaks rarely and in fragments.

Additionally, the use of Welles to play the violent Fagin splits the audience sympathies to confusing effect. Oliver and Brownlow appear on the page as less interesting characters, but one could hardly imagine the listener identifying with Fagin. Whereas the broadcast initially appears to critique capital punishment through Fagin, it then places the listener in the position of accepting it as his fitting punishment at the end of the broadcast. In these ways, the broadcast is at odds with itself structurally and thematically, although it is hard to interpret the effect of the actual broadcast from its only currently available form, the draft script.

In another scene of social critique, Judge Fang represents an unfair, uncompassionate justice system, with Fang mainly represented as a series of banging gavel sounds that override any attempts by Brownlow or the Police Officer to testify in Oliver's case. The bookstall owner does not come forward in the radio version to clear Oliver; rather Oliver tells his story about watching Dodger pick Brownlow's pocket himself, directly to the listener and to Brownlow. Brownlow offers to pay the fine for Oliver's crime and takes him away without external evidence as to his innocence. Oliver still faints at his hearing, which allows for a well-placed commercial break, after which we return to Brownlow's home and (along with the disoriented Oliver) try to learn more about our new surroundings. Narratively, Welles uses Dickens's short literary scenes to fit the space and design of commercial broadcast, but to disorienting effect in this production.

In the second half of the broadcast, the elements of social commentary are subordinated dramatically to melodrama via the character Nancy. Once Oliver is kidnapped back to Fagin's gang, the radio story departs radically from the novel, cutting Oliver's relationship with Rose, life in the country, and the revelation of his parentage. Instead, Oliver's attempt to break into the country house with Sikes lands him with an anonymous Doctor, and Nancy tells Brownlow where to find him. The key scene that is retained from the original, however, is Nancy's murder scene.

Nancy is the only woman in Fagin's gang in the radio script, and she has a maternal connotation from the first time Oliver describes her. The irony of Dickens's description of Bess and Nancy as "nice girls" is gone, replaced by the child's un-ironic view of Nancy: "She wore a red dress and a great deal of hair hanging loose around her neck. She seemed to me a very nice lady."[28]

With Nancy as an unambivalently sympathetic figure, protecting Oliver from Sikes's dog and telling Brownlow where to find him, the violence of Sikes's murder of Nancy is made even more outrageous and sensational to the listener. This scene puts violent melodrama very much at the front of the production, and is gruesome in its use of literary and audio detail.

> NANCY: Bill, dear Bill, you can't have the heart to kill me! Bill. . . . Bill
> SIKES: Let go of me!
> SOUND OF BLOW
> NANCY: Bill, Bill, for dear God's sake, for your own, for mine . . . stop before you spill my blood! I have been true to you, upon my guilty soul I have!
> SIKES: Let go of me, you devil, let go!
> SOUND OF CLUB ON HER FACE
> NANCY: Bill! Bill! SOUND OF ANOTHER BLOW
> NANCY: Bill!
> FINAL HORRIBLE SCREAM . . . THEN COMPLETE SILENCE.

The use of "complete silence" in radio is a powerful tool, as Welles's *War of the Worlds* broadcast would again prove. The specificity of the sound cues is startling (how does one create the sound of a "club on her face" in particular?) But one can also assume that the violence, familiar to Welles's listeners on *The Shadow*, may have been riveting to the audience. Welles was finding ways to thwart the censors and to exploit the gruesome possibilities of imagination. The very fact that listeners are not shown the details of Nancy's death allows them, with the help of audio cues, to imagine whatever scenario they find most horrifying.

Welles's adaptation of *Oliver Twist* may have been less finely crafted than his *Tale of Two Cities*, but he was clearly finding ways to push the conventions of sound use, literary adaptation, and narrative manipulation in ways that would very shortly catapult him to fame via his Halloween broadcast. In addition, he was emphasizing contemporary social critique in tandem with mass entertainment, just as he had on stage in the "Voodoo" *Macbeth* and antifascist *Julius Caesar*. This would be a persistent theme in his RKO cinema career, and ultimately maintaining the balance between progressive politics and entertaining art would test the limits of RKO's patience with Welles in his incomplete projects such as *It's All True* and *Heart of Darkness*.

Even before the sponsorship of Campbell Soup, *Mercury Theatre on the Air* was positioning itself as a showcase of auteur adaptation. In the buildup to the *War of the Worlds* broadcast, CBS promoted Welles first and foremost as an artistic master at adaptation of the classics. Dickens was a key author in Welles's collection of texts for adaptation, and only two weeks after *Oliver Twist* aired, it was highlighted with the earlier *Tale of Two Cities* in the marketing of upcoming shows. A press release on October 20, 1938, was titled "Works of Wells, Dickens, Ibsen to be 'Mercury Theater' [*sic*] Presentations." The release outlined upcoming productions, including H. G. Wells's *War of the Worlds*, and the November broadcast of *The Pickwick Papers*, to focus "principally on the famous court-room episode." It also referenced Welles's recent appearances "as 'Oliver Twist,' Sidney Carton in 'A Tale of Two Cities,' Brutus in 'Caesar' and Rochester in 'Jane Eyre.'" By representing Welles as the voice of Oliver (erroneously, according to the draft script, which lists Kingsley Coulton in the role),[29] the press release suggests that Welles was simply becoming associated with the voice of the lead in whatever masterwork he had adapted, an association that reinforced Welles's own desire to create an image of himself as both star and director, and to transfer this image into a lucrative Hollywood film contract.

But even as he used the classics to present himself as the quintessential first- person-singular author of his productions, Welles's work was heavily dependent on a complex negotiation with audiences, sponsors, and fellow actors. This transaction emerges clearly during his final Dickens adaptation of 1938, *A Christmas Carol*.

A Christmas Carol

A Christmas Carol differed from Welles's earlier adaptations in that he inherited this fourth and final Dickens production from his commercial sponsors, Campbell Soup. *First Person Singular* had now become *Campbell Playhouse*, and this would be the fourth year of their popular presentation of *A Christmas Carol*. As Guerric DeBona notes, Dickens became enormously popular in the 1930s, and *Christmas Carol* in particular emerged as a cultural icon.[30] The draft script for the show demonstrates a tight level of control anticipated by the sponsor, including casting the return of Lionel Barrymore as Ebenezer Scrooge. Lionel had been sponsored as Scrooge by Campbell Soup since 1934, although his brother John had to step in for him at the last minute in 1936 when Lionel's wife died.[31] The show was popular with the company, the audience, and Lionel, and the sponsor wanted to integrate Welles into this mix smoothly. The "Suggested Carol Opening" scripts the introduction for Welles—a critical part of his vision of performance, the moment that he felt established or lost intimacy with the audience. The script suggests, "Introduction from Orson Welles in New York—planting fact that this is

Campbell's Christmas present to the listener—that it's the fourth year of its presentation, etc. etc. (Welles—as Campbell's spokesman)." The script further anticipates the opening exchange between Barrymore and Welles—no improvisation required: "In introducing Barrymore, Welles makes use of the phrase we have used for three years, in describing him:—'America's grandest character actor.'" To which Barrymore would respond how happy he was to be there once again with, "as much respect and admiration as *I* have for Orson Welles—whom I might describe as '*Radio's* grandest actor.'"[32]

One could anticipate that this particular stage might be too small to share, that Welles would not take pleasure in subordinating his performance concepts (his own entertainment brand) to a soup company and its commercial traditions. Barrymore, suffering from a sudden illness, reportedly his crippling arthritis, never appeared. The actual performance concluded with a "Follow Script" announcement: "We are sorry that Lionel Barrymore, our Scrooge in past years, was not able to come to New York to be with us tonight but we hope that he will resume his pleasant habit next year." He did, in fact, and Welles would return from Hollywood to play narrator to Barrymore's Scrooge in 1939. But by then, radio seemed more a source of easy money than a forum for artistic experimentation for Welles.

Welles himself (in contrast to his RKO contract) was willing to share the stage when it served the purposes of what he considered good entertainment and good company. Almost exactly two years later he and John Barrymore would parody themselves as Shakespearean actors who were also vaudevillian hacks on the Rudy Vallee show,[33] and Welles promoted his Campbell Playhouse and later the Lady Esther series by bringing in other guest stars to lure audiences to the show. The Lady Esther series had weekly surveys by the firm Pedlar and Ryan to ascertain just which stars were crowd favorites, as well as to gauge Welles's own popularity. Anticipating this kind of commercial pressure even before he entered Hollywood, Welles prided himself in his hucksterism, confessing to *Time*, "I am essentially a hack, a commercial person. If I had a hobby, I would immediately make money on it or abandon it."[34] This statement stood in stark contrast to Houseman's attitude, which led him to refer disdainfully to their sponsors for the *Campbell Playhouse* as "the soup people."[35] But Welles's own path was leading him in a different direction from Houseman and the theater, as the *Time* magazine article summarized: "Nor does he want the Mercury to pin all its faith on the classics."[36] Late 1938 seems to mark a turning point away from the coauthored mission statement of the Mercury published by Houseman and Welles the previous August, which explicitly focused on making the classics available to the general public at a reasonable price.[37]

Despite shared authority and credit, Welles was emerging even at this stage as his own name brand. A May 1938 article in *Time* was, after all, simply titled, "Marvelous Boy." As Welles moved the Mercury Theatre onto the airwaves, radio permitted him to experiment with conventions of spoken word and perspective in a manner that powerfully enhanced the impression of a dominant, *singular*, and *personal* voice. Radio allowed Welles to experiment in ways that theater no longer offered, and he promised to "treat radio itself with the intelligence and respect such a beautiful and powerful medium deserves."[38] In a June 29, 1938, interview with the *New York Times*, Welles emphasized his interest in language-as-performance, explaining, "Language never lives until it is spoken aloud."[39] Radio offered an ideal medium to exhibit how his interpretation of language-as-performance would adapt from stage to screen.

Welles was courting Hollywood even as he juggled continuing stage and radio productions, seeking to widen his sphere of influence within the entertainment industry. In a speech to the National Council of Teachers of English in New York, Welles lambasted theater in favor of film, calling its entertainment value "vastly inferior to the movies."[40] Radio could do things that realistic theater could not, he argued in a draft manuscript of an article for *Radio Annual*: "A few words can conjure up a scene beyond the furthest extension of the powers of the boldest and most resourceful technicians."[41] Welles craved performance technology that could adequately convey his ongoing absorption with first-person perspective, and while radio offered possibilities that theater did not, film offered an even wider variety of possibilities for experimentation with narrative in word and image.

The Allure of Hollywood

Welles knew that ideas regarding the reinterpretation of the classics had a market in Hollywood, but he wanted to hold out for an offer that would give him artistic control over his works while securing the public perception of him as a budding star director—a dominant presence in the creation and marketing of a distinct brand of entertainment. The perception of Welles's potential to fill this role palpably increased after his *War of the Worlds* production on Halloween of 1938.

The concept of the auteur had yet to be articulated (and it is still being refined), but consumers were increasingly demanding identifiable, emblematic market personalities who transcended the role of "spokesperson." Welles had already emerged as a theatrical star by appearing on the cover of *Time* in May 1938 for the "Marvelous Boy" article. The article pairs Welles's name with both the classics and modern adaptation by captioning his cover photograph "George Orson Welles: Shadow to Shakespeare, Shoemaker to Shaw." This balanced coupling of popular culture and "high" art would become a hallmark of the Wellesian brand. Still, there were aspects to his growing legend that caused him discomfort. The article suggests, "He loves the mounting Welles legend, but wants to keep the record straight. Stories of his recent affluence [. . .] annoy him."[42] The ability to manage money eluded Welles throughout his Hollywood career, and initially he was looking for a film deal that would help finance his other projects as well as his personal lifestyle. He wanted an opportunity that matched his growing image and that would diversify his name brand entertainment.

Before the RKO offer in 1939, he had already rejected an MGM contract that required him to serve an apprenticeship under King Vidor.[43] He also rejected a 1937 offer from David O. Selznick but referred Selznick to Houseman as an able script selector and adaptor. Selznick's offer had not contained a high enough profile for Welles, who responded in a letter that he would be planning productions in which he would appear himself.[44] Sidney Howard, who worked with Selznick on *Gone with the Wind*, had also become aware of the work of Houseman and Welles, and even if he did not take time to spell either of their names correctly,[45] he did take time away from finishing *Gone with the Wind* to remark positively on their Federal Theatre production of *Dr. Faustus*. Howard additionally suggested that they try a modern-dress *Julius Caesar*, since he believed that "the best way to stimulate the writing of good modern plays is to keep the classics a part of what goes on."[46] Welles and Houseman did create a modern-dress *Julius Caesar* as their first play for the Mercury Theatre, and it opened to outstanding reviews on November 11, 1937, shortly after Howard's note. Welles was aware of the importance of knowing the right people to ensure the logistics of production, and he worked hard to enhance his budding Wellesian brand. As early as 1937, he was deemphasizing his creative reliance on Houseman and others to tap into the small circle of Hollywood executives like Selznick who could help secure a contract that would offer creative license as well as security—a type of deal that had eluded others in Hollywood.

By 1939 Welles had landed his contract with RKO, a studio known for its focus on creativity and independence in design,[47] and his contract stunned the media and Hollywood with its generous terms. The *New York Times* reported on August 20, 1939, "Every one of the thousands of actors who have passed through Hollywood during the last quarter-century has striven to get the same kind of a deal but no one else has succeeded."[48] When he ultimately went to Hollywood, he went in style, renting the home of Mary Pickford and Buddy Rogers, and creating a media stir over his starlike behavior. The contract was lucrative and lax in studio supervision, but it demanded a pace of production that would become a severe problem for Welles. RKO wanted Welles to reproduce the success of his radio reinventions of the classics, and to produce these films at a fairly rapid pace. After the debacle of the never-completed *Heart of Darkness*, however, RKO and Welles would shift their goals in diametrically opposed directions. RKO still wanted Welles to remake the classics, while he turned away from this strategy for a variety of personal and creative reasons, creating a breach that ultimately would force him out of his contract and label him a high risk for other studios.

The signs of potential conflict between Welles and the studio were present in his earlier relationships with sponsors and colleagues, and even in the very title of his series, *First Person Singular*. As James Naremore points out, "a more egocentric title one could not imagine."[49] He had developed a reputation as an enfant terrible by this point, and after the controversy over *War of the Worlds*, the media referred to him alternately as a baby genius or a demon: "Marvelous Boy" or "Bearded Bogyman"; "Child" or "Hobgoblin of the Air." Either way, the articles implied a decided lack of maturity and reliability.

Nevertheless, Welles held great commercial promise as an entertainer. He was a master of disguise, a mercurial magician able to move fluidly between the poles of genius and madman. He could play roles of almost any age and often delighted audiences with his flexibility (see Figure 2). Similarly, his radio work was the product of equal parts research, collaboration, improvisation and hucksterism. He would use much the same formula for his films, but cinema as a structure required more time and money to implement his approach.

In part, Welles's difficulty with RKO developed out of his interest in constructing narrative from a first-person-singular perspective. As discussed more fully in chapter 1, his interest in representing stream of consciousness, intersubjectivity, and deconstruction of reality contradicted his self-promotion as a commercial lowbrow entertainer. This unusual combination of characteristics became a hallmark of Welles's performances, one that Anderegg traces through his study of Welles, Shakespeare, and popular culture. Analyzing the ability of MGM's 1935 *David Copperfield* to bridge the span between "classic" and "popular," DeBona similarly remarks, "Dickens-ness" appealed to "leaders of industry, the Arnoldian intellectuals, the respectable middle class, and even the anonymous masses."[50] Welles was not only a significant contributor to a culture that mingled the huckster with the intellectual but also a product of it. To meet the demands of quick and yet quality production, Welles turned to the literary classics, as he had on stage and radio before.

Resisting RKO: The Economics of Experimentation

Through fall of 1939 and 1940, Welles was under economic pressure from a variety of fronts, even as the nation itself was feeling the pressure of upcoming war involvement. First, Welles's divorce from Virginia was causing financial strain; second, he chose to go on a lecture tour that underpaid him and took him away from Hollywood during a critical period in fall of 1940; third, *Citizen Kane* was proving controversial both in its provocation of Hearst and in its coauthorship controversy with Herman J. Mankiewicz; fourth, he was having great trouble negotiating the demands of Campbell Soup for his radio series; and finally, he was failing to fulfill the rapid-pace production that his RKO contract required of him. Both Welles and the studio realized that he had to start working immediately on a new idea that would rescue them.

Both the divorce and lecture tour put pressure on Welles in the fall of 1940, as his correspondence with his attorney, Arnold Weissberger, indicates. Virginia was seeking additional funds to send their daughter, Christopher, to private preschool, and Weissberger was trying to avoid the additional payments while maintaining the assertion that Welles was Christopher's sole means of financial support in order to challenge the draft, if needed. In response to Virginia's request for a hundred-dollar initiation fee and twenty-eight dollars a month for the school, Weissberger advised Welles that he would

> stall Virginia along by slow correspondence until the first numbers under the draft are called. If your number should be chosen, I think it would be feasible to offer to make the requested payments (which are relatively small)[. . . .] If, on the other hand, your number is not called, I will write Virginia that you have fulfilled your obligations to Christopher under the separation agreement.[51]

The controversy with Virginia continued during October and November 1940, and although Welles did eventually pay the preschool entry fee (against the counsel of Weissberger), he rejected Virginia's request for the monthly stipend after his draft number was drawn 5,283rd, making it unlikely that he would be called early or, in fact, at all. Weissberger remarked on the contrast between Welles's luck and that of Jimmy Stewart.[52] Welles's luck, however, was Virginia and Christopher's loss, and Weissberger deducted an extra hundred dollars from their rent support to pay for shipping household items to Welles, commenting to Welles that this would "be a sort of invisible reimbursement of your payment to Christopher."[53]

Welles's luck did not translate into skill at managing his income, and by mid-November he was in dire financial straits, unable to afford a thousand-dollar donation to the Hollywood Community Chest (a donation he seemed unwilling to make regardless).[54] His financial pressures were acute after his autumn lecture tour. The tour depleted his funds and distracted him at a time when he needed to cultivate connections and relationships in his new profession as a Hollywood film director-writer-star. Welles's assistant Richard Baer confided to Weissberger that the tour was an impractical failure that paid only forty-five hundred dollars, and

> took him away from something a good deal more important and even more productive from both an artistic and an income point of view. While we had first thought that the ten day intermission after the close of the picture [*Citizen Kane*] was not particularly serious, I cannot still feel that this is true.[55]

Desperate for cash after spending his last funds on a party for himself at the close of the lecture tour, Welles realized he had to start working immediately on a new idea for an RKO project, while simultaneously worrying about building up his cash reserves.

In this crisis, Welles returned to a familiar pattern—he looked toward the Mercury, Houseman, and possible adaptations of earlier projects for RKO. Welles wired Houseman on November 28, "Hope to come east for a Christmas week or so and see much of you. How about a job on your Campbell Playhouse? Every means of income, as you possibly know, has been cut off and I have no prospects whatever."[56] Weissberger was also growing increasingly nervous about Welles's finances and asked Richard Baer to "Please let me know what the plans are, if any, with respect to the second picture [in the RKO contract]. Is Orson likely to commence it before the first of the year? We cannot possibly approach RKO for reallocation of the contract payments until the second picture is under way."[57] Weissberger was even more emphatic by December 26, 1940, reminding Welles that

> we are in default for not having completed the picture [*Citizen Kane*] by October 1st, and for not having commenced the second picture by December 1st. If for any reason RKO should wish to take advantage of any breach on our part, it could readily use this[. . . .] I would propose we specify completion the first picture by February 1st 1941 [. . .] the second picture by April 1st 1941 [. . .] the third within 90 days after completion of the second.[58]

Welles needed a story idea fast, and if past patterns were a predictor, he would return to adapt one of his radio classics, an approach that would allow him to recycle a partial script and actors.

Welles and Houseman had brought up the idea for an adaptation of *Pickwick Papers* to radio executives representing Campbell Soup in New York at a September 29, 1939, meeting in which they assigned grades to possible story adaptation ideas. This preliminary meeting focused on adapting what they regarded as "classics," whether from present or past authors. They considered scripts ranging from *The Great Gatsby* to *Trilby,* and would later be involved with many film productions of these texts. For example, Welles's successful 1938 radio performance as Rochester was reprised in the 1944 *Jane Eyre,* an idea discussed at this meeting. Welles used two radio shows as sketches for *The Magnificent Ambersons,* one by the same title from October 29, 1939, and the earlier radio play *Seventeen* from October 16, 1938. Welles reportedly played the recording of the Mercury radio version of *The Magnificent Ambersons* to convince RKO president George Schaefer to produce it.[59]

At the September 1939 meeting, Houseman and Welles both gave an "A" to *Pickwick* as a story idea, and the main resistance seems to have been from two executives who had not read the novel but promised to listen to the recording of the October 1938 Mercury radio production, featuring Welles as Sergeant Buzzfuzz. The idea of adapting *Pickwick Papers* into a new medium remained interesting enough for Welles to suggest to reporters for the *Saturday Evening Post* six months later that he had "wanted to make Pickwick with W. C. Fields, but that great actor was under contract elsewhere."[60] Certainly *The Pickwick Papers* would have been a natural choice for Welles at this juncture. It offered an already completed scenario, coupled with the appeal of a major star already associated with Dickens through his success as Micawber in MGM's *David Copperfield.*

Why then didn't Welles use it? The answers are complex and several. The changes in Welles's life and his relationship with RKO over the next year suspended the era of classic adaptation for Welles and took his career in a new direction following his first released RKO film, *Citizen Kane.* Add the well-analyzed Kane controversy to the other disasters for Welles in the years between 1939 and 1941,[61] and it becomes apparent that Welles was no longer interested in translating the classics for the masses, despite RKO's hesitance to abandon a formula for economic success that they felt would result in larger profits.

RKO had hired Welles, in the words of Naremore, as a "jack-of-all-trades who would produce a picture a year, and though he seemed to have half the classic literature of the Western world on his list of proposed films, his stay at RKO was littered with rejected or abandoned scripts."[62] As late as 1940 both Welles and the media still thought his first RKO picture would be the adaptation of *Heart of Darkness,* although he was aware of getting a "bit of pushing around and stalling on the budget."[63] Between 1940 and 1941, there is an interesting pattern in the ideas that he picked up and then rejected. During this period he shifted away from his concept of routinely adapting the classics for the masses, although he did retain interest in adaptation. For example, he tried to get the title registration for *Jane Eyre* away from David O. Selznick in December 1940, two years after he played Rochester on radio and three years before he would play the role under Robert Stevenson's direction.[64] But he was also developing a greater interest in contemporary authors and unusual, experimental projects that foregrounded his other narrative interests: interrogations of subjectivity, primitivism, and the line between truth and fiction. In fact, until his 1948 *Macbeth*, Welles would not really bring a "classic" piece of literature to film as a director.

Instead, Welles's creative interest shifted to current topics of politics and identity, always themes of his adaptations. Specifically, he literally moved south of the border. This new focus on Latin America may have been stirred, in part at least, by his relationship with the Mexican actress Dolores Del Rio. As little as a month after the 1939 New York meeting in which he and Houseman had discussed adapting *Pickwick*, he was spotted carrying the book *Conquest of Mexico* into a New York City film meeting, though he deflected the question of it as a possible film project.[65] Even as his romance with Del Rio waxed and waned[66] his interest in Latin America increased, and over the next two years, Welles would propose several Latin American story ideas to RKO: *The Way to Santiago* (a.k.a. *Mexican Melodrama*),[67] a film that mingles the exploration of the first-person-singular perspective with that of national identity; *It's All True*, the unfinished Brazilian documentary discussed in depth in chapter 4; and *Unnamed Mexican Story*, a variation on agitprop focusing on class liberation of Mexico. In all these projects, Welles continued to explore the first-person-singular perspective that began with his radio series. But these story ideas also indicated a fundamental shift in Welles's thinking from his Campbell Playhouse era, during which he had focused on promoting himself as a reinventor of the classics.

By 1941, aggravated by increasing tension with RKO, Welles was ready to risk dissatisfying the studio by embarking on projects that deviated from the classics because original works would reinforce his image as star director and let his work appear undiluted by associations with other creators. In short, Welles was ready to risk originality, particularly after the volatile writing dispute with Herman Mankiewicz over coauthorship of *Citizen Kane*. Following the release of *Citizen Kane*, he would continue his exploration of the first-person-singular viewpoint without the same level of dependence on adapting classics. Isolated by the studio and the public, he came to believe that his best hope for success and artistic freedom came through accepting a certain amount of isolation and independence. His idea for *The Pickwick Papers* became outdated in that it would not feature him in the central role and would limit his new desire to be regarded as a creator of original screenplays rather than a master of adaptation.

Welles never adapted Dickens onto film despite the fact that he considered such a project both publicly and privately, and worked with Dickens more than any other author in the year preceding his Hollywood move. Nevertheless, Welles often drew on his large pool of radio adaptations as sketches for film projects, and he continued to cross-market his entertainment brand throughout his career. It would have been hard to make a new version of *A Tale of Two Cities* so closely following Ronald Colman's Academy Award–nominated version. On the other hand, it must have been hard for RKO to resist capitalizing on the other Dickens success in 1935, George Cukor's *David Copperfield*, starring W. C. Fields, and it does appear that the studio briefly considered a partnership between Welles and Fields for a version of *The Pickwick Papers*. Ultimately, Welles's *Pickwick Papers* did not get made for a variety of reasons, the least interesting of which is contract difficulty with Fields. Since Fields had been on loan from Paramount to MGM for *David Copperfield*, it seems unlikely that RKO could not have worked out this obstacle. The real impediment to this project stems from Welles's own developing Hollywood persona. *Citizen Kane* proved an educational experience for Welles, both disillusioning and redemptive. He emerged from the tumultuous years 1938–41 with a clearer perception of his own ambitions and aesthetic interest in the first-person singular as a means of modernist expression of alienation, as well as an increasing desire to explore psychological primitivism and the blurry line between reality and fiction.

Welles does leave us traces of his imagined versions of Dickens on film. The radio plays of 1938 are vivid entertainment spectacles in their own right, and certainly Welles strove throughout his career for intertextuality, integrating film clips into stage performances such as *Too Much Johnson* and *Five Kings*, and capturing his radio finesse with dialogue and sound experimentation in later films. His experiments with lighting, sound effects, and staging influenced each of the three main performance mediums in which he worked—theater, radio, and film—as well as his new favorite medium for performance of himself as a brand name, television.

By August 1940, Welles had mailed letters to leaders of religious congregations to gather reactions to his proposed *Life of Christ* project, leaving behind *The Pickwick Papers*. Juxtaposing the prospect of playing Christ with that of backing Fields's performance in *Pickwick*, it seems safe to say that

Welles chose the first-person singular over classic adaptation, an interest that is prophesied in an early typed journal entry probably written around his twentieth birthday: "we are all of us merchants of our biography, buying the future with our past."[68] Indeed, Welles bought his way into Hollywood with his adaptations of Dickens classics like *A Tale of Two Cities, The Pickwick Papers,* and *A Christmas Carol.* He bought his way back out again, however, with his commitment to creating himself as a brand name based on controversy and innovation, and this long-term investment in his image would cost him short-term box-office returns.

Chapter 3

Exploiters in Surroundings Not Healthy for a White Man: Primitivism and the Identity Detour

> The story is of a man and a girl in love[. . . .] There is an unhappy ending which we won't need to mention, man dies and the girl goes away unfulfilled. There are cannibals, shootings, petty bickering among the bureaucrats, native dances, a fascinating girl, gorgeous, but black, a real Negro type. She has an inferred, but not definitely stated, jungle love-life with our hero.
>
> —*Heart of Darkness* plot treatment

This passage, from the plot treatment for Orson Welles's first Hollywood film, *Heart of Darkness*, captures the 1930s fascination with the primitive, often seen in classic Hollywood cinema. But the passage also acknowledges the psychological complexity of white colonial desire for the primitive when it promises that in this film, "everyone and everything is just a bit off normal, just a little oblique—all this being the result of the strange nature of [the ivory industry's] work—that is, operating as exploiters in surroundings not healthy for a white man."[1] Guerric DeBona uses this very paragraph to argue for Welles's *Heart of Darkness* as a critique of fascism, a push for racially progressive politics, evidence of Welles's genius in adapting and complicating Conrad's modernist prose.[2] While DeBona's assessment accurately captures Welles's political goals, his view of primitivism was heavily rooted in the belief that the white male psyche would be rejuvenated through intimate contact with the primitive. Welles himself participated in this paradigm, often seeking creative rejuvenation through exchanges with the primitive, as did other modernist authors and artists. His genius, however, was that of the griot, a cultural storyteller able to assimilate the longings and fears of a group and convey them through a compelling narrative. Welles's primitivist dramas in the 1930s and '40s spoke for an anxious white collective, often exploring the shifting paradigms of white colonial desire and conquest.

Welles's stage, radio, and film narratives between 1938 and 1942 are key to understanding mid-twentieth-century American constructions of whiteness, because the increasingly popular acoustic performance of race on the radio used audience imagination differently than did the visual spectacle of blackness invoked on stage or in film. Welles is a unique artist in that he worked freely in all three media, offering unprecedented insight into the intersection of these performance forms. Radio offered freedom beyond that of visual media to interpret white fantasies of race, since radio performance enticed imagination through sound rather than spectacle. There were two main modes of invoking race in the disembodied sound of radio: realism and expressionism. Radio shows like *Amos 'n' Andy* invoked realism through mundane plots and dialect, even as they relied on the fantasies of white actors and audiences to generate audio blackface.[3] Welles, in contrast, evoked the mood of the primitive via suggestions of the supernatural and exotic. For Welles, race was the stuff of magic, not of everyday comedy.

Orson Welles molded his identity as a genius much as any showman or magician would: by taking raw material and transforming it unexpectedly before his audience's eyes and ears. He created his boy-wonder reputation by playing against the grain of the American public's expectations, manipulating its various fascinations with social collectivism, primitivism, and high art. His approach was predicated on and overtly interested in race—as an expression of the mysteries of identity and sexual power, but also as a political topic. Welles's white imagination incorporated and explored primitivist images, marking the intersection between modernist fascination with the primitive unconscious and popular fascination with the exotic.

Populist Modernism and the Primitive

Welles's radio work in the late 1930s and early 1940s reflects the growing cultural preoccupation with defining civilization—and the civilized mind—through its relation to the primitive. Welles's vision of the primitive, like that of many modernists of the 1920s, contains great ambivalence: while it maintains associations with alluring self-destruction, it is often the white male protagonist who cannibalizes or internalizes the primitive, rather than vice versa. Rather than functioning as a purely external signifier, the primitive reflects a needed and desired aspect of white (male) American self-definition. T. S. Eliot summarizes the explicitly aural associations of the primitive in his 1917 *The Use of Poetry and of Criticism*, in which he links "auditory imagination" to

> feeling for syllable and rhythm, penetrating far below conscious levels of thought and feeling, invigorating every word: sinking the most primitive and forgotten, returning to the origin, and bringing something back, seeking the beginning and the end. It [. . .] fuses the old and obliterated, and the trite, the current, and the new and the surprising, the most ancient and the most civilized mentality.[4]

Often, Welles's mass entertainment strategies follow the dramatic arc suggested by Eliot, taking a male protagonist into the depths of the primitive in order to bring him back to his origins and emerge newly "civilized."

Additionally, the clash between civilized and primitive is gendered as a male quest often acted out upon or through a female body, which represents either a white ideal of civilization or the dark allure of woman-as-terrain. Through the conquest of one or both of these women, the male protagonist is either made whole or destroyed, depending on his power as a patriarch and colonial adventurer. Thus the primitive comes to represent a type of emotional anarchy, a darkness within the white male protagonist that must be conquered.

The most elaborate example of this pattern is Welles's first RKO project, the unfinished film *Heart of Darkness*, based on a 1938 radio adaptation; but his protagonists undertake similar psychological quests in the 1939 radio drama "Algiers," his 1936 staging of a "Voodoo" *Macbeth*, and his 1938 performance in "The White God," an episode of *The Shadow*. In all these productions, the primitive appears in accordance with the model outlined in Freud's *Totem and Taboo*—as "a necessary stage of development" through which whiteness passes.[5]

Welles's level of involvement with these productions varied. In the case of *The Shadow* he served only as an actor, while he adapted, directed, and starred in *Heart of Darkness*. Certainly the level of complexity delivered in the Welles-authored narratives differs from those with which he was involved only as an actor, and (as DeBona suggests) the Welles narratives often contain an element of self-critique and skepticism about the mechanisms of entertainment that produce them.[6] Nevertheless, Welles's interest in primitivism positioned him at the intersection between the popular and the elite, the location of what Werner Sollors terms "populist modernism," a collectivist impulse that paradoxically integrates modernist fascination with "high" art and Western elitism.[7] Kobena Mercer calls populist modernism "a kind of surreptitious return of the binaristic oppositions associated with an essentialist concept of ethnicity arising in the very discourse that contests and critiques it."[8] Welles aesthetically rearticulates white fascination with the primitive even as he increasingly critiques it politically in the 1940s. A major difference between Welles and many of his contemporaries, however, is that his interest in primitivism coincided with a conscious effort to hire actors and actresses of color to perform his scripts. Thus his politics and art conjoined.

Colonizing Genius: Manhood and Nationhood in Welles's *"Voodoo" Macbeth*

Welles's *Macbeth* challenged conventional dramatic practice in several ways. It was radical in its casting choices, in its willingness to freely adapt Shakespeare to appeal to mass audiences, and in its focus on integrating music and visual experimentation. To a degree, Welles was simply channeling racial associations with primitivism from his surrounding culture—from his wife, Virginia,[9] the New York literati, and Eugene O'Neill, among others. Nevertheless, blackness and Harlem played pivotal roles in securing the public concept of Welles as master magician: "master" of internal and external darkness, "magician" testing the boundaries of conventional rules of marriage, race relations, and artistic production.

Welles's willingness to adapt Shakespeare into a modern context raised the question of whether to adapt the text to African American dialect, which risked creating a Tambo and Bones *Macbeth*. Ultimately, Welles chose not to adapt Shakespeare's iambic pentameter, but reviewers like John Mason Brown lamented his decision not to adapt Shakespeare's verse into dialect to make the language match "the locale."[10] Welles's explanation for why he chose this approach reveals the racism embedded within Welles's otherwise progressive political ideology. Reminiscing about the production in February 1942, Welles recalled,

> The negro with his virgin mind, pure without any special intellectual intoxication, understands the essence of the Greek theater better, which demands simplicity and the absence of artificial interpretations. I staged Macbeth by Shakespeare in Harlem, New York, by a cast of Negros [*sic*] and never had I the trouble to read or to correct speech and intonations. They discovered all themselves, with a prodigious intuition that they have in a high degree for the tragic theater. And this in the face of their never having read or heard speak about Shakespeare!"[11]

Welles's performance ideology emerged from the conjunction of several aesthetic movements and his 1936 "Voodoo" *Macbeth* reflected multiple anxieties inspired by legacies of turn-of-the-century racism in performance.

Blackness and the exotic flowed in two currents in the early twentieth century. The first, inherited from nineteenth-century sentimentalism, George

Frederickson labels "romantic racialism" in his work *The Black Image in the White Mind*. Romantic racialism offered stereotypical images of the suffering mulatta, the exotic black "buck," and the endearing Uncle Tom. Its affectionate condescension laid the groundwork for twentieth-century images of primitivism, particularly via modernist uses of race as metaphor and symbol. George Crandall elaborates on the twentieth-century tendency to fall back into the patterns of "romantic racialists" who used blackness to represent what seemed "tragically lacking in white American civilization."[12] Expressionism used romantic racial symbolism to evoke the internal emotions moved on to the external skin—thus the tragedy of race in dramas like O'Neill's *The Emperor Jones* (1920), in which the beating tom-toms and the jungle are tangible performance metaphors for Brutus Jones's own interior struggle of conscience and guilt.

Welles's early dramatic use of primitivism emerged from the conjunction of romantic racialism, expressionism, and populist politics. It added to the metaphors of the first two movements a concern with the social construction and political outcomes of racial identity. Nevertheless, his primitivism retained the romantic associations of blackness with dark passions and the supernatural or, as Marianna Torgovnick terms them, "our id forces."[13] For decades, blackness as a symbol of lost passion and of simplicity had made primitivism seem romantic and nostalgic to white audiences.[14] But, as Torgovnick notes, 1930s primitivism was criticized by fascists as a symptom of debased, promiscuous folk culture.[15] On the other end of the political spectrum, collectivists used primitive images to represent the vitality within unfettered sexual communion and the achievement of self-discovery and freedom through impulses that rejected fascist elitism.[16] This second paradigm fit not only the political and aesthetic needs of the Federal Theatre Project's Negro Theatre Unit but also the personal fantasies of Welles. It invoked the paradigms of romantic racialism, but with positive connotations.

The creation of the Negro Theatre Unit was controversial, and advance word of Welles's "Voodoo" *Macbeth* did nothing to reassure those who thought such a theater would do no more than provide a place for black actors to play out white fantasies of blackness. The appointment of John Houseman to lead the unit made it vulnerable to charges of racism from its inception. Houseman tried to alleviate the controversy by dividing the work of the Negro Theatre Unit into two categories: "work by, for, and with black actors and classical work performed by black actors but staged and designed by white artists."[17] In the second category, Welles's *Macbeth* mingled Haitian politics and voodoo imagery with Shakespeare,[18] unambiguously eliciting white fantasies of race but also offering credible jobs to black actors. The

Black Communist Party picketed Welles's rehearsals because of their fear that Shakespeare's tragedy would be transformed into a minstrel burlesque.[19] There was ample precedent for this anxiety, since popular skits like "Bones Plays O'Fellar" and "Dars-de-money" had been minstrel staples a generation earlier,[20] and radio shows like *Amos 'n' Andy* confirmed the enduring popularity of such minstrel images.[21] The question was whether black actors would be allowed to play characters with emotional depth, with the tragic dignity of the Macbeths rather than the superficial comedy of Tambo and Bones.

Justifiably concerned, audiences did not expect the convergence of 1920s expressionism with 1930s social agitation. In his "Voodoo" *Macbeth* Welles depicts blackness in classic modernist primitive terms: it is powerful, compelling, supernatural.[22] But it also contains a layer of psychological complexity not usually associated with primitivism. As James Naremore suggests, the tension between good and evil within a protagonist had long been a preoccupation of Welles's: he had explored the theme of liberal humanism versus "the demons of psychoanalysis and the supernatural" as early as his play *Bright Lucifer* in 1933.[23] Welles invokes the psychology of the supernatural in both *Bright Lucifer* and *Macbeth* by prominent use of an expressionist drumbeat.

Drumming Up Interest: Hecate and the Witches Take Center Stage

Like Eugene O'Neill, Welles used the expressionist drumbeat to reflect supernatural forces at work on the mind of his protagonist. The audio cue of the primitive drum captured the figurative pulse of the "primitive" within Macbeth and represented both an "authentic" Haitian feel and a white fantasy of the darkness of voodoo. He enlarged the cast to have a number of actors play voodoo women, witches, and voodoo men, as well as casting the classically trained Eric Burroughs[24] as Hecate, who played opposite an "authentic" voodoo drummer, Abdul. Welles literally placed the drummers, and thus the witches and Hecate, center stage:

> Before the curtain rises, drums and voodoo chanting in the darkness and the scene becomes gradually visible [. . .] Voodoo ceremony in progress. Half-circle of white-clad women celebrants—in the center, somewhat raised from the stage level, the three witches. To the left, the dark figure of Hecate. Distant low thunder and lightning.[25]

Hecate is given lines from both the witches and Macbeth himself, and even participates in Banquo's murder, making him a central character. Hecate presides over all the events as a master magician, making Macbeth's fate the product of dark magic, and the script describes Hecate and the three witches as "birds of prey" stalking Macbeth as their victim (1.2). Welles divides the texts into two acts in the draft script (three acts in the performance version), with each act framed by Hecate's curses. At the end of the first act, Hecate promises supernatural tortures for Macbeth will follow:

> I will drain him dry as hay;
> Sleep shall neither night nor day
> hang upon his pent house lid:
> (Drums stop)
> He shall live a man forbid!
> (A thump of a drum on the last syllable of 'forbid')
>
> (1.2)

Hecate often closes scenes, immersing the crowd in darkness and silence. He closes the first and last scenes by crying, "Peace," at which the "drums, army, music, voodoo voices, *all* are instantly silent" (2.6). Then he initiates his "spell," first on Macbeth, later on Malcolm, by crying, "The charm's wound up!" (1.1, 2.6; a line Welles chose to use to close his 1948 film adaptation of *Macbeth* as well). Like a ringmaster, Hecate controls the tempo of the production through chants and drums. In this way, the "Voodoo" *Macbeth* was as much an audio event as a spectacle, marking scene shifts and mood changes with aural as well as visual cues. It also channeled white fantasies of the exotic through the filter of claims of authenticity. The promise of an authentic Haitian voodoo experience[26] lies at the center of several critical reactions to the show and resonates in the memories of those involved with the production. The drumbeat simultaneously conjured modernist expressionism and quotidian Haitian existence, both the exotic and the ordinary.

Acting Out White Fantasies: Harlem Actors and a White Auteur

The drumbeat in particular recalled another white American dramatic genius. Simon Callow remarks, "The influence of *The Emperor Jones* was felt by many spectators, especially perhaps in [its] insistent use of drums. Welles, like many an artist[, . . .] stole anything that was germane to his purpose. He was not, in fact, a great innovator at all; he was a great fulfiller."[27] However, Welles's use of the drums to make transitions between scenes, to bridge events, and to control the audience's perception of the play itself extended beyond O'Neill's more decorative use of them, in no small part because of the creativity of the drummers themselves. Richard France calls Welles's drums transitional markers that created "the equivalent of a film dissolve."[28] Houseman praised the drummers for creating a "supernatural atmosphere [that] added to the excitement that was beginning to form around our production of *Macbeth*."[29]

While the vision of Haiti Welles presented was more fantasy than fact, the drummers gave the performance a dimension of authenticity. But their artistry was continually ciphered through layers of white fantasy, and absent a recording of the performance,[30] the drummers exist in critical discourse mainly as embodiments of these fantasies of the Haitian primitive.[31] Arthur Knight articulates the centrality of the drums to the production by saying, "No one who ever saw his *Macbeth* will forget the rhythmic pounding of jungle drums as an underscore to the mounting tragedy."[32] Indeed, reviewers at the April 14, 1936, opening were fascinated by the drummers. Failing to appreciate the psychological complexity of Welles's conception, they tended to see the show as a musical. Solidifying the fears of the Black Communist Party, as Callow points out, the word "amusing" keeps popping up in their reviews—a word not usually applied to Shakespeare's *Macbeth*.[33] The witches were a fascinating and disquieting point for reviewers, described by John Mason Brown of the *New York Post* as "mumbo-jumbo agents of a fearful witch doctor"; Macbeth himself was "a sort of Brutus Jones Macbeth."[34]

In the figure of the drummers, the "Voodoo" *Macbeth* fused the supernatural and metaphoric associations of black skin and primitive drumbeat with the aura of Shakespeare's genius. In this case, the Bard himself plays the role of T. S. Eliot's white protagonist, taken into the darkness of Haitian voodoo with his Macbeths and emerging the stronger (or at least the more popular) for it. Of course, Welles accompanied Shakespeare on this journey, and there is far more Welles than Shakespeare in the script. Using the tool of adaptation, Welles was able to mediate between the public's fascination with voodoo and its respect for literary masterworks to forge a work of populist modernism.

The major difference between Welles and earlier modernist dramatists who used primitivism is that his interest in the primitive coincided with a conscious effort to hire actors and actresses of color to perform his scripts, and the 1936 *Macbeth* was perhaps his most successful endeavor in this regard. The WPA "Voodoo" *Macbeth* featured a black cast at a time when a working actor of any race was a rarity. It provided steady work and good publicity for 125 players, a broad mix of respected actors and newcomers. Even the child actors got good press coverage.[35] Its collective production impulse contrasts with that of O'Neill's earlier *Emperor Jones*, which highlighted a single black actor and relegated other black actors to minor roles. Despite the communal impulse of the script, however, Welles-as-director often acted the role of colonial governor giving paternal guidance to his cast, a point that created resentment among some cast members. Selling himself as a genius-of-the-people, the youthful Welles acted out primitivist fantasies through his Haitian Macbeth, particularly through his relationships with black actors.

The Wellesian tales surrounding this production are many, and it is hard to separate fiction from fact, even in interviews with Welles. However, the tales themselves are evidence of the connotations of primitivism surrounding the production. Welles's erotic obsession with the primitive extended to Jack Carter, whom he described as "beautiful[, . . .] a black Barrymore." Welles seems to have bought into a cultural skin fetish that linked black skin to dark passions. To enhance the racial dimension of "Voodoo" *Macbeth*, Jack Carter and Edna Thomas reportedly darkened their skin with makeup for their roles as Macbeth and Lady Macbeth, although publicity photos and footage indicate that theirs was not the heavy blackface of Olivier's Othello (see Figure 3). In the folklore surrounding the performance, the essence of Carter's darkness was his bad-boy reputation. He was associated with a murder charge and the mob in Harlem—Houseman describes him as "a pimp, a killer, and finally an actor." In an interview with Barbara Leaming, Welles described his relationship with Carter in erotic terms: "'I seduce actors, make them fall in love with me' says Orson—and so it was with Jack Carter." Welles accompanied Carter on drinking forays into nighttime Harlem, engaging in a type of racial tourism common at the time among white liberal intellectuals.[36] Welles was translating T. S. Eliot's paradigm for the protagonist's cathartic use of the primitive from theory to practice. Through his relationship with Carter, Welles felt rejuvenated creatively.

Houseman endorsed the "curious intimacy" between Welles and Carter, admitting that it "proved of inestimable value to the project." In an interview nearly fifty years after the fact, Welles remembers nearly being arrested at a Harlem rent party with Carter, and returning home to call Houseman and embellish the adventure: "I intended to torture him [Houseman] . . . but when I realized it was giving him a little pleasure, I dropped it."[37] Whether or not Welles's anecdote is strictly factual, it reveals a fantasy that casts the two men with whom he associated most as superego/id, with Houseman representing white intellectual restraint and Carter black erotic desire. Welles often exaggerated his escapades with Carter to aggravate Houseman, with whom he had begun an unusually ambivalent artistic friendship.[38]

Welles's own longing for Carter's role as Macbeth was manifest when Maurice Ellis, the lead in the touring version, fell ill in Indianapolis and Welles himself took the stage in blackface.[39] Reminiscing about that performance, Welles said, "I was a much darker Macbeth than Jack was. I had to prove I belonged."[40] He also claimed that the audience did not recognize him in blackface, since at the time he was primarily known as a radio actor.[41]

Welles's understanding of blackness was that it could render him part of the anonymous throng even when he was playing the leading role in *Macbeth* and despite the fact that, even following his own logic, his famous voice should have revealed him readily to most audiences. Part of his love of disguise, blackface allowed him to escape his role as white intellectual and enter into the realm of undifferentiated masculinity (at least in fantasy), as had his racial and sexual touring of Harlem with Jack Carter. Welles's desire to "prove I belonged" to both Freud's primitive and civilized worlds, to straddle the domains of ego and id, would become a classic mark of his later work, and it reflects a cultural preoccupation with the realization of white genius via the conquest of the darker primitive. He highlighted an Oedipal interpretation of the Macbeths, saying, "Lady Macbeth *ought* to be the mother in the family to a weak-willed husband, and Edna Thomas was the mother."[42] Thomas, an open lesbian, did not really conform to the traditional Oedipal maternal role Welles assigned her, but Welles often conceived women's roles in two genres: Oedipal temptress or available ingénue.[43]

As for the most prominent reviewer of the day, Brooks Atkinson, Callow remarks that his review in the *Times* revealed his "(more or less) innocent racism."[44] To a contemporary reader, this variety of racism seems far from innocent, and the review also reveals the convergence of the homoerotic and the colonial in Atkinson's perspective. Atkinson praises the "sensuous, black-blooded vitality" of the witches and drools over Jack Carter as a "fine figure of a negro in tight-fitting trousers that do justice to his anatomy."[45] One cannot help but suspect the tom-toms were playing a bit too loudly for Atkinson, whose review reveals more about his own desires than about the performance. The critical fascination with the drummers continued as the show toured the country. Robert G. Tucker praised the production, saying, "It has the aspect of savagery and voodooism and the manner in which the uncanny atmosphere is created and carried on is the most impressive feature of a splendid production."[46] Even recent critics focus on the mediating power of the drummers. France sees them as an "aural counterpoint" to the visual spectacle: "The *primitive* violence of the drums [. . .] added dimension to the images of *civilized* violence onstage."[47] The military clashes of ambitious men, even the slaughter of a child, seem to be positioned culturally as violent by-products of "civilization," when in fact these acts erode the very binary of civilized/primitive. The presence of the drums troubles this binary, questions the categories themselves—by juxtaposing Bard and Abdul, Welles and Hecate, author and performer. Mainstream critics from the 1930s to the present seem satisfied that Shakespeare lost mastery of his text during the "Voodoo" *Macbeth*, that the performed adaptation utilizes the text without reproducing it. Instead it creates a new text, one that satisfies and challenges audiences through its ambivalence, and specifically through its use of modernist primitivism.

"Voodoo" *Macbeth* was an early experiment with Wellesian primitivism, a motif that reappeared throughout his career. Welles often associated the primitive with the ability to disappear into anonymity and to play erotically beyond the bounds of social convention.[48] Nowhere is this cultural preoccupation with the primitive as a vehicle for white genius more clearly manifest than in three of his early radio performances: "The White God" episode of *The Shadow* and his *Campbell Playhouse* productions of *Heart of Darkness* and "Algiers."

A "White God" in the Shadows

Between 1938 and 1939, Welles starred in two radio performances that explicitly took the listener on T. S. Eliot's rhythmic journey into the primitive for the sake of rejuvenating the "civilized mentality." "The White God" episode of *The Shadow* aired July 10, 1938, and "Algiers" aired as part of the *Mercury Theatre* series on October 8, 1939. The *Shadow* series was deeply rooted in Freudian concepts of the dark unconscious, opening each week with the brooding reminder: "Who knows what evil lurks in the hearts of men? *[resonant maniacal cackling]* The Shadow knows." Welles's presence was more widely received in *The Shadow* episodes, even if listeners did not know it was Welles, than in any other medium. His voice held a power over listeners that drew them into the fantastic adventures of Lamont Cranston, the invisible Shadow, and his sidekick, Margo Lane (Agnes Moorehead). The part was an ideal fit for Welles in that Cranston was debonair and yet had a darker side—he was both civilized and primitive. In addition, The Shadow matched up with Welles's ambition to be a magician, since the Shadow was an invisible protagonist who often used telepathy to trick his adversaries. The very invisibility of the protagonist suited the medium of radio, for what easier protagonist to imagine than one who is invisible? The broadcasts manipulated the listener's imagination with the same aural cues that Margo and other participants in the drama were given to understand where the invisible Shadow was and what he was doing, such as a slamming door or a sliding lock to mark an entrance or exit.

In "The White God," the Shadow is called to the South Pacific to figure out why fifteen ocean vessels have disappeared in an area known as the Graveyard of the Pacific. The Shadow quickly ascertains that a man referred to by natives as the "White God" has turned a volcano on the island into a giant magnet that pulls in ships and seaplanes. In a twist that endears this episode to any academic listener, the White God is actually the disgruntled university scientist Lloyd Carlin, who had assisted another scientist, Rudolph Hoyt, in his development of magnetic technology. Fired from the university, Carlin has now stolen the technology and used it to convince the natives that he's a white god. They are not the only ones who are convinced. As the natives are throwing his old mentor, Hoyt, into the volcano as a human sacrifice, Carlin taunts him, saying, "Since being dismissed from the university, I have become a God, a White God!" This episode, lasting only thirty minutes, lacks the complexity of writing and stylistic execution of Welles's Mercury Theatre productions, but it offers a glimpse into the popular concept of primitivism in the entertainment industry and suggests Welles's ability to take techniques and images from popular performances and recombine them into the multilayered, more ambivalent psychological narratives associated with modernism in his Mercury productions.

For example, the use of sound effects in this episode shows how closely aural stimulus ties to modern concepts of identity, even in a simple half-hour radio drama. By singling out tricks and slippages of aural imagination, even this episode of *The Shadow* interrogates linear notions of white subjectivity. First, the Shadow himself is a disembodied voice, androgynous in that he needs Margo Lane or another sidekick to embody his actions. In this episode, he controls the natives by throwing his voice to make it appear that Hoyt's daughter (who—fantastically!—survived a fall into the volcano and climbed back out) has a man's voice. As the Shadow exclaims, "A masculine voice coming from a reincarnated woman should prove quite a shock!"

The Shadow uses Miss Hoyt's body to enact his own desires. It serves as a proxy for male power as he competes with the White God for his subjects, the "primitive" island people. To counter the permeability and weakness usually associated with the female body, the Shadow asks Miss Hoyt to wear a concealed bullet-proof vest. As a result, she doesn't fall when Carlin shoots her, thus making the natives believe that she, too, is a god. Through Miss Hoyt, he instructs the terrified natives to bring the White God to her. When she worries that the natives won't understand the Shadow's standard English, he reassures her that he's really speaking to Carlin in a man-to-man contest of authority, dueled out via the body of a woman. The Shadow declares, "The girl is your new and only god!" In response, the listener hears frightened "native" cries and yells, accompanied by the omnipresent native drum.

The male power contest itself uses conflicted metaphors of the primitive/civilized binary, showing it is not really binary at all but a plural and shifting power matrix. In this case, the Shadow (darkness) is seeking to unseat the White God (the ultimate white patronymic) and usurp his control of the primitive. But the civilized arrives in the form of a dark "shadow" masked by the body of a white woman—a twist on the usual metaphor of the primitive itself as a dark mask. The battle between the Shadow and the White God becomes entirely about interpretation. He who manipulates expectation and understanding wields power, and women, natives, and nature are all mere pawns in this contest of meaning. By manipulating the aural imagination of the natives through his voice, the Shadow imbues himself with the traditional phallic powers of idealized whiteness: he masters Miss Hoyt's literally impenetrable body, and he controls meaning and subjectivity for the natives through the manipulations of her body and his voice. On another level, Welles manipulates the aural imaginations of the mass audience of the radio show itself, creating an illusion of threatening natives in the South Pacific from a New York radio studio but also revealing the fraudulence of his devices. Since the listener is in on the "trick" of Miss Hoyt's vest, we have to wonder what other tricks have been employed to deceive us as listeners. The only difference in the positions of the "primitive" audience and the modern radio listener is modern awareness of the instability of audio perception, in other words, a self-critical ear and wariness of technology.[49]

For his final trick, the Shadow must dupe more than a mere audience of natives. He must trick his white male counterpart, Carlin. The Shadow fools Carlin into ascending the volcano by pretending he is walking beside him. In a maniacal, nihilistic moment, thinking he is face to face with the disembodied Shadow, Carlin activates his "giant magnet" while he and the natives are at the lip of the volcano, leading to their collective destruction. Carlin mistakenly employs his phallic power (the magnet) because he is tricked by the Shadow's own phallic power (the voice). Our last aural images of Carlin and the natives are the sounds of their screams as they fall into the volcano, indistinguishable from each other. Carlin has become one with his primitive audience and lost his status as both white man and god. The radio audience, in contrast, retains its position as witness to modern entertainment, a position that depends on the knowledge that this parable of transgression and containment is ephemeral, a trick of technology.

The Shadow's intellectual contest with the White God for control of the primitive is probably not what T. S. Eliot had in mind in his discussion of primitivism and modernism, but the performance shows the lingering aesthetic effects of the association between primitivism and a diseased white mind. The Shadow is able to encounter the primitive, master it, and return to his origins. The demented Carlin, however, is toppled by his own aspirations, which leave him stranded in the primitive. The power of the primitive always threatens to turn on a weak patriarch.

This episode contrasts the Shadow's disembodied intellect with primitive physicality, as defined by a lack of intellect and preference for violent action. When the Shadow first sees the natives paying deference to Carlin, he observes, "The primitive mind is eager to believe anything that savors of the supernatural." But this statement hides the frame of performance of the show itself, in which hordes of "civilized" listeners huddle close to the radio, enthralled by a series that savors the supernatural in each episode. This audience would be duped into mass panic by Welles's *War of the Worlds* only a few months later. Titus Ensink has observed that the confusion of the listeners in *War of the Worlds* resulted from "interpretive ambiguity" in the structure of the text itself that led the listener to confuse activities within and outside the play text itself.[50] Hostility toward such ambiguity marks one difference between the mid-twentieth-century audience and earlier Victorian audiences, which were more likely to derive pleasure from the mystery surrounding tricks of technology.[51] In contrast, mass media tricks that were not easily identified and understood, like Welles's *War of the Worlds,* were open to criticism and censorship by the audience, which increasingly relied on radio as a method of disseminating news and factual information. But for Welles the magician, radio was an exciting new tool to play with narrative, and the manipulation of the eyes and ears of an audience was the ultimate trick.

An Oedipal Detour in "Algiers"

Much like the episode of *The Shadow* discussed above, Welles's performance of "Algiers"—an installment of the *Campbell Playhouse* series—leads listeners on an aural trip through fantasies of the exotic with a white, male protagonist seeking redemption. "Algiers" came at a key time during Welles's negotiations with Campbell Soup to continue the radio show despite his move to Hollywood and his film contract with RKO. His radio career, increasingly subordinated to his film aspirations, was still a major source of income and reputation, as his publicist Herb Drake indicated in a memo to Howard Benedict on August 2, 1939. Drake recounted that "at one time [Welles] was doing 12 or 15 other programs each week" in addition to *The Shadow,* and that the *Campbell Playhouse* was "extremely successful . . . placing 5th in some important manuals today" and winning many radio awards.[52] He also mentions that the theater season, with which Campbell Soup explicitly connected its show, was not "very hot," and he suggests that "we don't go any further mentioning *Five Kings* [Welles's adaptation of Shakespeare's history plays] now since Welles doesn't know what he's going to do with the damn thing." At this time, Welles was moving away from the adaptations of the classics that had been the focus of the *Campbell Playhouse* and toward materials he felt had greater mass appeal.

As a result, Welles wrote a great deal of correspondence in this year regarding radio story ideas, which were negotiated among himself, Houseman, and producer Diana Bourbon as a representative of Campbell's production agents, Ward Wheelock, Inc. This correspondence reveals increasing tensions between the New York theater focus of *Campbell Playhouse* and Welles's increasing interest in developing his role as a filmmaker. The fall broadcast schedule for the New York–based Campbell Soup show conflicted with Welles's Los Angeles–based RKO contract and shooting schedule, which he was already failing to fulfill. Houseman—uncomfortable with Hollywood, the film medium, and his relationship with Welles—wanted to return to New York and used *Campbell Playhouse* as an excuse, thus sparing himself further embarrassment.[53] Meanwhile, CBS and Campbell Soup were dabbling with the idea of promoting a radio book club by adapting at least one book a month for the show. This goal matched the original classics-for-the-masses mission of the Mercury Theatre but not the changing goals of Houseman and Welles.[54] Finally, Campbell Soup had a socially conservative agenda that did not match Welles's increasingly progressive political agenda. Correspondence between Welles and representatives of Campbell Soup on August 16 and 29, 1939, indicates that Campbell's agent, Ward Wheelock, Inc., submitted the script for *Liliom* to the Catholic Charities and Publicities Bureau on Welles's behalf because they were worried about offending the church. In September, they tried to control Welles's personal appearances and rejected his idea to employ his lover Dolores Del Rio as a guest star, instead suggesting Frances Langford. Wheelock wrote Welles, "1. You are trying to do too much. 2. We feel that your going on the air in any other capacity is a dilution of your efforts for us. 3. That you should be in New York on Friday morning as previously agreed."[55]

Welles countered Wheelock's strictures by arguing that his film contract demanded more independence from his radio show, as well as the innovation of recording some installments of the show in Los Angeles. Welles argued on October 2, 1939,

> My movie obligations require me to deliver complete and fully cut picture, ready for release by January 1st [. . .] last possible finishing date for actual shooting is November 15th [. . .] fairest arrangement would be for client to agree to Hollywood origination on those weeks during shooting time [. . .] with the exception of the Barrymore [*Christmas Carol*] broadcast [. . .] no reference to Hollywood should be made during the course of the program.

Into this power struggle came the radio performance of "Algiers" on October 8, 1939. The preceding week, Welles and Houseman had made Wheelock very happy with a broadcast of *The Count of Monte Cristo*, which Houseman had referred to in his telegram to Welles on September 19, 1939, as a "rich classic . . . Haha." He saw it as a book that Wheelock would consider to be classic and as a way of avoiding the "third bourgeois domestic story in row." Wheelock loved the show, commenting in his October 3, 1939, wire to Welles that it was "one of the best things we've ever done and the best individual job I ever heard on the air." Ominously, however, Diana Bourbon warned Welles two days later, on October 5, to keep Ernest Chappell "and our Hollywood office fully advised of all Playhouse developments." At this point, Chappell was Campbell's man in Hollywood and would be blisteringly chastised the following week for letting Welles run amok with "Algiers."

Welles vehemently defended the broadcast from a denigrating attack by Diana Bourbon in a message to Chappell on October 9, 1939. Welles dismissed the reactions of Bourbon and of the friends and CBS executives who had listened to it with her, rejecting what he viewed as their bourgeois values. He then reasserted his control of the broadcast event, arguing that his work was artistic rather than commercial and denying that Chappell or any representatives of CBS or Campbell should have significant impact on his broadcast. "Algiers" itself had been framed as an authentic slice of Casbah reality, delivered to your living room by a knowledgeable guide: Welles. Thus Welles fixed himself as the mediator between audience and sponsor and between imagination and reality. Making listeners comfortable with the exotic primitive tropes of modernism in American living rooms required a sense of narrative timing and framing. Again reenacting Eliot's journey through the primitive, Welles served as the medium for listeners to experience the Casbah—but only as a romantic imaginary locale, explored, overcome, and rejected within fifty minutes.

For "Algiers" to work as an identity detour in miniature, it first needed to be accepted by listeners as authentic. Welles prepared this effect a week in advance, reading to the audience about the actual Casbah at the close of the *Monte Cristo* broadcast. The following week, he opened the "Algiers" broadcast by reminding listeners of this description, saying, "Take my word for it, it's authentic, because, believe it or not, your humble servant has lived in the Casbah."[56] He then described it as one of "the wild and wicked cities of the world where anything can happen and everything does." It was "only a step" from the modern Algiers, but "when you take that step, you enter another world, a melting pot for all the sins of the world [. . .] and in that labyrinth Pépé le Moko is at home—and he is safe as long as he stays there."[57]

Like the earlier "Voodoo" *Macbeth*, "Algiers" uses aural cues to create the mood of a romantic, supernatural locale capable of driving its male protagonist into outlaw madness. The location became a key source of contention between Welles and Diana Bourbon. She complained not only of the expense of hiring "authentic" musicians but also of hearing Casbah street sounds in her own living room and being unable to follow the narrative because of them. Welles retorted on October 12, 1939, "you insist that the Casbah is background and I insist it is foreground."[58] While the commercial interests of CBS/Campbell Soup favored bourgeois domestic narratives—literally stories that would please Bourbon and her associates as they listened—Welles wanted to explore modernist expressionism and its psychic fragmentations, particularly through images and settings that evoked primitivism. "Algiers" was based on the 1938 Walter Wanger film of the same name, which was itself a remake of the 1937 French *Pépé le Moko.*[59] After these two movies the Casbah already held a reputation as a "notorious area of corruption and native depravity," and the popularity of the story depended on feeding the audience imagination for its "filthiness and vice."[60]

In her essay "Entering Freud's Study," Marianna Torgovnick assesses Freud's uneasy fascination with the primitive as it relates both to cultural history and individual identity. She notes that Freud "divides history into the categories female/male and primitive/civilized. He then allies himself with the 'triumphant' categories—civilized male."[61] However, she also notes that the rise of fascism destabilized these binary categories, since Nazi Germany eroded the concept of Western "civilization."[62]

Since World War II, the traditional formulation of a civilized, stable (white) ego has given way to an ambivalent, fluctuating model of identity in which the old alliances are still invoked but with less confidence. Identity in this model becomes a geographic territory to be contested, negotiated with, and ultimately conquered. Torgovnick asserts,

> The mature ego is identified with the imperial city-state, which will colonize primitives quite literally and colonize (in the figurative sense) many feelings, including feelings of free sexuality and oceanic oneness. The 'oceanic' must be 'ousted from a place in the foreground' because it would displace the individualistic paternal line [. . .] to which Freud wishes to trace civilization, its benefits, and its discontents.[63]

Thus, the chaotic, multiethnic, "oceanic" sounds of the Casbah disturbed listeners like Bourbon precisely because they were foregrounded, threatening linear notions of identity that were customarily represented by nonoverlapping dialogue, continuity of character, and indications of fixed masculine American identity—an obedient wife; a low, masculine voice; middle-class American accents; the familiar, patrician tones of Orson Welles. In her

October 9 letter, Bourbon calls the show "a sound-effects nightmare" and complains, "my guests got up in a body and went and sat in my bedroom where they couldn't hear the radio."[64] In addition, Welles had relocated "Algiers" as a parable of American identity, moving the ambiguity of the narrative one step closer to Bourbon and her friends by making it about an American couple touring Algiers. To Americanize the civilized/primitive paradigm, Welles chose New York rather than the original text's Paris to represent Western civilization, and the American characters nostalgically invoke familiar New York markers—Zabar's and Lindy's—to contrast the lawless Casbah (Welles would again relocate the narrative frame from Europe to New York in *Heart of Darkness*).

The broadcast drops the listener directly into the confusion of the Casbah. The American couple find themselves in an alley of thieves, looking at a bar from which the Algerian detective Inspector Slimane warns them, "Americans will be brought out feet first." A police raid and shooting ensue, all in the first five minutes of broadcast. "Algiers" featured guest star Paulette Goddard as Gaby, an American woman who becomes intoxicated by the romance of the Casbah and runs toward gunshots instead of away from them with her fiancé, Richard. She lands right in the middle of a male contest for power over the primitive, which will be fought over her body.[65]

Amid screams, gunfire, and orders to shoot on sight, Gaby is pulled off the street by Inspector Slimane, who murmurs in foreign tones, "Here you will be safe." She has just fled her tour group and Richard, a model of American capitalism who sums up the Casbah as "A lot of yelling, murdering savages."[66] He would prefer to be in the safely commercial Monte Carlo, having disembarked from their ship in Algiers only because Gaby wanted to see it.

Gaby is a symbol of Richard's wealth, and international jewel thief Pépé le Moko (Orson Welles) associates her with the diamonds she wears even in the Casbah. But she is also a symbol of American upward mobility who possesses an active financial ambition. Money is her occupation, and when Pépé asks her, "What did you do [. . .] Before the diamonds?" She replies, "I wanted them."[67] Revealing herself as a lower-class striver, she taps into cultural connotations of class Otherness that allow her to bridge the gap between the whiteness of moneyed Manhattan and the nonwhite Casbah. She shares the suggestive indeterminacy associated by Peter Stanfield with Hollywood's use of jazz in the 1930s and '40s by means of which "morally suspect, lower-class, sexualized women are represented as literal or figurative octoroons."[68] Thus she appears both as the ultimate commodity prize and as a transgressive force capable of either realizing or defeating the goals of male protagonists. She is a greater gamble than any to be found in Monte

Carlo, and three men compete to win control of her in "Algiers." The one who controls Gaby will control the narrative as well, becoming the author of the tale rather than a figure in it.

By the end, "Algiers" has become Slimane's story to tell; of the three men he is the only one who leads Gaby rather than following her. She lures Richard off the boat into Algiers and Pépé out of the Casbah. In contrast, Slimane pulls her off the streets and introduces her to Pépé; he also confines her to her hotel and eventually tricks her into leaving Algiers. Ultimately, he is the one who tells us that Pépé has been killed through the guise of an official memo of events. Like so many of Welles's narrators, Slimane has to compete for control of his text, but in the end he controls the narration and thus the listener's sense of history. Moving into the first-person-singular mode of storytelling, this episode writes itself simultaneously as a fictive personal history (Slimane's lived experience) and as a memoir encasing a moment of cultural history (the police report of an international political "event" that has happened in Algiers).

Slimane begins to take control of the narrative when Gaby leaves Richard during the opening police raid, which was planned by the visiting inspector from New York, Commissioner Hillier, and carried out against Slimane's advice. Slimane plays the situation against the grain, taking advantage of a temporary breakdown in white Western male power—the convergence of a bumbling police raid, a runaway fiancée, and an international jewel thief beyond reach of the law—to gain control of the narrative prize, Gaby. It is a shell game in which the sought-after object is ostensibly Pépé. His lawlessness represents a prohibited regression of the white subject, and his power lives only within the realm of the Casbah, outside systems of material meaning for American identity. He challenges traditional values like marriage and the law by stepping outside the bounds of American commerce and culture, in which "male sexual desire feed[s] female material desire—caught in an urban American web of class, race, and gender."[69] Pépé has transgressively chosen the urban milieu of Algiers over that of New York and "feeds" his bounty to his native lover, Ines.

Gaby's power, in contrast to Pépé's, is specific and material. She circulates as an object of exchange in the world of law and commerce outside the confines of the Casbah. Slimane steps into the gap of meaning and begins a cultural and psychological marionette show, using each of the three white intruders to control the others and bringing order from chaos by driving them from the Casbah (or perhaps by exorcising the Casbah from them). Gaby is drawn to Slimane's exotic world, and he uses her as the queen in a chess game, manipulating her to move the other pieces where he wants them and using Gaby's body as a proxy for Pépé's.

As Gaby escapes Richard amid the gunfire, we hear the noises that listeners like Bourbon found so disorienting: scripted sound effects such as "Native Screaming in pain as he is hit" and a "slight scream, medium off mike." Gaby is pulled into a different world, sliding from the rigid capitalist national ego into its ambivalently seductive id amid undifferentiated "Arabic Jabber." As the Casbah chaos recedes, Slimane enters as a new not-quite-reassuring voice: in formal but accented English diction he tries to soothe her: "It will soon be over, all this activity."[70] He has pulled her, however, into a refuge shared by the injured Pépé. Pépé is not native to the Casbah. Like Gaby, he is a New Yorker who willingly took a wrong turn, an identity detour. Eventually, she will seduce Pépé, and in the pursuit of her he will come out of the Casbah and encounter civilization and death.

First removing the complex colonial undertones of the French original, Welles's adaptation depicts Algiers primarily as a place of sexual and romantic fantasy. Exoticism remains expressionistic for Welles, as it was in the "Voodoo" *Macbeth*, but now embedded in the undifferentiated crowd sounds of the Casbah, which represent the psychic desires of his protagonists. This expressionist urge put Welles at odds with his sponsors, who complained of its expense. Bourbon pointedly asked Ernest Chappell on October 9, 1939, "They also tell me you had 9 native musicians and a girl singer. Is Orson paying for these [. . .]?"[71] The larger conflict, however, lay in the broadcast's thematic and structural challenges to bourgeois individual American identity.

American identity itself, embodied in Gaby's New York-ness, seduces Pépé out of his haven. Overcome with emotion, he exclaims to Gaby, "You know what you are to me? New York! The whole town, that's you! You're lovely—you're sensational! Do you know what you remind me of? The subway!"[72] In addition to the obvious phallocentric metaphor of Gaby-as-tunnel, this speech indicates that Gaby now signifies American civilization for Pépé. Embodying Stanfield's ambiguous figurative octoroon, her body shifts between the promises of primitive lawlessness and civilized power.[73] When contrasted to the darker body of Pépé's native lover, Ines, Gaby shines white. Gaby's allure is that of the ego reasserting itself over a wayward, childish impulse that is explicitly associated with the lawlessness of the Casbah. Pépé's struggle to choose between Gaby and Ines poses a choice between two concepts of himself: one embracing a capitalist Western worldview and associated with "maturity," the other turning toward exotic, alluring regression and labeled "deviant"—an Oedipal primitive that enjoys the exotic journey and thus defers the return home to engage the symbolic fathers of law and nation.[74] Hence Welles's assertion in the introduction to the broadcast that "in that labyrinth [of the Casbah] Pépé le Moko is at home—and he is safe as long as he stays there."[75]

Like Lloyd Carlin, Pépé has absolute power over the dark regions until he is disturbed by challenges from his original "civilized" world. In Freudian terms, his stay in the Casbah is a temporary regression, a rejection of his responsibility to assert ego over id and to take the prominent place of the father. It represents the location of great power for him, but only the temporary power of lawlessness. His stay there is a self-destructive regression, a seductive trap. He describes his time there to Gaby as "walking in my sleep" or being in a "hole," and to Ines as "like being in a grave."[76] Such a dark, deadly place inevitably cannot harbor him for long.

Gaby's appearance triggers Pépé's desire to return to the Oedipal quest of capitalist civilization, but too late. His compromised white identity is unable to survive outside the dark region, and his very ambivalence between the two spaces of primitive and civilized kills him. His divided attraction to both the classic symbols of civilized New York and the primitive sensations of his locale prove fatal. In contrast to Pépé, Inspector Slimane understands and excels at the rules of the game of power. In a twist of "The White God" plot, this time the native Slimane wins the battle with his white counterpart over meaning. Once again, however, the diseased white male ego is destroyed by its very divided nature. Unlike the protagonist of the French film version, Welles's Pépé is not a villain. Around Gaby, he seems more desperate than controlling and more tormented than violent.

The inspector is a key figure in both the narrative and the controversy the broadcast provoked. He is depicted as the director of the plot. When he uses Gaby to set up Pépé, turning white female seduction against the protagonist, he is also a manifestation of the symbolic "civilized" father. However, he is also a "native" voice. Like Gaby, his meaning shifts between primitive and civilized according to context and interpretation. One of Diana Bourbon's complaints about "Algiers" was that Slimane's voice was not masculine enough: "Whoever played Slimane was bad too[. . . . W]hy the high pitched piping voice? There's nothing in the script to justify the supposition that Slimane was a eunuch."[77] Welles responded,

> Is an edict to go out that Algierians [*sic*] are henceforth to be played with low voices? (There is considerable internal evidence and some justification in the French movie script and in the French performance of Slimane, for the assumption that he, Slimane, was a eunuch, although I take it that you meant that as sarcasm.)[78]

This debate over Slimane's effectiveness as a character centers on his masculinity and the manifestation of his sexual power via a voice on the radio.

Thus "high voice, small penis" becomes the performance equation that Bourbon hears, and this voice is particularly unsettling coming from a native man who defeats the savvy American hero. Interestingly, the highness of the character's voice operated as a type of blackface, rendering the real actor, Ray Collins, unrecognizable to Bourbon, despite the fact that he was regularly featured in *Campbell Playhouse* and *Mercury Theatre on the Air.* This cultural invisibility fit the character perfectly, since Slimane's power lies in his ambiguity, his shape-shifting ability to manipulate one power structure against another. Thus he controls Gaby by controlling Richard; he controls Pépé and Richard by controlling Gaby, and he controls his "civilized" superior, New York Commissioner Hillier, by controlling Pépé.

Welles vehemently defended Collins's portrayal and furthermore asserted on October 12 that any challenge to his players was a challenge to himself: "Ray was wonderful, and at this point I must protest against esthetic discussion between you and Chappell about performances by actors, over whose efforts mine is the sole authority." Like Slimane, Welles was struggling to maintain control of his narrative, competing with commercial interests and a collaborative production process to gather the components of the episode and show under a single name: Orson Welles.

As Slimane is introducing Commissioner Hillier to the Casbah, aural cues highlight his ability to manipulate elements of the environment. Slimane points out slaves from the Sudan, the Moorish architecture and commerce of the street, and the Arab women who are "slaves from the Grand Atlas."[79] All the while, there is "native" singing in the background, and we hear Slimane shoo away an Arab woman, who approaches to beg. Slimane is Hillier's and the audience's guide to the cacophony of the Casbah, introducing the white tourist to its exoticism even while keeping it at a safe distance. His ability to shoo away intruding forces acts within the narrative as the technological security of the radio operates in the listener's living room: the white bourgeois audience can experience the illusion of interaction without the complexities that would arise from any real cultural exchange—without intimacy, without touching or being touched. Ray Collins himself provides a further buffer, since our authentic Casbah guide is in fact a mere simulator of Algerian presence.

Further emphasizing Slimane's sense of control, the aural structure of the broadcast takes the form of a countdown to Pépé's arrest. When Slimane introduces Pépé to Gaby, he informs him that he has already marked the date of his arrest on his wall, "high up—where it reads black in the rays of the setting sun!" To catch Pépé, he has to lure him out of the Casbah, and he knows that Pépé will follow the bait of the white woman. As the inspector wryly comments, "the bait is taken. . . . for the fish to be taken, the bait must be jerked away."[80] Slimane jerks Gaby away by telling her Pépé is dead and putting her on a boat out of Algiers. When Pépé leaves the Casbah only to see Gaby sailing away, he runs toward the end of the dock, calling her name as if he will swim to her. The police shoot him. As he dies, Slimane apologizes to him, explaining that they had to shoot him so he would not escape; he in turn explains that he *has* escaped, at least spiritually.

Physical death becomes psychic reincarnation in this tale of the Oedipal primitive. Pépé's time in the Casbah was a digression—as the audience's has been—and to attain a white male identity, he must both seek the (white) girl and die for her. In the paradigm of white consciousness trapped by a detour into the primitive, death is preferable to regression. The story functions as a cautionary parable, a type of patriarchal corrective. Pépé could not have returned to white civilization without threatening its very structure. Detours into the primitive are dangerous things, and those who linger too long, like Lloyd Carlin and Pépé le Moko, risk losing not only their identities but also their lives. Such detours are more safely simulated via whiteness, wrapped in buffering layers of technology and fantasy that entice and entertain without risking mutual contact.

A Familiar Other: Going Native in *Heart of Darkness*

One of the most famous stories using the paradigm of white consciousness lured into and destroyed by primitive regression is Joseph Conrad's *Heart of Darkness*, and it was this text Welles chose for his opening RKO project. A generation before Francis Ford Coppola adapted Conrad's tale as a metaphor for white American colonialism in Vietnam, Welles chose Kurtz and Marlow to embody his vision of divided American consciousness. Welles strongly identified with the characters in *Heart of Darkness*, which he performed twice on the radio, first as part of the *Mercury Theatre on the Air* (November 6, 1938), then again seven years later as part of the series *This Is My Best* (March 13, 1945). Houseman remembers that Welles saw "Kurtz as a young man rather like himself, with a fiancée who was rather like Virginia."[81] In many ways, the film was to be a visual manifestation of his concept of first-person-singular narration, with Welles originally intended to play both Marlow and Kurtz, thus focusing the film very plainly on the externalization of an interior moral conflict. In the plot treatment, Marlow is described as "'the first person singular' (An American 15 years older than Kurtz)."[82] By stipulating a difference in ages, Welles set up the story as that of a white man's struggle between youthful desire, which Kurtz acts out on native bodies, and mature restraint, represented by the nonsexual relationship of Marlow with "The Intended"—who in Welles's version comes up the river with Marlow in search of Kurtz. Like

Margo and Gaby, the Intended acts as an icon of whiteness, drawing the protagonist back from his identity detour in the heart of darkness.

The terrain in Welles's film was to be an exotic, unspecified locale, not necessarily Africa. A three-page plot treatment submitted by Herb Drake describes a jungle river of "no particular continent or island. It is just a place of mystery."[83] It would be the setting of an Everyman's moral dilemma. Welles postulated that "there is something waiting for us all in the dark alleyways of the world," and he marks this dark world as non-European: "aboriginally loathsome, immeasurable, and certainly nameless." In other words, the locale would be as far as possible from his audience's concept of "home."[84]

As in the "White God" and "Algiers" radio performances, Welles sought to portray an "authentic" fantasy of the primitive, depicting native consciousness as an abstract, undifferentiated force capable of seducing the white visitor, and using footage and sounds that had come to signify primitive cultures for the audience. The process of constructing the "darkness" in *Heart of Darkness* was one of collage. Welles sent a variety of assistants to research media images of the primitive and bring him the best snippets for his project. He sent Richard Baer to the Los Angeles County Museum "to make a survey of all the primitive races of the world" with the idea of creating a "'composite native.'"[85]

This "composite native" would be pieced together from images in previous performances, creating a familiar Other based on sights and sounds of "primitive" cultures that fit the fantasies of the white American public. RKO memos indicate that Welles sent research assistants to search stock footage of Africa and jungles for location shots. Notes from August 15, 1939, show he paid twenty-five hundred dollars for one hundred feet of film from *Dark Rapture* (although he later complained that it showed only insects). He reviewed a variety of other jungle films as well, in part to avoid the costs of location shooting but also to create a collage vision of Hollywood's ideal primitive setting. A flurry of memos from his assistants to RKO in fall 1939 yields a list of studio films reviewed by Welles for his *Heart of Darkness* project: *Cannibal Caravan, White Woman, Baboona, Jungle Madness, Crouching Beast, Congorilla,* and *Sanders of the River.* He was primarily interested in straight center shots of a jungle river, and these seem to have been largely unavailable, but he did order excerpts with masks, chants, dances, and the sounds of medicine men. Welles also culled images from his earlier stage and radio productions, and from the script for his radio *Heart of Darkness* in particular. The film cast was largely composed of Mercury actors, plus Jack Carter from his "Voodoo" *Macbeth.* Conversely, many actors hired for the film were promised radio roles as part of their contracts.

As an author, Conrad seems a better fit than Dickens for a cinematic adaptation by Welles because he shares Welles's ambivalent fascination with capitalist imperialism and race relations. As Patrick Brantlinger has noted, there is an interesting connection between Conrad's era and Welles's, in that nineteenth-century imperialism "prepared the ground in which fascism and Nazism took root[.]"[86] If one theme recurs throughout Welles's work at this stage in his career, it is an aversion to fascism, and as Michael Anderegg notes, the antifascistic theme is the only connection between Welles's first two proposed films for RKO.[87] This was a theme Welles had taken from stage to radio to screen. His 1937 stage production of *Julius Caesar,* described as an "allegory of fascism," was widely praised by critics of the time.[88] The proposed films *Mexican Melodrama* and *Smiler with a Knife*, as well as his 1945 radio broadcast of *Heart of Darkness*, all depict the dangers of fascism.[89]

The "Revised Estimating Script" for *Heart of Darkness* demonstrates a clear focus on fascism and eugenics, as well as a debt to the narrative structure and expressionist primitivism of the earlier Mercury Theatre radio performance. The principal feature shared by the radio and film adaptations was the representation of primitive culture via the sound of drums, native dances, and songs, juxtaposed with an extremely complex construction of storytelling itself. Conrad's *Heart of Darkness* uses a bifurcated structure that is associated with modernist interrogations of subjectivity, and Welles worked the theme of the divided self into his critique of fascism.[90]

The first problem of adaptation was how to handle the divided self in narration, particularly since Welles wanted to make the film a first-person narrative. In the novel, we are told the story of Kurtz through a nameless narrator who introduces Marlow, who in turn relates his encounter with Kurtz. Marlow tells a story that is an interrogation of storytelling and is placed against a background of imperialism, violence, eccentric genius and exploitation—all issues that not only fascinated Welles but also were at the heart of his negotiations with RKO. He was vividly aware of how the concept of individual genius could be celebrated both commercially and culturally, even as the "genius" himself was being exploited by "the Company."

The radio version's awkward use of Welles as an opening narrator (labeled "author") is replaced in the film script with an introduction by Welles-as-himself, to be followed by his performance as both Marlow and Kurtz. The 1938 radio version is quite short, taking only half of the one-hour broadcast.[91] Yet, despite the short amount of time he had to tell the story, Welles delayed the start of the narrative to praise Conrad's work in his own voice, calling it "a deliberate masterpiece, or a downright incantation, a fine piece of prose work at the least. Its best aspects are an artful compound of sympathy for humankind and a high tragical disgust." This preface prepares the listener to contemplate the meaning of Kurtz's final words—"The horror. The horror"—by raising the prospects of both sympathy and disgust well in advance.

The question of what so horrifies the horrifying Kurtz draws varying responses from critics—is the tale a critique of imperialism, or a reproduction of it? Is Kurtz horrified by himself, by death, by his encounter with "primitive" civilization, or by the lies (personal, imperial, and capitalist) that facilitated his encounter? As Brantlinger suggests, this debate is rendered irresolvable by the structure of the original narrative, which is heavily imbedded in the "double, contradictory purpose" of modernist impressionism that Frederic Jameson deems "schizophrenic."[92] Welles's adaptations reproduce these ambivalences and ambiguities and update them to a modern political context.

The material contexts of Welles's film, however, were far from ambiguous in terms of their racism. From the audio and visual symbolic representations of primitivism, to the pay structure of the racially marked roles, the overall structure of the film was racist. Guerric DeBona asserts, "Welles deploys the side of Conrad's modernism which wants to 'make us see,' but he rejects the Other side of fascistic, racist modernism in which whiteness is validated through blackness."[93] But while it is true that Welles was averse to racism and fascism politically, the material conditions of his art reproduced patterns of both racism and oppression. For example, Welles's use of unnamed stock characters like "Native Woman" and "Flogged Native" allowed white actors like Welles and Dita Parlo (tentatively cast as the Intended) to have extended screen time and receive elevated salaries, while his pursuit of cheap stock footage of the "Dark Continent" from pictures like *Sanders of the River* positioned black characters as two-dimensional stock characters.[94] His movie was not to be so very different from the other "jungle films" of the day.

If the *Heart of Darkness* radio broadcast is any indication of what the film might have become, Welles would have used markers of primitivism similar to those in his "Voodoo" *Macbeth*, "The White God," and "Algiers." The radio broadcast was peppered with Welles's usual expressionist referents: beating drums, "native" chants that sound suspiciously like Southern spirituals, and the sounds of white racial fantasies of blackness generally. The racist context of the film becomes even clearer in the elaborately specific project contracts, scripts, and correspondence. As Brantlinger again points out, the fictional voice in *Heart of Darkness* that could critique imperialism most forcefully would be that of Kurtz's Congolese mistress, who "though described in glowing detail, is given no voice[. . . .] Kurtz's black mistress knows all; it's unfortunate that Marlow did not think to interview her."[95] The same marginalized and silent black female presence is imbedded in Welles's script, only this time we have evidence of her "value" to the commercial narrative through salary estimates. The contrast between white and black femininity is rendered more explicit in Welles's film, since "The Intended"—given the name Elsa in the film—would have a substantial part and be played by Parlo with a possible salary of twenty-five thousand dollars. In contrast, "Native Woman" was never cast and was expected to be paid seventy-five to a hundred dollars. Her small part in the novel was even further diminished in the screenplay.

In film production, unlike most literary production, "author" and "text" are explicitly regulated within a commercial, capitalist context prior to production of the text itself. When RKO put pressure on Welles to cut costs in the winter of 1939, the parts of the movie the studio wanted to cut first were precisely the ones that interrogated subjectivity, fascism, and race relations—the roles to be played by actors of color and Welles's own deconstructive introduction. By and large this was not a censorship initiative but rather a budgetary choice that was prompted—ironically—by the rise of European fascism.

The first whiff of economic trouble with the picture came in a September 15, 1939, telegram to Welles from George Schaefer. Trying to assess the impact of the "European situation" on the movie business and concerned about curfews in London and theater closures in Paris, Schaefer warned that

> People are hesitant to congregate in theatres both in France and England[. . . .] I must make personal plea to you to eliminate every dollar and for that matter every nickel possible from Heart of Darkness script[. . . .] we should confine ourselves to a top of five hundred thousand dollars[. . . .] won't you please therefore go over your script and eliminate every dollar possible.[96]

Welles seems to have wanted to please Schaefer, and in his notes for a responding telegram he promised "every effort will be made to keep 'Heart of Darkness' within or below budget[. . . .] confidence is expensive. I'm trying very hard to be worth it."[97] Nevertheless, his December 12, 1939, budget estimates reflect anticipated costs ranging from $984,620 to more than $1 million. In an effort to cut the budget, salary reductions were planned. Elsa (still uncast but identified in handwritten notes as "Parlo") had a salary cut from $25,000 to $22,000. The lowest-paid roles received salary cuts as well: "Native Woman" (sometimes referred to as "Savage Woman") had a salary reduction from $150 to $70, and "Flogge[d] Native's" salary was cut from $467 to $116.[98] Jack Carter maintained his $1,000 as "Half-Breed" or Steersman, which came to approximately $200 a week, a comparatively high salary. Almost all the other actors' salaries were maintained or slightly increased, and all white actors were paid more than the highest-paid black actor, Carter.[99] In contrast Welles's line item for acting (not including directing and supervision) was $30,000.[100] The shooting schedule, dated November 28, 1939, indicates that George Coulouris, as "A Portugese,"[101] a role of similar stature to Jack Carter's Steersman, was getting $1,000 a week, guaranteed for five weeks (and he had already been paid $5,666 in preproduction). Native Woman was scheduled for only two days of shooting, eventually reduced further to one day, while "Flogged Native" got three days shooting and four days idle, for a total of seven days. Apparently, it took much longer to portray on-screen interracial violence than on-screen interracial love.

Shooting white romance, in contrast, took both time and money. Elsa was budgeted for thirty-two days shooting and thirty-six days idle for a total of sixty-eight days, the most shooting days and most idle days of any actor listed (Welles was not assigned days). The material racism underlying this project is stark. Welles's film could not avoid racism in its means of production, much less in its on-screen representations. So how does one reconcile the inherent racism of this Hollywood production with the progressivism of its author-director? Perhaps the answer can be found in the similarity of Welles's film to its literary source, since both are bedeviled by ambiguities regarding their potential as either revolutionary or reactionary propaganda. Brantlinger observes that Conrad's text was politically progressive in that its critique of imperialism came out prior to most similar critiques. This observation would apply to Welles's critique of commercial exploitation and race relations as well. But Brantlinger adds, "As social criticism, [Conrad's novel's] anti-imperialist message is undercut by its racism, by its reactionary political attitudes, by its impressionism."[102] The same can be said of Welles's film: his political intentions are undermined by the very structure of his narrative and the means of its production.

We can understand how critics like DeBona see Welles as attempting "to free us from racial ideas of the primitive."[103] But Welles's interrogations of subjectivity, of modernization in the form of science (particularly racial classification), and of fascism, fall short of challenging modernist primitivism. The real hope that this Conradian narrative could be redeemed from its inherent political ambivalence would have been its emphasis on self-critique. Kurtz, for example, is a critic of his own text who undermines his treatise on humane race relations by writing "Kill all the brutes" at the end of it.[104] With this sudden, irrational revelation of hatred, he undercuts the very concept of rational narrative and reveals the schizophrenic "I" behind the text. This narrative "I" is haunted by lust for the primitive and repulsion from it.

Welles's introduction, which features the electrocution of the audience, is the technical equivalent of Kurtz's revealing statement in his manifesto, "Kill all the brutes!" But Welles's statement occurs in the prologue, preceding his text, and the viewers (readers) are positioned as both brutes and victims. First, the prologue calls attention to the brutal manipulation of the viewer by technology. Then Marlow's preparations for his journey bring out scientific disregard for humanity—the viewers experience their own heads being measured along with Marlow in preparation for their role in scientific study. The viewer is quickly positioned to read her visual journey with a sense of irony and skepticism.

Racial exploitation is enabled by the idea of a fascinating "primitive" that helps define the civilized in opposition, and this opposition is established in both the novel and the film by the juxtaposition of Kurtz's native mistress and the Intended. The script leaves no doubt that the Intended and Native Woman were designed to fascinate the viewer, and that this fascination would be key to the commercial success of the film, despite the fact that the actresses' unequal salaries did not reflect their characters' comparable narrative value. The plot summary describes the Intended as a major factor in the marketing of the film, establishing a heteronormative racist model that represents civilized love in contrast to primitive desire. A revised plot summary on September 15, 1939, promised, "We don't know who she is yet but she is going to be a great beauty . . . virginal quality. The girl is to be sexy without waving her hips around. She is to have a calm, half-smiling face, perhaps over a full bosom, for instance. In a sentence, the girl is eager but unfulfilled." Similarly, in an undated character list, Elsa, listed only as "girl," is described as representing "love" and required "to make us believe she is in possession of that flame."[105] In the heteronormative, capitalist equation of desire, girl = love = commodity.

"Native Woman" contrastingly receives no description at all and is given little value in terms of salary or screen time. She has no motivation as a character, no personhood. She simply represents silence, the forbidden, the unconscious—the darkness at the heart of the narrative. She acts as a double for the Intended: like Ines and Gaby, they are a pair in which one must be denied for the other to be embraced.

In contrast to Native Woman, Jack Carter's character is given depth through his status as "mixed," making him a marker of the tragic failure of whiteness, the fear of and desire for miscegenation. "Mixed Breed" is described in the character list as

> The expatriate, tragic exile who can't remember the sound of his own language. He might have been a chief but [was] brought into slavery

> and demeaned in the services of elements he doesn't understand; a wild, proud beast born in a cage, he will never even guess why he is miserable.[106]

This tragic mulatto cliché character reflects the legacy of romantic racialism. The character's alliance with whiteness, however, gives him a higher monetary value within the means of production than a black female character. Although the Intended and "Mixed Breed" are two-dimensional stereotypes of white patriarchy, they are both awarded the ability to speak, and they speak to the experience of whiteness. Native woman has no such language. Both in the novel and in each of Welles's adaptations, she remains in silence and darkness, at the heart of the narrative but marginalized by the mechanisms of production, with few lines and a low salary. She is to be seen, not heard or paid.

The eye that does most of the seeing was to be Welles's. He at first intended to play both Marlow and Kurtz and to open the film by introducing himself to the audience as a first-person guide preparing to take them into the heart of darkness. In both Conrad's and Welles's tales, the first-person approach to engaging the audience emphasizes the psychic rather than the geographic nature of the journey. "Perhaps," as Patrick Brantlinger argues about the original text, "it matters [. . .] little whether we say the story takes place in Leopold's Congo or in some purely imaginary landscape."[107] Welles makes this imaginary landscape explicit by refusing to ground the action in a specific time and location and by using Marlow as a literal "eye" for the audience. The mirroring function of Africa in the original text is manifest not only in the physical similarities between Kurtz and Marlow in Welles's film script but also in the role of Marlow as a camera or mirror for the audience.[108] The other characters speak to the audience through Marlow, who is supposed to act as a register for the audience's emotions, a sort of funhouse mirror that can mediate or distort the image reflected in it.

Audience engagement was key to the success of the narrative and key to the studio pitch to make the film. The camera was to embody Marlow's gaze and thus that of the audience, steering viewers while Welles narrated via the soundtrack. When Kurtz spoke, it would be "straight into Marlow's camera eye."[109] Critics tend to see this as an awkward and limiting strategy for the portrayal of Marlow,[110] but it would have maintained the psychological focus of the narrative and kept Welles in place as mediator of the narrative, a role that was key to his RKO contract and his budding reputation as an auteur.[111]

Despite the racist dimensions of its production, the film marks Welles's first attempt at using cinema for political critique. In it he links fascism to an unhealthy interest in exploring the metaphorical darkness at the center of the story. He suggests again, as in "Algiers," that the identity detour, although enormously compelling, will kill you. In an early scene, Marlow has his head measured with calipers by a doctor in preparation for his trip. Since Marlow *is* the camera, the effect is that audience members are getting their own heads measured.

> DOCTOR (cont'd) I always ask leave, in the interests of science, to measure the crania of those going out there.
> MARLOW'S VOICE: And when they come back, too?
> [The Doctor hastily lowers his props.]
> DOCTOR: Oh, I never see them . . .[112]

So we set out with Marlow on a journey from which we know we won't return, suspicious of the commercial and scientific voices that sponsor the journey. Framing the journey as an interrogation of subjectivity, Welles forcefully positions the audience as the subjects of the film through the prologue (further discussed in chapter 1). While this positioning of the viewer adds a layer of self-criticism to the film and represents a gesture toward solidarity between civilized protagonist and primitive background, it does little to undermine the structural racism at the core of both the story and the film. The narrative itself suffers from the marginalization of the nonwhite perspective and a fascination with primitivist tropes like cannibalism and the supernatural, not to mention those ever-present tom-toms.

Welles's film is fascinating, however, in its ability to adapt the narrative ambivalence of the original text into mass media. Welles exhibits the same uneasiness with modernity and with the very tools of his own narrative production that Conrad deploys. Welles's ambivalence operates continually in two registers: within the narrative and in the external process of production (Welles's relationship with RKO and his use of cinematic technology). Structurally, the prologue performs the same layering effect as does Conrad's first, nameless narrator, who introduces us to Marlow and his story. The prologue illustrates Welles's own idea of collage, which tests the conventional notions of authorship and adaptation. Even in the prologue, expressionist references to whiteness are juxtaposed with the jazz sounds of darkness, constant reminders of Marlow's split identity. Just as Kurtz's murderous outburst undermines his rational analysis of conditions in the Congo, structural racism consistently undermines Welles's own resistance to fascism and espousal of populist politics. Finally, like Conrad, Welles retains a suspicion that his two protagonists, the narrator, and the author himself are all linked to the lies and propaganda circulated by the Company. Ultimately, his doubts would proliferate and destroy the film itself. Both Welles and RKO eventually became so suspicious of the ambiguity of the narrative itself that they shelved a project that might have proved to be as revealing and controversial as the novel from which it was adapted. In particular, his development of two techniques, first-person collage and expressionist primitivism, would have shed light on his emerging performance aesthetic as it developed concurrently on stage, radio, and film.

First-Person Collage in *Heart of Darkness*

In the original *Heart of Darkness*, we meet the narrator in the fog of the Thames. Just as he did with "Algiers," however, Welles makes *Heart of Darkness* into a parable about New York and American identity. We meet our narrator after seeing a collage of pictures and sounds from Manhattan, with echoes of African American culture setting the tone for the blackness-within-whiteness of the production: "In Central Park, snatches of jazz music is [*sic*] heard from the radios in the moving taxicabs."[113] Robert Spadoni suggests that the "throb of tom-toms foreshadow the jungle music of the story to come."[114] The collage represents Marlow's consciousness, for he, much like Pépé, is a displaced American whose national psyche is fragmented between binaries of civilized and primitive.[115]

Next Marlow is shown at a map shop on "an empty business street in some Central European seaport town." He decides to make the journey to the Congo and is sent for a physical examination with the head-measuring doctor, who also establishes Marlow's national and racial identity, referring to him as a "Good Nordic type" and telling him that he's his "first American" patient.[116] But these proclamations of who he is (and by extension, who the audience is, since Welles asserted in the prologue that this experience is happening to viewers via the camera's gaze) are undermined when Marlow chances to meet Elsa. She is walking toward the camera and thus toward the viewer's and Marlow's gaze:

> *As she comes closer and closer we see she is very beautiful. There is a look of recognition on her face. Finally she comes face to face with* CAMERA. *Both stop. She fills the frame, looking directly at the lens. The look of recognition on her face fades and changes to one of slight embarrassment.*
>
> ELSA: I'm sorry.[117]

Marlow's identity is to be bifurcated not only through geographic dislocation—an American working for Europeans in Africa—but also through his physical similarity to Kurtz. The tangible presence of an observer, Elsa, throws Marlow's identity into crisis. Through her awareness of Marlow's similarity to Kurtz, her every look undermines the concept of "I" that is so central to the narrative and to Welles's formulation of "eye = I" laid out in the prologue. If our eyes are not "I's," then who are we?[118] The answer is another collage or pastiche, the self as the product of cultural bricolage.[119]

Audio Expressionist Identification

As the film proceeds, we hear the expressionist sounds of two competing worlds: that of white civilization, represented by Elsa and classical piano music, and that of the dark primitive, represented yet again by native drums and sometimes by their more intimidating and contrasting partner, silence. References to whiteness are juxtaposed with the sounds of darkness to give us constant reminders of Marlow's split identity.

When Marlow encounters Elsa again and is formally introduced to her, she is at the Company's base camp, listening to her friend Eddie play the piano and remembering when she and Eddie first met in Venice. Like Gaby, she is instantly allied with white civilization, including money. She and the music provide a stark contrast to Marlow's first impression of the primitive wilderness outside the colonial camp:

> Marlow's Voice: "outside the silent wilderness surrounded this cleared speck on the earth, great and invincible, like evil or truth—waiting patiently. The river—glittering, glittering—flowed broadly by without a murmur [. . .] the silence of the land went home to one's very heart—a great silence around and above. Perhaps on some quiet night—the tremor of far-off drums—*Sound of drums*.[120]

The central elements of Welles's *Heart of Darkness* are strikingly similar to those of "Algiers." The sounds of the Casbah are replaced by drums, but again the Girl is a tool used to lure a white male consciousness that has "gone native" out of dark chaos and back into white civilization, even though it will be lethal for the man to leave the darkness. Instead of the "civilized native," Slimane, Marlow manipulates the Girl and the natives to master the tale and emerge as the final narrator. Like Slimane, Marlow is a hybrid of primitivism and whiteness. And just as in the radio episode of *Heart of Darkness*, Welles himself provides a rhetorical frame for this journey by introducing himself as the master "author" of our experience, a position made all the more explicit by the prologue, in which he visualizes his power over the audience by feeding us as caged canaries, firing a gun at us, and electrocuting us in the death chamber.[121]

Elsa's role is central to Welles's adaptation. She not only accompanies Marlow for most of his journey but actually draws him a map of the river and its stations, cautioning him that the stretch of river past Station 3 "is unexplored[. . . .] There are cannibals. Mr. Kurtz is somewhere here." Elsa also links Kurtz to European fascism. She says, "There was no good reason for sending him to the Dark Country—except to get him out of Europe;" "He's just a demagogue in a uniform to a foreigner, to somebody who doesn't know him."[122] But the narrative is more complex than pure antifascist propaganda, since Kurtz does not embody pure fascism or unmixed whiteness.

Rather, both Kurtz and Marlow acquire power through their ability to incorporate darkness into whiteness without becoming darkness itself, and this is the model of masculinity Elsa celebrates. Mere whiteness in a "dark" locale shows itself to be ineffectual, easily burned (literally) and victimized. Marlow seeks to balance himself between ineffectual whiteness and savage darkness. As he discusses his uneasy interaction with the cannibals, he articulates a desire to distance himself from the unsavory whiteness of the Company. Excessive whiteness in a man is associated with fascism and also with weakness—for example in the likes of the head-measuring Doctor and De Tirpitz, the leader of Station 2, whom Elsa describes as a "bad blue blood."[123] After killing Carbs and the Steersman, the cannibals (displaced from the boat to the jungle in Welles's version) approach the boat, but only to ask that Marlow and his men bring the "bad tribes" back for them to eat. Marlow wonders aloud,

> Why they didn't go for us—I don't know. They were thirty to five[. . . .] It occurred to me I might be eaten by them before very long, but I admit that just then I saw—in a new light, as it were—how unwholesome the Company men looked, and I hoped, yes, I actually hoped, that I wasn't quite so—so *unappetizing.*[124]

The darkness that Marlow must master is represented aurally by drums and silence, as in the earlier Wellesian performances. Marlow often narrates reflectively over the sound of the drums: even in the boat, "the drums are heard over soundtrack." Like Hecate, whose incantations silenced the drums to demarcate scene breaks in the "Voodoo" *Macbeth,* Marlow often talks over the drums just before a dramatic moment or a scene change. For example, as Marlow's party reaches the last outpost of civilization, Station 3, "the rhythm of drums changes. It is now even more violent, even faster, even louder, as we DISSOLVE." They have entered the territory that Elsa earlier warned "is unexplored[. . . .] There are cannibals. Mr. Kurtz is somewhere here." As they move into this uncharted territory, the Steersman, looking at the jungle, warns, "Those in there—they know that magic."[125] Steersman, as a "half-breed," can articulate the supernatural powers of the primitive because he has intimate knowledge of darkness.

The Steersman, Kurtz, and Marlow all straddle categories of light and dark. White fascists like De Tirpitz continually misinterpret darkness and therefore fail to master it. Discovering that the natives have steel-tipped arrows, De Tirpitz cries, "The natives are getting civilized quick. This was the stone age until just lately!" The more perceptive Marlow identifies the source of this "civilization," concluding that "Mr. Kurtz had taken a high seat amongst the devils of the land—I mean literally—DISSOLVE OUT."[126] Even while maintaining the traditional association of the primitive with the infernal, Marlow recognizes Kurtz's hand. He is able to locate the point of intersection between civilized and primitive precisely because he and Kurtz both mark this intersection.

Several structural choices make the nature of Kurtz and the horror of "going native" appear tangibly to both the boat crew and the audience. First, there is the opening of the story in Manhattan, during which Marlow talks directly to the audience and brings the narrative "home," so to speak. Second, Marlow and the crew encounter Kurtz's barbarity in the form of human heads mounted on poles, and some of them are white human heads. De Tirpitz remarks, "That's how Kurtz and the rest of them got their power back in Europe. This shouldn't surprise you. You've seen this kind of thing in the city streets."[127]

Marlow and De Tirpitz seem at first to interpret Kurtz very similarly, but the divergence in their perspectives becomes clear when they encounter Kurtz himself. Marlow, the hybrid American, is revealed as Kurtz's doppelganger, while De Tirpitz, the "bad blue blood" from Europe is shown to be a weak substitute for Kurtz. Marlow's meeting with Kurtz is a type of mirror moment, an encounter with subjectivity and moral ambiguity as articulated through racial metonym, and Kurtz recognizes it as such. Marlow still shares the camera's perspective, taking the audience with him into the subjective encounter as well. Kurtz and Marlow meet in a temple covered with skulls, and Kurtz is seated on a throne. Kurtz asks for a cigarette and reaches out "below frame of camera. He brings his hand back with the cigarette in it [. . .]."[128] In effect, the audience has just handed a murderer a cigarette.

Kurtz acknowledges the power of the mirror moment and recognizes his encounter with Marlow as a portent of death. Like Pépé, he has regressed too far to return.

> KURTZ: I'm dying—(*he looks keenly into lens of camera, straight into Marlow's eyes*) You're American. What's your name?
> MARLOW'S VOICE: Marlow.
> KURTZ: I'm Kurtz. You look like me—a little—

On the words "a little" CAMERA MOVES BACK SLIGHTLY *and* LOWERS A TRIFLE *from the extreme closeup of Kurtz' face, indicating that Marlow has stepped down and back. Kurtz settles back on his throne.*

KURTZ: (*looking straight at Marlow*)—The image of God—I can use you.[129]

Several key terms of Kurtz's identity as both man and god are put into play in this scene: the personal name, the national name, an act of self-identification, and a comparison of subjective agency to omnipotence. In this place such naming categories are contested, thrown into doubt and then reasserted. Kurtz and Marlow are both in a no-man's land, literally. They are operating beyond the bounds of traditional identity politics. They form an alliance as Marlow gives helpful answers to Kurtz's questions and pairs Kurtz and himself as an *us* versus the *them* of his own boat crew. This moment shifts the poles of us/them, white/black, and civilized/primitive binaries, since it is suggested that white fascism is a worse thing than the feared black cannibalism. De Tirpitz is audibly one of *them* (civilized white men), and when Kurtz hears his voice he asks Marlow, "How many more of them?" Marlow answers, "Six—counting me." To which Kurtz, acknowledging their alliance, responds, "I'm not counting you. You'd never understand."[130] Kurtz's perspective separates Marlow from white civilization, a shift in perspective Marlow is just starting to make.

Echoing Marlow's earlier repulsion from whiteness when looking through cannibal eyes, Kurtz assures him that neither he nor the cannibals will eat the crew because "The superior races are not very palatable." Kurtz and Marlow are both capable of distancing themselves from the indigestibility of other whites, but only Kurtz goes the extra step of allying himself with the cannibals. Nevertheless, it is De Tirpitz rather than Marlow who is shown to be a bastard son of Kurtz's highly unusual style of leadership. True, Kurtz is *part* fascist, but as the Intended has already told us, it would be a mistake to locate his hybrid power within the confines of fascism. De Tirpitz, on the other hand, is a true European dictator. Kurtz greets him as a son and places him on the throne, crying out, "The first real dictatorship!"[131] Kurtz knows, however, that De Tirpitz will fail to rule the primitive darkness under him. The next time we see De Tirpitz is when the natives carry his head out on a pole as Kurtz is leaving on the boat. De Tirpitz's fascism is a poor substitute for the more complicated hybrid power of Kurtz.[132]

Welles presents Kurtz in *Heart of Darkness* as similar to Lloyd Carlin in "The White God." Explaining his power to Marlow, he says,

KURTZ: "I'm more than a hero already. Not to you, of course—to my people. [. . .] My race,—the superior race. For them I'm more than a god. I'm every one of them. Think of it, Marlow. I'm a whole nation's long, golden dream[. . . .] Everything I've done up here has been done according to the method of my Government.—Everything. There's a man now in Europe trying to do what I've done in the jungle. He will fail. In his madness he thinks he can't fail—but he will. A brute can rule only brutes."[133]

A brute can rule only brutes, and a white god can only show light against a background of darkness. Kurtz's aspirations to rule the world are unrealizable outside the heart of darkness. He can succeed only in the jungle. In addition, once Kurtz crosses the psychic color line—represented by a gendered color line via the body of Native Woman—he is unable to make the transition back to whiteness and survive. When he looks at Native Woman on his way out of the jungle, he not only rejects her but is repulsed by her: *"Kurtz turns his head slowly to her and looks her full in the face, an expression of psychic hang-over—of exhausted lust, cosmic disgust. [. . .] Kurtz looks away from her, forward—and the litter proceeds past camera right as we—DISSOLVE OUT."* Hers was the specific body on which he practiced his power over darkness, but it is also the body that taints his psyche to the point of death. Once she is taken by Kurtz, he cannot fully remove himself from her. In fact, his body is her geographical territory. A sexual cannibal, she has invaded it and conquered his whiteness. As he departs she makes her way through the crowd of natives and offers him a lament that turns to a curse as she summons a deadly storm: *"She comes out to the bank, further than the rest, and stretches her arms toward the boat."*[134] The girl can still be made out through the gunfire smoke as lightning from a thunderstorm comes up behind her. The thunderstorm starts a fire in the jungle that spreads until it totally surrounds the boat, and Kurtz's final words, "The horror," refer to the storm itself. Kurtz dies during the storm, and his lifeless body is tossed into the river. Native Woman ultimately reclaims Kurtz by ruling the jungle and its dark magic.

Kurtz loses his power when he moves outside the deepest realms of the jungle, just as Pépé loses his power when he moves outside the Casbah, but Kurtz does not lose the power to haunt his double, Marlow. After Kurtz's death the camera perspective shifts as though we are being carried on a stretcher. Marlow's encounter with Kurtz, and with the heart of darkness within the psyche, literally makes him ill. The audience experiences this illness through distortions of perception and a mixing of visual and audio cues. One shot (described as "tricky") shows us Marlow's delirium through cannibal eyes: "Understand that Marlow is now coming down with a fever. In other words he sees things. This is the first thing he sees. Instead of a piece of meat on the plate, Kurtz is on the plate now, and as Marlow stares at the plate, Kurtz crawls off of it and off the frame."[135] Kurtz haunts the film as an apparition, appearing often accompanied by the sound of drums that conjure visual images.[136] Marlow next sees Kurtz with Elsa.

> I saw him again.—Months later, at the foot of the river—I saw him. With Elsa.—I saw those eyes—that wide immense stare condemning, loathing the whole universe—piercing enough to penetrate all the hearts that beat in the darkness.[137]

Marlow's voice-over conjures a silhouette image of the jungle procession with Kurtz on a stretcher, which merges into the image of the river, as *"Into the music [creeps] the suggestion of drums."*[138] Marlow contemplates these sights and sounds, filtering the audience's impressions:

> MARLOW'S VOICE (narrating) Yes, he lived then before me. The vision entered the house with me—the stretcher, the phantom-bearer, the wild crowd of worshipers [. . .] the beat of the drums, regular and muffled like the beating of a heart—the heart of a conquering darkness.[139]

Whiteness returns only when the remedy for this acoustic and visual darkness, Elsa, enters and brings her love-song waltz, which is faintly heard on the soundtrack. The desirable mixture of white European civilization and primitive darkness is once again achieved through the white female body, which appears as a psychic antidote to the dangerous seductiveness of Native Woman. As Elsa remembers Kurtz and his noble character, *"Imperceptibly, the waltz has merged into music reminiscent and suggestive of the jungle, ominous but also sorrowful and very faint."*[140] Elsa does not embody hybrid power, but rather enables it within the psyche of the male protagonist. Like Miss Hoyt and Gaby before her, she provides the medium through which the protagonist can conjure the sights and sounds of a whiteness asserted over darkness, forcefully subordinating the primitive within the psyche of civilization.

The final scene in Welles's *Heart of Darkness* emphasizes the ambivalence of this hybrid power in terms of a conflict between truth and illusion. It is a power based on manipulation rather than epistemological accuracy. Marlow lies to Elsa, just as Conrad's Marlow lied to the Intended, saying that Kurtz's last spoken words were her name. But Welles's Marlow also turns the question of truth on the audience: *"Marlow looks into lens of camera, straight into the eyes of the audience"* and asks, "Should I have told her the truth?"[141] To appropriate Brantlinger's assessment of Conrad, Welles "questions or mocks his own voice, his own talent for fiction making, for lying."[142] Finally, Welles's Marlow asserts the necessity of the lie of whiteness, saying, "I couldn't. I couldn't tell her. It would have been too dark—too dark altogether—(*pause*)."[143] Truth lies silent in the shadows of the white lies of civilization, a critique of whiteness within the ambivalent heart of darkness.

The September promotional pitch to RKO had acknowledged *Heart of Darkness*'s complex exploration of white sexual and racial fantasy, specifically promising to show

> two moderns who have a hell of an adventure in the dark places of the earth. The idea is, more or less by implication, that this is the Goddamndest relation between a man and woman ever put on the screen. It is definitely NOT "love in the tropics" [. . .] Everyone and everything is just a bit off normal, just a little oblique—all this being the result of the strange nature of their work—that is, operating as exploiters in surroundings not healthy for a white man.[144]

Distancing the film from the sentimentality of romantic racialism (*not* love in the tropics), the plot treatment instead places it in the context of a curious and tentative critique of the exploitive nature of whiteness. The exploration of the dark primitive at the heart of whiteness is labeled abnormal, "oblique" and "strange," as well as "not healthy" for the white protagonist.

"The White God," "Algiers," and *Heart of Darkness* all explore the theme of diseased white consciousness tainted by fascination with and yet failure to master the primitive. Invoking T. S. Eliot's auditory imagination, each performance fuses fantasies of primitivism with political references to modern life, positioning them as inextricably linked. Rather than being "shockingly unorthodox in its treatment of racial themes,"[145] *Heart of Darkness* invokes a tradition of modernist fascination with the primitive as a means of self-expression, coupled with a tentative embrace of populist politics and self-critique.

The Commercial Limits of Wellesian Primitivism

The downfall of the film seems to have been mainly fiscal. The censors had few problems with the script, and Joseph Breen's response to it refers only cursorily to the racial imagery, asking Welles to "please take care to avoid any possible inference of miscegenation" and to watch the representations of native dress, since "the breasts of the women must be covered at all times.[146] But Welles was taking too long to film and spending too much money. The movie failed to promise a profit—the first requirement of any Hollywood studio, particularly in the nervous wartime setting. Despite Welles's promise to Schaefer to cut costs, a series of December memos indicates extreme tension between RKO and Welles over the budget. On December 7, 1939, Eddie Donahoe sent Welles information on the budget of *Swiss Family Robinson*, which had been cut down to $596,000. Donahoe said, "These figures probably drive you nuts which they rightly should, but I only sent you this information so you won't feel so bad about making eliminations in *The Heart of Darkness*[. . . .] it certainly isn't a hopeless task." The meeting Donahoe and Welles had just attended with RKO had not gone well. *After* making budget reductions they anticipated a budget for *Heart of Darkness* of $984,620 and a shooting schedule of eighty-three days.[147] In other words, he was producing his first film at a rate roughly half as fast and twice as expensive as comparable projects under way at the time.[148]

Welles's failure to work within the rigid commercial confines of the studio system may, in fact, be one of his greatest legacies to independent film makers. His disdain for conventional methods of script production and shooting left a rich inheritance of experimentation to those who followed. It was also, however, enormously frustrating to those who sought to regiment the financial conditions of filmmaking. The difficulty of getting Welles to work within the profit model of commercial production was described by his attorney Arnold Weissberger in a letter to Richard Baer:

> I should like to make clear to you the reason for the financial jam which now exists. As you know, most large money earners in Hollywood [. . .] are kept on fairly stringent budgets and are told what they may and may not spend. Orson does not like to conduct his affairs in that way[. . . .] The expenses are incurred first, and then we have to see that payment is made in the best possible way. All along the chief difficulty has been that Orson's expenditures have anticipated his income so that he has always been in the red. Had there not been this unexpectedly long delay in the moving picture, sufficient funds would now be on hand to have gotten Orson straightened out[. . . .] I have been to see Schaefer and am trying to get him to agree to advance us some of the movie money before shooting actually commences, but most of that will at once be used up when Columbia repays itself for these advances."[149]

This detailed explanation demonstrates that Welles found himself in trouble with *Heart of Darkness* not because his vision of race relations was too progressive or his notion of narrative too experimental but because he refused to work within the economic conventions of classical Hollywood filmmaking. RKO eventually had to cover the $160,000 Welles had already spent on the film and shelve the entire project.

Welles's use of the primitive in stage, radio, and unfinished cinema narratives is fascinating in its rearticulation of modernist primitivism through the perspective of romantic racialism and in its attempt to represent a divided first-person singular. His vision, however, was far from revolutionary within the context of literary tradition. The same critique that Patrick Brantlinger offers of Joseph Conrad could easily apply to Welles: "Conrad must have recognized his own complicity and seen himself as at least potentially a Kurtz-like figure[. . . .] the African wilderness serves as a mirror, in whose darkness Conrad/Marlow sees a death-pale self-image named Kurtz." Welles embraced Kurtz's form of heroism, which consisted of "staring into the abyss of nihilism."[150] Like Conrad, Welles was a master at questioning or mocking his own narrative. Had it made it to the screen, this self-critical, ambivalent film would have posed an interesting challenge to modern viewers. Marlow would have embodied a psychological struggle over racist imperialism and fascism. But he would also remain an unrepentant liar, and lying within the framework of first-person storytelling conjures the abyss of modern identity as a constantly performed and renegotiated act: as the lie expands outward from selfhood to cultural and national identity, the modern tips ever toward the postmodern. Eventually the quest for Truth detours into the pleasures of fiction. Welles's ambivalence toward the lies of fiction would remain a preoccupying theme of his work, nowhere more so than in his next and final unfinished RKO project, the ironically named *It's All True.*

Figure 1. Orson Welles, 1938, in a promotional photo for *Heart of Darkness*.
Photograph by Louise Dahl-Wolfe; courtesy of The Lilly Library, Indiana University, Bloomington, and Collection Center for Creative Photography, University of Arizona. © 1989 Arizona Board of Regents.

Figure 2. Welles in make-up to play the role of Kurtz in *Heart of Darkness*.
Courtesy of The Lilly Library, Indiana University, Bloomington.

Figure 3. Jack Carter and Edna Thomas as the Macbeths in the 1936 WPA production.
Courtesy of The Lilly Library, Indiana University, Bloomington.

Figure 4. Welles in a publicity still for the Rio project.
Courtesy of Richard Wilson–Orson Welles Collection, The University of Michigan Special Collections, Ann Arbor.

Figure 5. Welles and Jiminy Cricket in a promotional photo for the 1941 Lady Esther CBS radio series. Courtesy of Richard Wilson–Orson Welles Collection, The University of Michigan Special Collections, Ann Arbor.

Figure 6. Photographic still from *It's All True.* Courtesy of Richard Wilson–Orson Welles Collection, The University of Michigan Special Collections, Ann Arbor.

Figure 7. Welles with a Brazilian crowd. Photographic still from *It's All True.* Courtesy of Richard Wilson–Orson Welles Collection, The University of Michigan Special Collections, Ann Arbor.

Figure 8. *Jangadeiros* for the "Four Men on a Raft" section of *It's All True.* Photographic still courtesy of Richard Wilson–Orson Welles Collection, The University of Michigan Special Collections, Ann Arbor.

Figure 9. Photographs of *jangadeiros* from the beach of Iracema.
Courtesy of The Lilly Library, Indiana University, Bloomington.

Figure 10. Grande Othelo cooking. Photographic still from *It's All True*.
Courtesy of Richard Wilson–Orson Welles Collection, The University of Michigan Special Collections, Ann Arbor.

Figure 11. Publicity photograph of Welles arriving in Brazil on February 9, 1942.
Courtesy of Richard Wilson–Orson Welles Collection, The University of Michigan Special Collections, Ann Arbor.

Chapter 4

R Is for *Real*: Documentary Fiction in *It's All True*

> As readers or viewers we also believe that the texts we engage with are "true *as stories*" (and no less "true" for being "stories").
>
> —Linda Ruth Williams, *Critical Desire: Psychoanalysis and the Literary Subject*

While the narrative mode discussed in the previous chapter depends heavily on imperialist binaries of white/black, good/evil, and civilized/primitive to engage modernist primitivism and couple it with romantic racialism, Welles's use of ethnicity in narrative held a different nuance when he attempted to distance his work from "fiction" and portray it as "reality." His final failed project for RKO was the Pan-American film *It's All True* (Figure 4). Although this project went through a variety of incarnations, it remained preoccupied at every step with exploring the gap between truth and fiction in cinema, and its narrative structure was indebted to the style of simulated news reportage that Welles had developed on the radio. In fact, when we look for clues regarding what the final film product might have resembled, one of the best sources is the November 1942 *Hello Americans* radio broadcast regarding Brazil.

Originally conceived as a trilogy of stories centered on North American tales of conquest, Welles shifted the focus of *It's All True* to South America following his arrival in Brazil. The project is inextricably linked to the political climate of its time, developed in large part as anti-Axis, pro-Ally propaganda.[1] Welles embarked on the project at the behest of both RKO and its shareholder Nelson Rockefeller, who conceived of the project as a possible entrée into new Latin American markets in the wake of European theater blackouts, and as a patriotic endeavor on behalf of the "Good Neighbor" policy aimed at securing Pan-American alliances in World War II. These overtly commercial and political goals, however, led to an innovative narrative goal on Welles's part:

to create a polyglot visual narrative, dependent on no single language but rather on music and image, and thus accessible to audiences of any class and culture. The nonlinear narrative ambitiously sought not only to represent but also to create a postcolonial Pan-American identity.

This ambitious attempt to explore postcolonial identity was problematically told via a white North American visitor to South American culture, one of a set of conditions that contributed to the project's failure. Wartime politics and travel restrictions limited studio supervision, allowing Welles to operate in comparative isolation in Brazil and freeing him to explore his philosophical and political aspirations on film. His experimentation, however, did not serve RKO's more conventional entertainment goals, creating friction between Welles and the studio. In addition, he was unable to dislodge himself from the position of privileged observer of his subjects, particularly the *jangadeiros*,[2] and his narrative attempt at unstructured, polyglot truth ultimately failed. The film itself was relegated first to RKO's film vault and then largely to the open sea.[3]

Critical discussions of this unfinished film tend to explore its artistic value and hypothesize about what it might have looked like in its finished state. Equally interesting, however, is the study of this project as it currently exists: on paper, on film, and in folklore, still conceptual rather than realized. It represents ambitious concepts regarding narrative experimentation and the ultimate rejection of these concepts by Hollywood, the governments of Brazil and the United States, and even Welles himself. As Catherine Benamou points out, Welles's suggestion that this picture would act as a type of magazine feature departed from the very concept of individual authorship toward an "author-function" that is destabilized and unfixed.[4] Describing his concept in a prologue to a plot treatment titled "Carnaval: Treatment for the Film Itself," Welles says,

> This is a picture divided into several parts. It is not, however, an arbitrary selection of short subjects, nor is it vaudeville.
> This is a new sort of picture.
> It is neither a play, nor a novel in movie form—it is a magazine.
> CARNAVAL as a sequence in this picture can best be understood if we consider it as an item in a magazine—as a feature story, not as a short story.[5]

While this prologue echoes that of *Heart of Darkness* in its desire for experimentation with narrative form, it goes even farther by rejecting the concept of traditional authorship. The concept for *It's All True* exaggerated Welles's previous adaptation and shooting strategies by operating without a fixed script and improvising a highly collaborative production. The project challenged cultural values of the time, including RKO's desire for quick commercial success and mainstream conventions of entertainment narrative.[6] But it also tied back to a cultural fascination with "documentary expression" that had emerged via fictionalized historical accounts like the *March of Time* radio series.[7] When Welles experimented with documentary fiction, however, he also tended to disrupt concepts of linear narrative and meaning, often disorienting his audiences. Sometimes, as in *War of the Worlds*, this audience disorientation could be labeled a success. At other times the audience resisted his experiments. For example, Welles conceived his new Lady Esther radio series as an "almanac" featuring the character of Jiminy Cricket as Welles's interrupting and questioning sidekick (Figure 5). As Jeff Wilson points out, audiences responded tepidly at best to this narrative experiment. Surveys revealed that audience members found his shows "confusing," "scary," and "weird."[8]

The very mechanisms of production were set against a project that simultaneously experimented with the concept of visual narrative, pushed the envelope of contemporary politics and race relations, and reworked traditional production concepts of the sequence of casting, scripting, directing, and editing.[9] Welles was crushed not by the studio system or the political climate but by his own production strategies, scripting process, and the aesthetic goal of documentary fiction, which were at odds with the equipment, finances, people, and political milieu that he needed to transform the film from concept into product.[10]

Merging Politics and Fiction

It's All True represented a new incarnation of Welles's recurrent preoccupation with documentary fiction. To make the classics compelling to a modern audience, Welles had repeatedly infused his stage and radio adaptations with cultural politics. For example, he revived his successful stage adaptation of Shakespeare's *Julius Caesar*—charged with references to modern fascism—for his radio show with the result of stirring contemporary political opinion. The potential power of this conjunction between narrative experimentation and political meaning fully emerged in his *War of the Worlds* broadcast, which successfully exploited an American culture of prewar fear and created "truth" from fiction for many listeners.[11]

Specifically, Welles used a widely recognized news-media format that was associated with truth but that he deployed for the purpose of fiction. The conjunction of a format associated with truth and a fictitious content created powerful confusion in his audience in terms of their interpretation of his audio cues. When tied to the contemporary political climate and told from the limited point of view of a first-person narrator, the strength of this confusion increased to the point of panic.[12]

For Welles, the panic he created with *War of the Worlds* helped solidify not only his career but also his concept of the power of fiction to reveal emotional truths and to focus the political consciousness of an audience. He had played with the idea of art as political commentary throughout his career, but with the advent of World War II his antifascist leanings took on a new public and commercial importance and infused his literary endeavors. Antifascist themes link several of his productions that otherwise have little in common, such as the 1935 stage adaptation of *Panic,* the RKO detective film *Smiler with a Knife,* and his unfinished *Heart of Darkness.* This interest in wrapping contemporary political reality inside literary vehicles became manifest in a desire for political legitimacy within the fiction of many of his productions. In the case of the Rio project, as was true in his earlier studies of the "primitive," this sense of authenticity connected to ethnographic representation, often conveyed both aurally and visually.

Welles relied heavily on sound to make the audience feel they were experiencing an authentic cultural difference. For example, in his "Voodoo" *Macbeth,* he hired drummers to create a sense of "real" Haitian voodoo at work in the theater. In his radio play "Algiers" he incurred the wrath of his sponsors by similarly spending a great deal of money on musicians to recreate "authentic" Casbah sounds. For *Heart of Darkness,* he sent his assistant to the library to research anthropological traits of "primitive" cultures in the effort to create a "composite native."[13] *It's All True* represents one more step in these inclinations through its intended concept: to visit a culture during a ritual moment of celebration, Rio's Carnival, and then to re-create this culture in great detail both in studio and on location, focusing in particular on its music.

Carnival itself holds a revolutionary connotation, even within its own culture, as a time of inversion and exploration of class power and difference. Stephanie Dennison and Lisa Shaw explain the multitiered manifestations of Carnival that Welles sought to capture with film and music:

> In the first years of the twentieth century three separate carnivals were held in Rio de Janeiro: firstly that of the poor, largely Afro-Brazilian population, in the central Praça de Onze district [. . .] secondly, that of the middle classes in the Avenida Central [. . .] and thirdly, that of the wealthy, white elite, which centered on lavish costume balls.[14]

Welles wanted to capture the beauty and celebration of a multiclass, multirace Pan-American identity, and what better place to explore this boundarylessness than Rio de Janeiro during Carnival?

It's All True represented a culmination of Welles's efforts to merge contemporary politics and fiction, but it also represented the tragic limitations of such acts of simulation, which are inherently corrupted by the means of their production. Welles's effort resulted in the drowning of the Brazilian national hero, the fisherman–political activist Jacaré, during a "simulation" of reality. In an effort to manufacture the spectacle of social liberation, Welles endangered the body of his cinematic subject, which in the case of documentary fiction is all too real. Despite earnest attempts to compensate the family of Jacaré and to turn the film into an homage to the lost fisherman,[15] he created an unintended narrative reality from his efforts to assert ethnographic authenticity. His film became submerged in studio reluctance and red tape, and parts of it were literally thrown in the ocean by the studio, making it the last of his unmade RKO film projects.

It's All True is fascinating in its overt rejection by the political entertainment culture that created it. Between Welles's arrival in Rio at the beginning of 1942 and Jacaré's death during filming in May, the local media, the governments of both Brazil and the United States, and RKO all lost enthusiasm for the project and for Welles himself. The ambitious structure of the proposed film employs each of the narrative styles discussed in previous chapters—first-person narration, serialization, expressionist primitivism—with the goal of creating a new genre of documentary fiction highlighted by the title of the film. If *Heart of Darkness* promised an element of self-referentiality, *It's All True* put self-critique of white subjectivity at the heart of the narrative structure itself, consciously eroding the gap between signifier and signified, revealing the seams between truth and fiction.

Traditional Melodramatic Scripts for the Rio Project

Whereas traditional, classic Hollywood films tended to use the sights and sounds of exoticism to reinforce whiteness, Welles wanted to use *It's All True* as a challenge to studio concepts of audience, narrative, and distribution. The difference between his "script" (or lack thereof) and studio expectations is clear in the draft script "Rick's American Bar," a story idea for filming in Rio that follows a formulaic storyline familiar to RKO executives.[16] This script gives a good idea of what the U. S. government and RKO expected from their political entertainment: a shallow critique of American racism and South American fascism, surrounded by a traditional melodrama. The protagonist in this script is Dick, a young military American pilot (read "good American") who meets a refined but greedy and self-centered former American plantation owner, Marybell, who is obsessed with segregation and diamonds (read "bad American"). The film depicts the emancipation of slaves in both the United States and Brazil as a product of beneficent white liberators. White femininity in particular is positioned in relative privilege to enslaved blackness. One shot describes the white hand of the empress handing blacks an order of the abolition of slavery in Brazil in 1888. Marybell is also a figure of privilege, but she rejects desegregation and admits to Dick that she moved from Georgia to Brazil to avoid abolition and be able to own slaves. She even confiscates books from one of her slaves who has been named after Abraham Lincoln and refuses to observe the tradition of freeing slaves who find diamonds over 18 carats.[17] As a "bad" American, she rejects ideals of democracy and enfranchisement, and symbolizes American racism displaced into a South American context.

When Brazilian emancipation does arrive, Marybell becomes a landlord of sharecroppers, exploiting black workers in Brazil. Her own children eventually reject her, marrying native Brazilians and refusing to enter her house. Doubtless this promiscegenation subplot would have limited the film's appeal in the segregated American South, and in the 1942 radio piece for *Hello Americans*, all similar miscegenation references were explicitly removed from draft scripts, in favor of the themes of democracy and modernization in Brazil. "Rick's American Bar" represents American capitalism and racism in a critical light, since Marybell ultimately chooses commerce over family and sends her husband away in search of the diamonds. The viewer gets an instructional lesson in all Marybell has lost through racial segregation, symbolized by her lust for diamonds. At the end of the film script, we learn that the bartender who sent Dick to meet her is actually her estranged husband, Charlie, who ostensibly sends her diamonds from the jungle every month. In "reality," Charlie sends her fake diamonds from the ACME Novelty Glass Company to assuage her greed.

With all the depth of a Warner Brothers cartoon, we see that ACME glass is a means for the good, moral Charlie to appease Marybell without capitulating to her racism and greed. The film is a none-too-subtle exhortation for wartime sacrifice and honor, as well as an exploration of the tactics of collaboration and betrayal. Viewers could praise the simplistic Dick, who visits the homes of strangers in the hope of good Southern home cookin' and returns the diamond hidden in his pocket to the racist old lady who put it there. Dick and Charlie keep Marybell's illusions alive while critiquing her perspective, judging her racist exploitation without disrupting it. Similarly, the film would have offered a toothless critique of American white imperialism.

This rejected storyline focuses on the critique of the stereotype of Southern racism and the embrace of jingoistic American ideals of honesty and tolerance through a traditional white male perspective. The script ignores Brazilian subjectivity and the realities of Brazilian quotidian life. It simply relocates white imperialism against an exotic background, and in a direct reference to the white European nature of its perspective, the one prominent black character in the script is Marybell's faithful servant, Othello.

Despite the shallowness of "Rick's American Bar," we can see several connections between it and Welles's concept for *It's All True.* Welles seems to have had little to do with this script, but it evokes several of the actual project's preoccupying themes: the definition of wartime American responsibilities against a Pan-American background, the exploration of lies versus truth in narrative, and the positioning of white experience filtered through a black facilitator (in the final script, our guide to the samba section of the film would be the musician Grande Othelo).

Another wartime adventure appears in a draft script also written for (but not by) Welles. This script apparently was inspired by a conversation Welles had with the unspecified author[18] and shares many traits with *Citizen Kane,* namely an interrogation of identity told through a retrospective attempt to piece together one man's reality. It also shares with "Rick's American Bar" the preoccupation with wartime American responsibility and confusion about reality. The revised version of this untitled script stresses that it's not really a war story, since "More than 90% of the action takes place in Rio de Janeiro in the winter of 1942" during Carnival. It promises to use "five full reels" of actual footage of Carnival, implicitly gathered by Welles on his trip to Brazil. This treatment opens with the statement, "A man and his identity are not easily separated. When it does happen, the most basic of all emotional conflicts is involved . . . the denial of life itself."[19]

Like *Citizen Kane* and *Heart of Darkness,* this film would interrogate the emotional life of identity, how it is constructed and destroyed, specifically through white male heterosexuality. Our protagonist, Michael Gard, is a wartime pilot like Dick, but he is battling amnesia after a crash of his fighter jet in Belgium. He remembers the apparent death of his mistress, Ludmilla Koren, a Jewish refugee pursued by the Gestapo for documents her father had. But this will not be Michael's final reality, and facts are withheld or distorted through the narrative as told by the wounded and disoriented Michael. As the plot treatment suggests, "Since we are not telling the story in straight-line narration, we are apt to court for ourselves more confusion than is necessary or desirable." The main idea is to create a compelling lie at the center of the film that will motivate the audience's sympathies and nationalistic spirit: Ludmilla has supposedly been chased down and killed during Carnival, thus infusing the previously neutral Michael with anti-Axis passion. Michael and the audience share a limited perspective, and "[a]ll through the picture Michael and the audience must believe the girl is dead."[20]

Michael's national and personal identities are united in his memory of both Ludmilla and his role as a fighter for the United States. He learns his name, nation, and marital status at the same climactic final moment of the film, when he looks down at his dog tags, and sees (with the audience) "Lieutenant Michael S. Gard, U.S. Army Air force . . . (he looks up, whispers) next of kin—Ludmilla Gard, wife."[21] The story is politically progressive in the sense that Michael and Ludmilla marry across religious boundaries, again raising the taboo miscegenation motif. But the narrative still fails to engage Brazilian subjectivity. Instead, it is common Hollywood studio melodrama, starring familiar white subjects once again displaced against an exotic background.

The approach Welles wanted to take is far more radical than either of these scripts, in both structure and content. Structurally, Welles wanted to attempt a type of pastiche that embodies postmodernity, bringing together fragments of narrative from a variety of sources and mixing various perspectives with suggestive and contradictory aural cues of narration and music, interrupting his role as narrator with Brazilian voices, sounds, and music. Benamou locates as many as seven potential scripted episodes for the film that emerge between June 1941 and September 1943, with three Latin American episodes most tangibly developed.[22] Most later versions of the conceptual framework for the film include one episode focused on Mexico and already partially filmed by Norman Foster, another portraying Brazilian life through Rio's Carnival, and a final segment to be filmed in Peru.[23] The Brazilian portion of the film would itself have multiple layers, featuring the *jangadeiros'* revolutionary sailing trip to Rio but relocating it in time to the eve of Carnival to create a transition from their story to a cultural examination of samba during Carnival.

The samba portion replaced a segment of the film intended to explore African American jazz,[24] marking a shift in Welles's exploration of the primitive and the exotic. Up to this point, Welles had primarily used images of blackness—either African or African American—to symbolize the primitive or the exotic, but with his Rio project, he began to focus on Latin American images of exoticism. Brazil provided an excellent transitional locale for this paradigmatic shift in Welles's career and reinforced his fascination with borderland cultures like Moorish Spain and the American Southwest in which ambiguous, racially indeterminate identity has more resonance than do simplistic black-white binaries.[25] Peter Stanfield suggests that mainstream Hollywood traditionally uses jazz music and blues on soundtracks to give a sense of "urban primitivism" by adding "a smearing of blackness on a world otherwise imagined as white."[26] But increasingly Welles perceived American identity as a collage of smears, still placed on a white background, but holding multicolored hues. *It's All True* was positioned by Welles and his handlers as a challenge to the superficial tactic of urban primitivism, as a more authentic look into samba culture, resonant of a newly emerging Pan-American identity.

As in *Heart of Darkness*, however, the methods of film production were exclusionary and therefore could not easily challenge a paradigm of white exploitation. The filming of *It's All True* depended largely on dramatic reenactment and thus utilized the traditional mechanisms of mainstream Hollywood film production, even as it aligned itself with the genre of documentary rather than fiction. Unable to catch much of Carnival on film due to technical, logistical, and personal problems, Welles restaged it. He also staged the arrival of the *jangadeiros* as they sailed into Rio, which had happened months earlier and in fact provided the inspiration for their inclusion in the film via a *Time* magazine article on December 8, 1941.

From *Ambersons* to Rio: The Concept of *It's All True*

There were several reasons for choosing to do *It's All True* on the heels of *The Magnificent Ambersons*. Herb Drake outlined these reasons in a letter to Tom Pettey on February 4, 1942. Personally, it was a good fit, since Welles planned to include his love interest at the time, Dolores Del Rio, in the "Brazil epic." It was also seen as aligning Welles with the rising nationalist tide of war interest, especially since it represented a partnership between Hollywood and the government as part of the "Good Neighbor" policy. In an inflated description of Welles's mission, Drake asserted that he would be the "most important Hollywoodite working for hemisphere solidarity."[27] This goal of Pan American unity achieved through propaganda films is reiterated in government and studio documents and would reappear in the *Hello Americans* broadcast as well. The trip to Brazil would also get Welles out of Hollywood, where according to Drake he had "been considerably oversold [. . .] the past few months, newspapers are a little tired of Welles activity, we need a lull." In addition, the whole shooting schedule was anticipated to be short, "four or five months altogether."[28] The project was seen as a quick and easy method of "handling" Welles, which correspondence indicates was a stressful project for RKO as well as for his own lawyer and publicity men.[29]

In contrast to these pragmatic reasons for selecting the project, however, Welles was drawn to a Pan-American narrative for aesthetic and political reasons of his own that were often at odds with the motivations of RKO and the U.S. government. Welles wanted to use film to examine lower-class Brazilian life as well as upper-class life, studying Carnival as a momentary intersection of class and race (Figures 6 and 7). Although Welles set out to critique the concept of "'free' and 'enslaved' territories throughout the Americas as a whole," he was confronted by the fact that neither the Brazilian propaganda office nor RKO was comfortable addressing topics of racial and class diversity.[30] The mere filming of subjects like the political agitation of the *jangadeiros* and the contrast between upper- and lower-class Carnival was controversial. On May 5, 1942, Pettey wrote to Drake that Welles was shooting a great deal of carnival footage dealing with lower-class, black Brazilian life. Pettey worried that although the film would "make a great musical," he "had to lie and lie for the last two or three weeks to keep the local reporters away from the studio . . . If they ever got in and saw some of the Rio shanty life we are doing they would write Orson out of town. So far we have had only one or two bad stories."[31] Pettey seemed to think Americans would enjoy the depiction of Rio's primitivism through voodoo and poverty,[32] but he feared Brazilian media would resent the depiction of Brazil as exotic or impoverished.

The criticism surrounding the Rio project resembled the reactions to Welles's "Voodoo" *Macbeth* in that it came from two opposing sources: traditional segregationists who were uncomfortable with any representation of black life, and racially progressive Brazilians who feared that they would be fetishized as exotics in an American travelogue. Reactions in the Brazilian media show people were unhappy that Welles was filming the poverty of the *favelas* in particular. Both *Diário da Noite* and *Meio Dia* complained in articles published the same week that Welles was showing an unseemly side of Brazilian life. *Da Noite* complains, "The filming of the favelas was not appreciated," while *Meio Dia*'s strong indictment of Welles criticizes his representation of Carnival because "only negroes appear."[33] The latter article goes so far as to suggest that Welles seek help from the Departamento de Imprensa e Propaganda (DIP) to avoid a film in which "only black people figure, as though Rio were another Harlem[.]"[34] A month later, after Jacaré's death, Gatinha Angora complained even more aggressively in *Cine Radio Journal*: "They let him film, to his delight, scenes of hills, no good half-breeds, at sambas which are not always 'Brazilian,' but full of music known all over the world; [and the] filthy huts of the 'favelas' which infest the lovely edge of the Lake."[35] As Benamou suggests, *It's All True* elevated subjects that "from a white North American point of view appear as 'profane' to the level of the sacred."[36] But the subject of lower-class black life appeared to be equally profane to a number of Brazilians as well.[37]

Welles challenged the social and racial bias of both cultures by visually elevating the impoverished black populace of Brazil, and his coverage of the *jangadeiros* in particular challenged mainstream politics regarding class and race. Welles incorporated heavily throughout the *jangadeiros* section the

Christ imagery of fish, cross, and fisherman that are so familiar to Western literature.[38] However, he also unintentionally exploited the very population that he purported to celebrate. The *jangadeiros* section of *It's All True* became indicative of the difficulties of the project in balancing an attempt at ethnographic entertainment that would also educate the viewer, an early form of "infotainment" now popularized by a variety of media outlets like the History Channel. It also shows Welles's inability to dislodge himself from the position of privileged viewer, a shift that, had he made it, would have moved his film from the realm of exploitation to that of revolution.[39]

Jacaré and the Tragedy of the *Jangadeiros*

The heart of Welles's film was the political confrontation between the four *jangadeiros* (Manoel Olimpio Meira, Jerônimo André de Souza, Raimundo Correia Lima, and Manuel Pereira da Silva) who sailed into Rio de Janeiro to confront President Vargas regarding greater civil rights. Unlike the Carnaval sequence, the *jangadeiros* story had a concept for specific shot sequence and would "star" the *jangadeiros* themselves, letting the most famous, Jacaré (a nickname given to Manoel Olimpio Meira) narrate his own story. The story line outlines twelve scenes designed to introduce the dangerous lives of these rural fishermen to the American public. Sequence four was to show a drowning, and sequences seven to eight the finding of the body and funeral. The scene features Jacaré's mother, sister, and niece mourning a fictitious character, whom Benamou interprets as becoming a metonymic stand-in for Jacaré following his death during the filming.[40] Welles planned to bridge the *jangadeiros* storyline and the Carnival storyline by restaging the *jangadeiros*' arrival in the Rio de Janeiro harbor as though it occurred on the eve of Carnival rather than in the previous autumn. Undoubtedly, the fictionalized version of the *jangadeiros* would have been romanticized in Welles's finished product, but it still held the potential to let poverty speak for itself, a revolutionary concept for mainstream Hollywood.

Of the existing film footage that remains, the *jangadeiros* shots are the most beautiful sequences of the film, with striking photography of the people themselves and their oceanside lives at Ceará (Figures 8 and 9). This part of the film was planned to feature Jacaré, the most famous of the four *jangadeiros*, talking directly to the audience about his life and political beliefs. The script depicts an articulate, persuasive man who does not romanticize poverty as do many descriptions written by the Welles film company[41]:

> JACARÉ: In my time I have wept. You might think, looking at my ugly sunburned face, that that is not possible. But I know what it is to get home and see the children hungry. We throw a few remains of fish

> on the fire, the wife fries them, and the tired body throws itself on bed until dawn, when the jangada has to leave. If it rains, the roof leaks and wets everything. It is misery. My man, to live like this is not worthwhile."[42]

Welles was insulated from this type of poverty, even though he was very interested in representing it in his film. During a preliminary visit to Fortaleza March 8–11, 1942, Welles stayed at the Jangada Club, which his interpreter Mathilde Kastrup described in her journal as "swanky as any yacht club, merely preserving the outward aspects of a rustic beach club."[43] He participated in a staged sailing race on a log jangada raft and saw the *jangadeiros'* homes after dark, returning to the hotel to dictate details of the film script. Then, according to Kastrup, "The DIP [the department of propaganda] crowd took charge."[44] The Welles visit was a staged event, superficially engaging the poverty that surrounded him; he remained a tourist filming a travelogue—a goal he had explicitly rejected at the outset of the project. On the basis of his limited view into the *jangadeiros'* lives, Welles exclaimed,

> I have never seen more colorful, adventurous people anywhere in the world. To me these are truly Brazilian people. I love the way they live and their happy, carefree approach to life. I think the jangadeiros sequence will be the high spot of our film[. . . .] The day before I got there I was told that one of the jangadeiros had been killed while racing his boat. The 45 minute race in which I took part resulted in a serious injury to one of the jangadeiros in the very next craft.[45]

Unable to remove the lens of white privilege, Welles misreads the lives of the *jangadeiros* and deciphers them as moving scenery—equivalent to the parrots or monkeys he invokes in his later *Hello Americans* radio broadcast. Their poverty is carefree; their injuries are an adventure, a good story. This diminishment of the *jangadeiros'* complexity and humanity didn't bode well for their working conditions on his film, and within three months Jacaré would die while reenacting his revolutionary protest sail to Rio.

The accounts of Jacaré's death vary,[46] but it appears that on May 18 or 19, 1942, the *jangadeiros* were being towed to a beach to film the reenactment of their sailing trip to Rio. They were towed to the wrong beach, and as the film crew waved them toward the shore, a wave capsized their raft, throwing all four men into the ocean. Jacaré was the only one to drown. The reactions to his death in the mainstream Brazilian media seem to see his loss as the tragic result of collisions between fiction and truth, capitalism and communal life, North and South America.

Austregésilo de Athayde wrote in *Diário da Noite*:

> Jacaré died at the edge of the beach, in an adventure without grandeur [. . . .] Better had they [the *jangadeiros*] all stayed on their dunes in their little carnaubastraw houses, without ever having seen the allures of Babylon, without meeting the American movie people [. . .] without knowing Orson Welles.[47]

A day later in *Da Noite* Berilo Neves wrote, "It is a grave error to transplant Reality to Fiction, legitimate heroism to the fleeting legend. [. . .] The jangada of the Northeastern caboclose does not fit into the narrow environment of the cinema lens."[48] Most incisively, however, *Correio da Manhã* published a column honoring all those who have died working in the cinema, pointing out that the majority of these are stunt men whom nobody knows. Jacaré was treated as another low-paid, expendable "extra" in the industry, and the article rightly prophesizes that "[t]he film, however, incomplete, will not be finished because Jacaré—a true hero—had no double to risk himself in the dangerous parts of the film."[49]

When Welles returned to Fortaleza for filming after Jacaré's death, he made a greater attempt to connect with local culture and have an authentic exchange with the community, in part because he had lost his RKO funding but also because he strongly felt Jacaré's loss.[50] But still, as Benamou notes, the social and cultural conflicts surrounding the *jangadeiros'* poverty "were swept from our view" in the filmmaking process.[51] The revolutionary concept of this portion of the film was undermined by the structure of the filming itself, from the staged excursions into the *jangadeiros* community, to the pay and working conditions of the *jangadeiros*. Ultimately, although Welles was able to push the boundaries of cinematic tradition conceptually and thematically in the desire to represent Jacaré's perspective, he was operating within a deeply hierarchical, capitalist commercial system that treated Jacaré as a relatively inexpensive commodity.

The Carnaval Sound: Possibilities and Obstacles to Marketing *It's All True*

Like the *jangadeiros* section of the film, the Carnaval sequence held innovative potential. It sought to develop the sense of aural pastiche and to represent the sheer diversity of Brazilian samba music, but it nevertheless lacked an overall Brazilian subjectivity. Despite Welles's desire for authentic representation and his effort to hire "a team of Brazilian journalists and intellectuals" as research consultants, the production was still generated within a conventional Hollywood production system.[52] Welles was constantly balancing his own interest in exploring taboo images of miscegenation, class warfare, and carnivalesque rebellion with the publicly stated mission of his project, to support Allied jingoism. Added to the inherently political conflict within his film, there was also an aesthetic conflict. In part because of his interest in adapting literary texts for media performance, Welles had long been interested in exploring the intersections between modernist literary forms and the emerging forms of mass media narrative in radio and film. One hallmark of Wellesian media narrative is an ability of the performance to call attention to the mechanisms of its own production, to demonstrate a sense of self-awareness and critique often associated with a modernist aesthetic and rarely associated with the emerging "classic" Hollywood cinematic narrative. As Miriam Bratu Hansen argues, "Modernization inevitably provokes the need for reflexivity."[53] When there is no attempt to resolve the ambivalence at the heart of modernist critique, then art tends to lean toward the pleasure in fragmentation and dissolution that is associated with a postmodern aesthetic. Because of the unfinished state of *It's All True*, it evokes the postmodern pleasures of nonlinear narrative collage, denying attempts to reconcile its contradictions or the multiple voices and images within its narrative.

In her study of classic Hollywood and the modernist aesthetic, Hansen outlines the traits commonly associated with the classic Hollywood film and suggests ways in which American film systems are able to incorporate and absorb evolutions in cinematic narrative. According to Hansen, Hollywood film has traditionally been associated with a sense of narrative unity that masks "process and fact of production," celebrating instead the psychology of individual characters and formal harmony.[54] But she also suggests that the emerging system of classic Hollywood cinema transcended these formal expectations, flexibly incorporating challenges to formal unity and harmony as they emerged, embracing self-critique. She sees American classic cinema as "a regime of productivity and intelligibility" that also functions as "a scaffold, matrix, or web that allows for a wide range of aesthetic effects and experience" rather than a rigid universal system.[55] Welles's experience with RKO suggests that the Hollywood system did embrace experimentation, conflict, and disharmony but only to the extent that such experimentation promised commercial and political viability.

The stakes were high for American cinema in this era, and the studios were each trying to establish a coherent reputation for a certain narrative style that would promise them a niche of the consumer market. This quest for commercial viability drove studios to create unique cinematic languages of image and sound that audiences would come to crave—specific genres, directors, and stars that could be recirculated to consumers with reliable profitability. RKO had invested in Welles as a potential image of intelligent experimentation with media entertainment. The cinematic language in *It's All True* was experimental, to be based on image and sound, rather than on written dialogue, but Welles still wanted this new language to be commercially appealing. As Hansen again suggests, "whether we like it or not, American movies of the classical period offered something like the first global vernacular."[56] Welles wanted precisely to create this type of global vernacular, a combination of sound and image that would transcend spoken language and appeal to a polyglot Pan-American identity.

One central identifier of the Wellesian narrative is its ability to incorporate modern ambivalence and awareness of metanarrative within its structures, whether on stage, screen, or radio. Even in his 1936 farce *Horse Eats Hat*, Welles delighted in startling the audience by breaking the border between stage and auditorium. He staged "accidents" in which his actors would fall into or be exposed to the audience, perform "spontaneous" musical numbers during intermission or extend the stage action into the auditorium to dismantle audience expectations of the division between performance and reality.[57] In almost every Wellesian production, there are moments designed to encourage audience disorientation, whether through the fake news bulletins in *War of the Worlds* or the proposed direct-address prologue to *Heart of Darkness*. Welles sought to disorient the audience once again in his Rio project, announcing in a Mercury press release on May 5, 1942, that the film would "be comprehensible to the eye and not necessarily the ear of the audience."[58] Specifically intending to experiment with sound in his film, Welles wanted to use music to deconstruct the visual images. This aural focus perhaps explains why, even after the failure of the film, his *Hello Americans* radio broadcast about Brazil captures many of the issues, themes, and even narrative techniques that Welles articulated as goals for *It's All True*.

Jazz and samba. Welles intended to use music to evoke an emotional response through correlative aural experience, and his concepts for the *It's All True* soundtrack often connected samba with jazz. His shift from African to Latin American topics moved him to the edge of a postmodern aesthetic, still projecting tenets of modernism but also beginning to revel in the disintegration of boundaries and binaries. Welles liked the rhythmic, hybrid connotations of both samba and jazz, and after he decided to forgo the African American jazz section of the Rio project, Welles transplanted his ideas regarding jazz in the United States to samba in Rio. His choice to focus on samba rather than the more bourgeois Brazilian carnival marches reflects his interest in the samba's association with the rhythmic *batuques* and *lundus* and with a history linked to African slaves. "The hills" of samba emerge as recurrent images in several drafts of both the film and radio scripts for the Rio projects. The radio version played a samba excerpt, and then in all draft and broadcast versions, scripted Welles to deliver the line, "Dig that rhythm, you cats. That's the Amazon and the Congo talking." For Welles, samba represented the coming together of Africa and the Americas, a polyglot music that represented his fascination with the primitive, but with the potential for polyglot oneness rather than binary division.

Welles wanted samba music to represent the potential for Pan-American unity, a shared language of music that would unite human experience across boundaries of class, race, and language. He opens his Carnaval plot treatment by exploring the relationship between samba and American jazz:

> Our Carnaval picture opens in the hills, in this huge conservatory of the samba[. . . .] Rio's kinship to old New Orleans is pointed out. The analogy is pursued, and we come to the conclusion that these cities are closer than they seem on the map, that between American Jazz and American Samba there is much in common.[59]

Both types of music were of interest to Welles in their spontaneity, their unscripted ability to blend various traditions across lines of class and race, and their public appeal. Thus samba served as the central metaphor for the Rio section of *It's All True*. The film was driven by sound as much as by its visuals, and he planned to employ sound to flout Hollywood expectations for conventional narration. In his "Carnaval" plot treatment, Welles asserts, "Music, as I have said, is the basis of our picture."[60]

"Amelia" and "Praça Onze." In both the film project and the early concepts for the radio version of *Hello Americans*, Welles incorporated two sambas in particular: "Saudades da Amélia" and "Adeus, Praça Onze." Both of these sambas share a sense of nostalgia for the simplicity of premodern sensibilities and were carnival hits in 1942.[61] The first, sung to a woman who is not Amelia, longs for the simplicity and poverty that the former girlfriend Amelia represents. The singer accuses his current girlfriend of superficial materialism and longs for the days when Amelia would willingly starve for him:

> You only think of riches and jewels,
> Everything you see you want
> Oh, how I long for Amelia—
> She really was a wonderful girl.
> Sometimes she went hungry with me.
> She thought it lovely not to have anything to eat."[62]

"Praça Onze" strikes a similarly nostalgic note, but for the city itself. In a draft script after Jacaré's death, Welles compares its tone to that of "My

Old Kentucky Home."[63] It laments the death of pre-Vargas Rio, since the destruction of the Praça Onze, a traditional gathering place, was part of the Vargas plan for modernizing the city[64]:

> I'm going to finish with Praça Onze
> There will be no more Samba school, no more
> Cry tamborim
> Cry all the hill.[65]

Individual and cultural death reappear throughout both the radio and film versions of the Rio project, evoking the imperialist nostalgia of primitivism, but with interplay and depth that was missing in his earlier primitivist projects. *It's All True* attempts to capture the voices of a culture that is increasingly threatened by modernization, aware of its own seduction into capitalism and urban development. Dudley Andrew notes that "disintegration" is a key theme of the Wellesian brand, and that "characters, knowledge, entire ways of life are undermined and collapse over the course of his films."[66] But this disintegration can also be seen as dissolution of the individual into the collective, a symptom of political absorption that isn't necessarily negative and can be revolutionary. As Benamou points out, *It's All True* returns the individual "to the state of collectivity" in each segment.[67] The *jangadeiros* return home; Grande Othelo returns to the hills, taking samba with him at the end of Carnival. In this way, the structure of the film mimics its themes: the film offers a documentary exploration of a collective culture through various individuals who are foregrounded temporarily (Jacaré and Grande Othelo,[68] but also Welles himself). Self-exploration still appears as cultural tourism, but the balance of this piece leans toward postmodern pleasures in dissolution or disintegration, as well as in self-reflection.

As the rushes for the film returned from Rio to Hollywood, the studio executives became concerned. The film lacked any marks of the "classic" cinematic unities—no lead actor, no written script, no character development. The film Welles sent back looked, even by his own account, like "[t]housands of feet of apparently repetitious material of people dancing and more people dancing, thousands of feet of crowds and more crowds."[69] Asked by RKO to provide at least a plot treatment for *It's All True*, Welles reluctantly agreed but attached a lengthy prologue to the script describing his aesthetic goals for the picture. Welles emphasized three necessary aspects of his artistic vision: (*1*) Samba music would act as the central "language" of the film; (*2*) to capture the spontaneity of Carnival, no script or recognizable stars should be involved; (*3*) the model for his narrative would be a blend of journalism and entertainment rather than fiction.

The Wellesian voice. RKO could accept the first of the three goals, but the lack of stars and the film's experimental form would prove more problematic. The samba sound could be sold to Hollywood; Welles's further reluctance to script his brand-name voice met with studio resistance. He told the studio in his plot treatment, "it hasn't been possible to approximate the actual wordage."[70] But Tom Pettey, soothing conventional Hollywood, promised to bind the lush visual and musical images of Brazil within Welles's narration, saying, "Over it all will be the Welles voice."[71] He quotes Welles as explaining in a lecture to the Rio cultural society that the film would "be four or five stories with me doing a lot of talking to make them hang together."[72]

Catherine Benamou describes Welles's conceptual shift in *It's All True* as turning away from the model of a director toward that of a feigned "deliberately naïve" collaborator.[73] In particular, his voiceover would be used to deceive the audience, as Pettey explained:

> The Welles voice has been heard throughout the earlier parts of the film which has turned into what the audience suspects to be a travelogue. Suddenly, just as the audience tires, the voice fades out and the cameras turn from the scenic beauties of Rio de Janeiro to a group of pretty girls at Copacabana."[74]

At this point, the camera would shift to the image of the *jangadeiros* coming into the harbor, and the narrative would move from travelogue to revolutionary representation of the underclass.[75] But this experimentation with the use of Welles as narrator would have moved him from trusted authority to trickster figure, setting his voice at odds with the documentary truth-telling form. Even though this type of fact/fiction erosion is now a recognizable hallmark of the Wellesian brand, experimentation with the famous Welles voice, coupled with other experimental strategies, made this film difficult to sell to the studio.

If the unscripted ambiguity and dissonance made it harder to sell the film as a Welles vehicle, so did Welles's plan to share the narration with Brazilian figures like Donna Maria, whom his plot treatment suggests would help explain the samba lyrics. The self-reflexivity present in earlier projects was foregrounded in *It's All True*. Welles's voice would be interrupted, challenged, and generally reduced as a primary point of identification for the audience. In one scene Welles is told by an interpreter that the Brazilians he is filming "say the camera is staring at them." As Benamou points out, this can be seen as "an exposition of the division of labor involved in shooting, and a violation of a cardinal taboo in Hollywood practice."[76] It is also reminiscent of the prologue to *Heart of Darkness* in which he forced the audience to experience the position of caged canaries or electrocuted convicts. In both these projects Welles highlighted the violence inherent within the act of filming, of capturing the body on film.

Similarly, Welles often used his voice to invoke the violence of narration. As Phyllis Goldfarb describes Welles's use of sound in narration, it "calls attention to itself, and reflects on the medium that has promulgated that convention."[77] Much like the experiments with dialogue he was using in his radio series, Welles intended to present himself as participant rather than an authority in his own film. To capture the multiple styles and forums of Carnival samba in his film, he rejected coherent narrative in favor of ethnographic pastiche. He explained that the Carnaval sequence "was to be entirely unrelieved by story (or what is generally considered story)" and yet "above all, it had to be entertainment."[78] With this final sentence, Welles tries to balance the aesthetic and the commercial. In the prologue to his plot treatment, he repeatedly attempts to reinscribe his experimentation within familiar terms for studio executives, but without apparent success.

There were other structural challenges to the studio's marketing of the film as well. Just as Welles refused to use his own famous voice to position himself as a "star," he refused to use recognizable actors in the project:

> no actors were brought to Rio, no big names were made available to the picture, none of the usual cast of characters was present to build around. Finding new people, therefore—Brazilian people—and using them effectively and correctly, was one of our biggest jobs. Yet we always had to remember that this Carnaval part of the picture was less about individuals, or musical numbers, or dances, than about Carnaval itself.[79]

Although the film would not use recognizable Hollywood "stars,"[80] it hoped to create new Brazilian stars. Welles promised that the musician Grande Othelo would act as the central figure and image of the film, leading the viewer from scene to scene (Figure 10). In addition, he positioned Grande Othelo as a potential Hollywood discovery:

> Remember that name. It belongs to the performer himself and this isn't the last time you will encounter it. This is only his first American picture, and he's a big hit in it for sure. Othello likes to be compared to Mickey Rooney, but he's closer to a young Chaplin or Jimmy Savo.[81]

Welles used Grande Othelo as a counterargument for his lack of structure, a familiar image to classic Hollywood—the discovery of a potential big star. Additionally, Welles promised that the introduction of samba itself would be lucrative for RKO, that "[a] movie about Samba couldn't be better timed[. . . .] It adds up to this: R.K.O. controls the market on Samba."[82] Welles balanced his radical experimentation and politics with promises of traditional consumer popularity to appease the increasingly nervous RKO executives.

"Shooting a storm": Unstructured Carnival style. Welles's second argument for the unstructured shooting schedule and style of *It's All True* was that Carnival itself could be captured cinematically only through a strategy of spontaneous filming coupled with dramatic reenactments of key scenes or moments. Benamou describes his strategy as modeling the film "stylistically and structurally upon the ritual of Carnaval itself—its theory and practice."[83] Tying his unorthodox scripting style to the desire for ethnographic authenticity, Welles argued that his expensive habit of shooting many repetitive reels of film was necessary, since "the problem of shooting Carnaval may be compared to the problem of shooting a storm. We often had no choice but to set up our camera and grind away until we got something useable."[84] Again rejecting the rigidity of a linear script, Welles argued, "Our Carnaval film will have a script only after its completion in the cutting room. It must also be explained that no story line exists or can exist—no important narrative pattern involving personalities and human events."[85] He emphasized that this style had been accepted before he left for Rio, that "It was understood by all concerned before I left that carnaval would be shot on the cuff."[86]

In this way, he equates the spontaneous scripting with the "authenticity" needed to convey Carnival. The lack of Hollywood actors and script support the journalistic, magazine feature goal of his filming. This is not to say, however, that *It's All True* was journalistic reportage. The "truth" Welles was interested in was clearly manufactured, a trait made much more obvious in the eventual *Hello Americans* broadcast where Welles responds to a fictitious listener who asks if he's broadcasting from Brazil, "by short wave" by saying, "No—dramatic license. . . . This broadcast comes to you by dramatic license, from the first place you think of when you think of Brazil . . . from Rio de Janeiro."[87]

Welles sought to create a brand of documentary fiction that probed the concept of truth, and he freely admitted that many scenes of Carnival were reshot and reenacted. He suffered no illusions of art separate from politics or commercial viability, admitting, "we knew almost at once that it would be necessary to restage many episodes and customs of Carnaval[. . . . T]he Department of Press and Propaganda offered to see that anything we might want to restage would be put together again at any time convenient."[88] There is inherent ambivalence in Welles's goals to record accurately and yet to create entertaining "scenes," and *It's All True* openly treads the boundary between fact and fiction, critiquing itself even in its creation.

This model of fictitious, ambivalent reporting was not new to Welles's filmmaking, nor was it new to the American modernist narrative. Welles's narrative position in *It's All True* mimics that of the reporter Thompson in *Citizen Kane.* As Robert Carringer notes, Welles is an evidence gatherer whose search for authority, like that of Thompson and Nick Carraway in *The Great Gatsby,* "is undermined by the very process of searching."[89] These news-gathering narrators become less confident of their missions as they learn more of their subjects, according to Carringer.[90] As in *Heart of Darkness,* the ultimate object of the modernist quest is unknowable, elusive, and perhaps even dangerously alluring and self-destructive. Welles positioned himself at the nexus of the unknowable exotic in *It's All True,* eschewing a fictitious character in favor of himself as narrator but also submerging his individual role into a polyglot Pan-American collective. This proves a dangerous strategy in classic Hollywood filmmaking, which prefers an identifiable director or star to draw in viewers at the box office. It also proves the malleability of the classic Hollywood narrative, however, in that as David Boardwell and Kristin Thompson suggest, the system can adapt and absorb deviations in its traditions, regulating "what may violate it."[91] Ultimately, this flexibility allows Hollywood cinema to absorb "idiosyncratic auteurs like Orson Welles."[92] Welles was working to build a new type of classic cinema language, one that would challenge familiar cinematic tropes while still incorporating aspects of traditional Hollywood. In his journal of the Rio experience, Tom Pettey quotes Welles's ambition:

> I'm going to do something that has never been done before and probably never will be repeated. I'm making a picture that is neither a travelogue, a documentary film, a boy meets girl romance nor a glorified newsreel. It's going to be a new medium of entertainment[.][93]

But of course even this quote was circumscribed within the Hollywood production method; Pettey's journals were sent to Mercury publicist Herb Drake and to columnists Hedda Hopper and Erskine Johnson, among others. However revolutionary the concept of narrative for the Rio project, it was taking place within the Hollywood studio system for political and commercial purposes. In this way, the project is more revolutionary in its unfinished state.[94]

The Carnival footage that remains from *It's All True* juxtaposes the various classes and locales of the samba balls, moving between private clubs and public squares. The styles of samba are also contrasted: big bands versus local sambas from the hills.[95] Thus the Carnaval segment as it remains can be seen as a site of "reconciliation of national, regional, class, and racial difference."[96]

This assessment would probably not be possible, however, if the film had been edited for final commercial release. Two bodies of evidence seem to suggest that a finished studio version of the film would have circumscribed its oppositional, diverse images within linear, commercial finality: notes regarding the economic and political trajectory of the film, and the production process that resulted in the final script for the *Hello Americans* Rio broadcast.

"Playing with a Purpose": Art and Propaganda in Brazil

The prewar politics that spawned *It's All True* were fundamentally at odds with the prewar economics that motivated RKO. Benamou summarizes the irreconcilable tension between the diplomatic and cinematic missions for *It's All True* by saying, "[T]he war formed both a *precondition* for the development of the Latin American project [. . .] and a *pretext* which RKO executives considered using for discontinuing the shooting in Brazil."[97] Welles, as diplomat, was supposed to bridge North and South American cultural differences. Welles as director was supposed to market these differences to an American audience. This created "fissures in studio-government collaboration at the material levels of production and distribution."[98] In other words, the two entities that encouraged Welles to embark on the Brazilian project had fundamentally opposing goals. Although the project was initially conceived to address the overlapping needs of the government and RKO, increasingly Welles was perceived by the studio as elevating his role as goodwill ambassador over his role as director of a marketable Hollywood film.[99]

Welles's appointment by Nelson Rockefeller as a goodwill ambassador refocused the film project on the question of why North Americans should be interested in and (financially) invested in South America.[100] The Office of the Coordinator of Inter-American Affairs (CIAA),[101] Motion Picture Division, created in October 1940, suggested that projects like Welles's would "further the national defense and strengthen the bonds between the nations of the Western Hemisphere" and invested more than $20 million in feature pictures.[102] The CIAA invested significantly in Welles, even agreeing to insure the "producer against loss up to 30 per cent of the total production cost, but not to exceed $300,000." Schaefer invoked this subsidy to reassure investors that the project was worthwhile.[103] In this way, Welles's mission was primarily political, and the local media reports of his arrival offer a picture of him being met by more politicians than fans, with none of the screaming girls who greeted Tyrone Power on a similar trip (Figure 11).[104]

In addition, the Mercury publicists worked hard to position Welles as an authentic member of the Brazilian community rather than just another exploitative tourist from the North. When Welles arrived in February, he told the media that he was almost born in Rio, and downplayed his efforts to avoid the draft by saying, "In the first place my number has not come up. . . . And in the second place, even if I did want to serve as I did want to voluntarily, I would not be accepted because of my health exam[. . . . T]he work I am doing here is much more important than keeping guard over highways"[105] Pettey's April 2, 1942, correspondence describes Welles as "one of the city's most impressive landmarks" and promotes the story that Welles was drawn to Rio because his parents honeymooned there: "'So,' said Orson, 'I was conceived in Brazil. I must go there and make a motion picture among my people.'"[106] Thus Welles and his publicity men tried to position him diplomatically as both patriotic and personally loyal to Brazil—the embodiment of a Pan-American identity.

But the proposed propaganda function of the film was fundamentally at odds with its concept as an authentic examination of Brazilian life, since the presentation of the Vargas regime as a desirable partner of the United States required "'democratic' whitewashing."[107] Welles's radio broadcasts from Brazil at the time supported his diplomatic propaganda function, and even the *jangadeiros* section of the film could be interpreted as supporting a positive image of the Vargas regime, since it provided an example of the "regime's positive' achievements in the direction of democracy."[108] Welles was perceived as more successful in his diplomatic mission than his cinematic project, and the CIAA commented as late as April 1942 that "Mr. Welles' presence in Brazil has had a most satisfactory effect, both with the public and with the Brazilian Government."[109]

On the government's side, the CIAA had two goals: to bring rural communities into contact with urban communities and "to disseminate pro-Ally information."[110] The lectures that Welles delivered to the Rio cultural society and other entities during his stay in Brazil were seen as part of the latter half of this diplomatic mission, as were his radio broadcasts from Brazil. The *jangadeiros'* tale fit the former need, offering a visual image of the rural meeting the urban as they sailed into the Rio harbor, and giving the sense that Brazil was moving toward democracy and modernization, two concepts designed to appeal to mainstream American audiences. The death of Jacaré complicated this mission for Welles, and although he stayed in Brazil as a goodwill ambassador until August 1942, both the film project and his diplomatic effectiveness waned with the drowning of Jacaré.

Even before Jacaré's death, however, RKO wanted to pull the plug on Welles's project due to budgetary concerns and the sense that he was running amok without studio supervision.[111] Benamou attributes part of the budgetary concern to RKO's own financial crisis in 1941 and 1942, forcing them to move from "'high quality,' 'artistic' features [. . .] to low budget, crowd-pleasing series" like the Tarzan films.[112] Welles had been hired under the assumption that he would be a prestige director, not a crowd pleaser, and this shift made his Wellesian brand an increasingly bad match with RKO. The budget crisis made the studio assert more creative control over all their directors, not just Welles, but their increasing desire to intrude on his always independent creative process put their goals for the Brazilian project squarely and irrevocably at odds with his. Benamou interprets the CIAA as being more pleased than RKO with Welles because RKO wanted to quantify Welles's work product in terms of hours, money spent, and potential for profit, whereas the CIAA preferred to think of his diplomatic mission in the context of increased communication between the cultures.[113] Therefore, activities that seemed wasteful to RKO—like simply mingling socially—were seen as positive to the CIAA.

The liberal, unstructured concept for *It's All True* could not have been tried at a worse time for RKO. Welles's unscripted filming technique resulted in 66,134 feet of Technicolor footage and (only about a quarter of it from actual Carnival, the rest of it staged) and 19,414 feet of black-and-white footage by May 4, 1942.[114] While certainly they were saving money on acting salaries by hiring locals, not stars (Jesús Vásquez Plata,[115] the child actor in the "Bonito" section was to be paid sixteen dollars a week), they were also hiring casts of chorus girls and crowds of extras to reenact Carnival. Welles's total expenses by June 29, 1942, were $678,185. In particular, he paid the Urca casino a large amount to stage Carnival sequences and tended to spend anywhere from a thousand to fourteen thousand dollars a day. Welles's grandiose plans were often scaled back by RKO, including his plan to "live with the *jangadeiros* in Fortaleza for several weeks."[116] Communication back to RKO was expensive as well, and UP correspondent Frederick Othman describes Welles working from his "headquarters at the Casino de Urca, where four jazz bands play constantly" and chatting "with the boys here at RKO via telephone at $6 a minute—and if you don't think the facts in this dispatch cost a pretty penny, then you're not an RKO stockholder."[117]

Welles's Mercury public relations team strove to reassure RKO and the public that Welles was a serious diplomat and creative genius rather than a North American playboy on a profligate spending spree. Editorial changes to Pettey's March 31 missive reflect a desire to downplay Welles's reputation as a child-genius who is out of control in favor of building a more responsible image of him and suggesting that the filming delays were due to a cultural slow pace rather than to his own disorganization.

> One of the most charming things about Rio de Janeiro is that it is the sort of place that makes Orson Welles seem normal. In fact there

> are times when it makes Welles appear ~~very adult~~ *positively* business like[. . . .] He has been in Rio more than ten weeks and ~~is just getting started in production~~. The Cariocans feel that he is hurrying things a bit, but shrug and say, "he is not as eccentric as most North American businessmen who want to do everything in a week."[118]

Pettey's public relations placement worked, and was picked up by Othman, who wrote that Rio is "the one place which makes the mighty Orson seem normal. There are times when the city even makes him appear adult and business-like."[119]

Nevertheless, the childlike playboy image was still an integral part of the Wellesian brand, the id to his genius-businessman ego. Pettey describes him on April 2 as a

> boy named Orson who was in a new country populated by happy, care-free people who liked to play. Orson the indefatigable worker, became Orson the untiring playboy[. . . . T]hen one night he went to work and presently discovered he had been playing for a purpose. In those two weeks he had worked out the plot for his picture, learned the habits and customs of the people and had gathered enough material for movies, radio shows and a book.[120]

In this passage, Pettey manages to align Welles's inner child with the primitive "childlike" Brazilians, evoking the binary associations that the project purportedly attempted to transcend. Trying to bridge the gap between his diplomatic and cinematic missions, Welles promised, "When I tie the stories together with my commentary the people of all the Americas will know at least something of the habits and customs of their neighbors. They are going to be entertained, too."[121] This oxymoronic desire to sample Brazilian culture from the position of diplomatic insulation without falling into the traditional studio paradigm of shooting travelogue proved impossible to achieve. Ultimately, it seems likely that Gatinha Angora's concerns were realized:

> Each time the robust and handsome fiancé of "del Rio" points his cameras to so-called "picturesque" spots of the city, we feel a slight sensation of uneasiness, perhaps, like a vague warning of the evil which will come later[. . . .] Yes, because experience has unfortunately already taught us the point reached by the thirst for curiosity of these American technicians who visits us [. . .] lots of talk, lots of praise for our land, our people, our customs, and then, when we have occasion to see on the screen a film on a South American subject, we have that disaster which we all know."[122]

The Brazilian people were not allowed to escape the violence of the colonial lens, even though the fragmented narrative structure of the unfinished film offers glimpses and aural fragments of Brazilian life, the finished product would very likely have had to capitulate to RKO's commercial concerns. To become a viable market commodity, *It's All True* would have been reeled in, literally, in the editing room.

Hello, Americans! The Radio Rio Project

Of course, it is very hard to argue for what might have been, but the best evidence of how the editorial process tended to erase the revolutionary content of Welles's work, along with portions of its revolutionary structure, is the evolution from draft to final copy of the radio version of the Rio project, broadcast on November 15, 1942, after Welles's return from Brazil. The radio broadcast was drafted and revised during Welles's time in Brazil, with an early draft script dated March 1942. Catherine Benamou calls the *Hello Americans* radio shows "the most direct forms of appropriation by Welles" of *It's All True* material.[123]

Many of the same tensions reside within the *Hello Americans* radio broadcast as within the film, and several elements remain intact through all copies of the draft into the broadcast version. For example, the radio broadcast retains Welles's vision of samba music as the central "language" of the performance, as well as the use of a multivocal blend of journalism and entertainment. It also treads the line between documentary and fiction, invoking the type of genre blending familiarized in *March of Time* and other historical-fictional blends of the era. However, as the script was revised for broadcast, it also eliminated several of the revolutionary structural and thematic components that Welles originally intended to be central to his film. It turned away from attempts to capture the unique voices and multiple perspectives of ordinary Brazilian citizens, instead using voices and perspectives that were familiar to Americans. The broadcast version represented the Brazilian voice through the singing of Carmen Miranda, capitulating to the commercial desire to sell a "hot" commodity through a known star and propagating the exact exoticism that the Brazilian media had feared.

An early draft for the script dated March 6, 1942, reflects Welles's original ambition to include a polyvocal critique of the Northern perspective on Brazil. The script opens with Welles's voice introducing the samba. In an attempt to address the concerns of the Brazilians who saw samba as an undesirable public representation of Rio de Janeiro, Welles promised that samba would show

> another side to Rio. Not a seamy side—not at all, even if chic isn't the word for it. No, indeed, if Rio's back yard isn't exactly gala, it's even

> gayer than Rio's front lawn. There isn't a jazz-smith up North who could ever express it. It's set to music but the music's all its own—rich, deep, Brazilian. It comes rolling down to Rio from the hills, it throbs in the streets, everybody dances to it—it's called samba.[124]

Undermining the univocality of his narration, he is interrupted repeatedly by Brazilian voices labeled simply "1st voice" and "2nd voice." These two voices challenge oversimplifications that Welles asserts about the cultural life of Brazil and reflect the multiple perspectives on Brazilian life that Welles's research team had collected and translated from local media. Specifically, the voices argue over the origins of samba, whether it was born in the hills or the city. One voice focuses on the popular conception of samba as born from the folk tradition of the hills, while the other sees the hills as a place that marginalized urban groups temporarily escaped to when necessary: "It is this way, Sr. Welles: as the Police were distressed with the noises made by musicians in the city late at night, they arrested them without pity. This is why they took refuge in the hills where Police could not reach them. The Samba belongs to the city, to all Rio."[125] In later versions of the script, however, the conversations with these dissenting, "authentic" voices are cut, so that Welles controls the narration. As narrator, he periodically enters into brief dialogues with other figures who present American consumers with commercial products from Brazil—Carmen Miranda, architecture, parrots.

The script retains the central concepts of *It's All True.* For example, it emphasizes the parallels between samba and jazz. However, the broadcast eliminated the complexity of dissent within Brazilian culture and the conflicting interpretations of samba within that culture. Even in this draft script, the section of the dissenting voices is marked out, creating a cut from the line "That's the Amazon and the Congo talking" to Welles saying "I'd like to remark that Samba, like some wines, doesn't seem to travel very well."[126] The revised version waters down the Brazilian cultural debate over samba even more and presents samba simply as a potential export for Americans who like jazz and other "exotic" pleasures. An insert to the draft presents the American voices of a mother and her two children, "Junior" and "Girl," who talk about all the delightful things you can buy at the festivities surrounding Carnival.

> GIRL: They have so many beautiful costumes, for a long time I couldn't make up my mind whether to go as a gypsy girl, a Hindu, an Hawaiian, or Minnie Mouse. We finally decided, though—mother and I both went as Baianas. They're all the rage.
>
> JR: Baianas are natives of Bahia.[127]

The children educate the American consumer regarding what exports to buy from Brazil—what will be "all the rage" in terms of exotic accessories from South America—and evoke familiar North American images, Mickey Mouse and gypsies. Following the exact pattern of the proposal for *It's All True*, Welles goes on to introduce samba music, discussing with a voice labeled "Linda" the lyrics to "Amelia" and "Praça Onza," the same two sambas represented in the film version. But then Welles is interrupted once again by a voice labeled "Brazilian."

> BRAZILIAN: Sr. Welles, excuse me, but I'd like to raise an objection.
> WELLES: Certainly, Sr.
> BRAZ: Is it not possible you give too much emphasis to our Carnival?
> WELLES: How can your Carnival be over-emphasized? [. . .]
> BRAZ: "Now don't you think it would be wrong for you to give your country the impression that our country does nothing but laugh and sing?
> WELLES: [. . .] if we learn your songs, we'll get to know you better. Music doesn't need to be translated. As for laughter—I'd like my people to hear your people laughing. It's a very beautiful sound. Laughter isn't what you'd call a luxury. Just now it's a necessity. Don't worry: I'll tell about your schools and factories and your magnificent new cities—this isn't just one broadcast; this is part of a whole series. But, Sr., laughter is the first attribute of civilization and I want my countrymen to know how civilized you are . . ."[128]

Welles uses the Brazilian dissent to silence it, but it is still represented in this early draft. Later drafts exchange the Brazilian voices for more American voices, which share impressions of Brazil from the point of view of the privileged tourist, there to consume products and return home, rather than attempting to represent any of the conflicts inherent in simplifying a culture down to a one-hour entertainment broadcast.

The broadcast version of "Brazil" focuses on two themes comforting to the American listener in a wartime era: democracy and modernization. It keeps an opening from an earlier draft in which Welles's monologue is interrupted by a jingoistic American, saying,

> I love my country without you telling me to, and so does everybody else. Okay? . . . What do you mean by saying the show you're doing is only for Americans who talks [*sic*] English. Everybody in America talks English.
> WELLES: I've got you there. I was just saying it's easy to forget how much

> America means when you got on the phone. You say we all love our country, and of course that's true. But do we all love America? Do you realize what America means? (Music: Sneaks In)[129]

Welles then patiently guides the listener in an aural equivalent of drawing back a camera into a long shot of the Americas, moving out from "our neighborhood" to "our state" to "our new nation" to "America—two continents—One continent with a canal. Our half of the Globe, Our portion of the earth. The new world."[130] This version retains the concept of the interrupted narrative but uses it to reassure the skeptical American audience rather than to represent the complexity of the Brazilian subject. It also introduces Carmen Miranda to the script as the voice of Brazil, a change that was retained in the broadcast version. The marketing vision for RKO's cinema project and the CBS radio broadcast were similarly dependent on using big-name stars and familiar commodity images to hook audiences. Both forums accepted experimentation only to the extent it didn't disrupt the commercial potential of the broadcast or its wartime propaganda function.

To emphasize the themes of democracy and modernization, the broadcast script introduced several American voices identified by their occupations—architect, businessman, writer, etc. These roles are kept in the final November 15, 1942, broadcast, which opens with the skeptical American followed by a dialogue with Carmen Miranda in which she introduces the audience to the exotic instruments used for samba, emphasizing their African origin and their use of catskin.[131] Then Welles shifts to a marketing campaign for Brazil as a potential investment for North Americans:

> WELLES: . . . Brazil is a big country—a very big country. . . . There's a lot to like—and a lot to tell: there's history and legend and romance. Most people don't care very much for statistics. It depends on what interests you. For instance, if you're a businessman—
>
> BUSINESSMAN: That's what I am—a businessman. I'll tell you something about Brazil: This country is three million square miles of the biggest wealth potential on God's green earth. . . .[132]

This version emphasizes Brazil's modernization and economic potential, moving from Businessman to a mining engineer who talks about gold and diamonds—"big ones too."[133] He is particularly interested in manganese for steel. The character "Explorer" argues with "Sociologist" about the demise of the jungle as it is consumed for construction and the advancement of civilization. An architect and his wife are focused on how to bring Brazilian goods home with them:

Architect: My wife wants to take at least two dozen parrots back home with us. Me, I'm an architect, and I'd prefer some of the Baroque Colonial buildings I've seen . . .[134]

Welles: That's quite a problem, moving large buildings from one country to another. I think it's been done, tho. . . .[135]

The most heavily edited dialogue between the draft and final versions are the lines of a character titled "Writer." In the draft script, he says he likes the "Skyscrapers and voodoo"[136] of Brazil, but in the broadcast version, "jungles" is handwritten in over "voodoo." The images of primitivist modernism are replaced with the commodities and resources that are valuable to the wartime effort—technology, minerals, energy. In both the draft and final copies, "Writer" is drawn to the interracial identity of Brazilians, but only a hint of this aspect of Brazilian life makes it into the broadcast version. Several lines about intermarriage and mixed racial identity are cut, but the final script keeps the writer's assertion that "Portugal's the melting pot of Europe," and that therefore "a drop of real Brazilian blood is an honest to goodness drop of all mankind's blood."[137]

In typical Wellesian self-reflection, the broadcast concludes with Welles ruminating about "the committee of blind men who investigated the elephant." Each describes just the portion of the body he can touch, and therefore all are wrong:

Welles: . . . Each expert had a different version of the truth—depending on which section of the elephant's anatomy he happened to grab. Now, I don't pretend to be able to see any better or any more than anybody else who might try to describe these countries, but I promise I won't concentrate solely on the trunk or the tail or the tusks—or natural resources or Indian war dances or butterflies or Big Business. It's not easy, but I am going to try to outline enough so you can fill in enough to get some notion of what the other half of America really looks like.[138]

This would have been an ambitious goal for the broadcast series, to return to the serialization format he had perfected on radio during 1938, but to use serialization to build intercultural understanding.[139] The structure of this broadcast mimics aurally many of the visual goals of the unfinished *It's All True* in terms of employing a polyvocal, documentary fiction format, as well as incorporating themes of Pan-American identity, antifascism, prodemocracy and racially progressive politics. But as the editorial process for this broadcast shows, much of the revolutionary power of the film would have been lost as it moved through the editorial and distribution process.

Welles might try to reassure us, as he did the Brazilian skeptic in the March 6 draft script, "Don't worry: I'll tell about your schools and factories and your magnificent new cities—[. . .] I want my countrymen to know how civilized you are . . ."[140] But why not let the Brazilians decide what aspects of the culture they would prefer to equate with civilization?

Mainly because industry publicists thought they could sell images of the laughing, happy simplicity of Brazilian life. Pettey had tried to tap into this image in his March 31 entry in his Rio project journals, which tried to resituate the negative press about Welles's high-profile speeding and partying in Brazil by saying, "If Welles goes tearing about town in a high speed automobile as he does on shooting days, the natives leap out of the way of the fenders and laugh. They are accustomed to leaping and laughing."[141] Pettey depicts Welles as the life of a party that all of Rio is attending: "it was really Orson's carnival. Before he arrived in Rio there had been little enthusiasm of the pre-Lenten festival. It was wartime, the people were not interested in celebrations."[142] Pettey attempted to resituate the communal event of Carnival into a first-person-singular Wellesian event, and this type of consolidation of cultural experience into the Wellesian brand was far from a radical act.

Welles's interaction with the Brazilian community seems ambivalent, at times making connections but also alienating many people. Not only did resistance to his presence in Rio appear in the local papers with increasing frequency during his stay, but he also began to have problems with his own crew. Pettey reported on May 5, just days before Jacaré's death, that Welles was getting harassment from the RKO home office. He complains, "Welles is quite difficult[. . . .] He has had so much publicity he feels that he can push any of the newspapermen—Brazilian or American—around and that he is above criticism. He'll find out."[143] This ominous warning would be fulfilled just days later, after Jacaré's drowning, when Welles's support from the press, the government, and RKO disappeared. Sadly, this letter from Pettey indicates how futile Jacaré's death may have been. He says, "It looks like we have spent a lot of time on the Jangadeiros for no purpose as I hear by the grapevine that the studio has called off that part of the film."[144] The grapevine apparently had not given Welles the same message, and the filming continued on May 18, resulting in Jacaré's death.

The failure of *It's All True* could be best summed up by a Brazilian voice: that of Enéas Viany, who wrote a piece in spring 1942 titled "They Think It Is but It Is Not." Viany argues that the North American perception of Brazil is that "we speak Spanish and can only dance samba." But he argues that Brazilians are equally at fault for this misperception, since he has "colleagues who place the name of Carmen Miranda on the same level as [pianist] Guiomar Novais, [sociologist] Gilbert Freyre or [opera singer] Bidu Sayao."[145]

In a sense, Welles is correct in his assertion in the prologue to the Carnaval plot treatment: "It cost a lot of money for us to come down here[. . . .] The only way that cost could be justified was for us to make here a picture and not a travelogue, to make a Carnaval Sequence which would define, in itself, the difference between a documentary and a feature story[. . . .] The time and the money haven't been wasted."[146] Precisely because *It's All True* remains unfinished, and because its production is so well documented by Welles's own crew, the media, and the governments of both countries, this project left behind a wealth of information on the attempted formation of transnational identity, the commercial exploitation of South America by North America, and the patterns of narrative experimentation in both radio and cinema at midcentury. Had the film been finished, probably much of its complexity would have been erased in an effort to create a seamless commercial product.

One of the draft scripts for *It's All True* seems keenly aware of the tensions within the process of the project's development and touches directly on several of the issues that would ultimately sink the project. In this draft script, undated but written before Jacaré's death, Shifra, the script girl (based on Shifra Haran, Welles's assistant), introduces the *jangadeiros* story to Welles when he complains that they need more stories of real people or they'll never finish the picture. After calling him a "fat wreck," Shifra gives him a sheaf of papers that she has had translated to English from Portuguese. She tells him of the *jangadeiros'* trip to Rio and says of the papers, "That was written by Jacaré. He's their leader. I tell you seriously, Orson, he's one of the great men of the world."[147] Welles, moving seamlessly from *being* the first-person singular to *representing* it, reads the words, "'My name is Jacaré. I was born on the beach at Iracema in the province of Ceará—' As he continues we FADE OUT."[148] Welles's first-person singular here merges into Jacaré's identity, tying together the two personas at the center of the film, foreshadowing how closely the fate of the project would be tied to Jacaré.

In addition, this version moves from the *jangadeiros* to Carnival by using President Vargas as the transitional figure. In the transitional scene, introduced by samba music, Welles visits with President Vargas in his office, and they talk about the *jangadeiros*. The ending resonates with the past's haunting blindness to the future. Vargas says he wishes Welles could have met the *jangadeiros* when they were in his office and comments reassuringly, "As you know their story has a happy ending."[149] Sadly, nothing could be further from the truth.

It's All True offered an ending for Welles and RKO as well, but not a happy one. By the time of this final RKO project, Welles had moved away from the Mercury Theatre classic adaptation strategies and had begun to explore the boundaries between truth and fiction, when combined with the first-person singular. The resulting entertainment forms were too progressive for mainstream Hollywood to accept as commercially viable. Increasingly, Welles would move from Hollywood insider to exile, eventually removing to Europe and taking on increasingly Quixotic projects. This shift from the role of American propagandist to expatriate critic (and occasional Hollywood heretic) gave Welles his lasting legacy. Although his years at RKO produced more "unfinished" than finally edited and marketed projects, his complexity of vision and desire for experimentation with the blurry line between fact and fiction would become the true legacy of the Wellesian brand, and would have enduring effects on mass media entertainment. We see his legacy today in the "confessional" booths of reality television, the laughing audience of "fake news" shows, and the proliferation of fragmentary texts on Internet sites like YouTube. The twenty-first century is truly an era of Wellesian pleasures—not the elite pleasures of auteur cinema but the mass media pleasures of fakery and fraudulence, and of self-referential images that encourage the audience to unravel these forgeries and delight in their revelation.

Afterword

Wellesian Legacies—What, If Anything, Do Mel Gibson, Stephen Colbert, and Steven Spielberg Have in Common?

The Wellesian brand has helped establish at least two images that resonate in contemporary American media culture: the star director and the concept of "truthiness." This final section examines twenty-first-century manifestations of these themes that intrigued Welles in the earliest stages of his career, and suggests why they retained such cultural relevance. When we compare these two entertainment legacies, the Wellesian concept of "truthiness" appears to have had an even greater impact on American culture than does the advent of the star director.[1]

The first part of this chapter examines the legacy of directorial branding, using two contemporary director-driven films that initially recall early Wellesian projects. The first movie, Mel Gibson's *The Passion of the Christ* (2004), shared many of the ambitions and obstacles of Welles's own proposed Christ project but ultimately circumvented mainstream studio barriers to become a huge economic success. The second project, Steven Spielberg's adaptation of *War of the Worlds* (2005), shared many strategies with Welles's famous adaptation but had a much less immediate impact on its audience than did the 1938 radio broadcast, despite being a box-office hit. Controversy helped fuel the success of both these projects, although the controversy surrounding Gibson's *Passion of the Christ* can be understood as emerging from a post-Holocaust perspective, while Spielberg's adaptation of *War of the Worlds* can be attributed to its post-9/11 context.

Over the course of the twentieth century, the Christ project became a type of American cultural touchstone through which budding star directors (in the case of Mel Gibson, a star actor already) could establish themselves.

Directors ranging from Cecil B. DeMille to Martin Scorsese took on the challenge of adapting a Christ narrative, with varying degrees of commercial and artistic success. Much like the Holocaust film, the Christ narrative addresses a topic of historic and spiritual importance in an attempt to assert artistic control over archetypal narrative. The assumption is that if the male director (for mastering the master narrative seems to be a primarily masculine preoccupation) can assert creative control over such a culturally central narrative, then he has achieved technical, commercial, and artistic excellence. In this way, the Christ narrative represents an artistic opportunity for the auteur and a commercial opportunity for the star director. The director highlights his individual interpretation and domination of a culturally collaborative narrative, and if successful, he is rewarded with an increase in filmmaking reputation and commercial status. In Gibson's case, *Passion of the Christ* was a huge success, eventually grossing more than $600 million worldwide.

Although one of the reasons Welles abandoned his Christ project was religious controversy, this same controversy was one of the major reasons for the success of *The Passion.* Gibson chose to center his Christ project in the contentious tradition of the passion play,[2] and images of Christ's suffering were cited as a main reason for the box-office draw of the film in terms of their "realism." However, these images also proved highly disturbing to a broad cross-section of the audience. Ultimately, *The Passion* appears to have been a short-term success for Gibson, since he has been unable to build on its popularity.[3] Thus despite the fact that Gibson brought to fruition a film project Welles was only able to conceive, he has failed at this point to establish himself as a directorial brand.

In contrast to Gibson, Spielberg has successfully established himself as a market brand, capable of promoting his films through the association with his own name. He is perhaps the most powerful director of his era, able to "green-light" projects that are associated with his name even as a producer. Though Spielberg is unarguably a star director, critics still debate his entitlement to auteur status based on artistic merit. Spielberg's artistry has a distinctly commercial bent, and as Warren Buckland notes, "Spielberg's brand image is closely linked to his internal auteur status [. . .] ."[4] By first forming Amblin Entertainment and later DreamWorks, Spielberg also created a marketing structure for films that were associated with but not by him. Both companies were closely linked to Spielberg himself through their logos—much as Welles's work was always clearly identified by his voice. The Amblin logo directly invoked Spielberg's signature film, *E.T,* and as Buckland observes, the later DreamWorks logo incorporated the moon imagery of Amblin to convey "an idyllic, idealistic, sentimental Norman Rockwell–type image of America—another universal image of lost childhood experience."[5] Amblin and DreamWorks acted as mechanisms to present Spielberg's vision of cinema and successfully extended his brand to incorporate the work of others. DreamWorks espoused goals similar to that of George Schaefer and RKO in Welles's era in that both studios wanted to promote prestige directors. DreamWorks saw itself as a space for creative filmmaking driven by personality and talent, particularly for directors "who have their own vision and imagination, and do not require constant guidance."[6] Thus DreamWorks was able to attract "directors such as Robert Zemeckis, Ridley Scott, Woody Allen, and Sam Mendes."[7] Spielberg emerges as an auteur's financier, a director who has moved into the realm of producing other director's works and who is able to imbue the work of others with his own directorial brand.

If Gibson inherited Welles's penchant for controversy, Spielberg inherited his gift for visual "magic." Spielberg's personal brand of filmmaking emphasizes spectacle, which is often equated with the "magic" of cinema. Buckland describes Spielberg in language reminiscent of those who emphasize Welles-as-magician. Spielberg is "the conjurer who has mastered the art of entertaining via technical virtuosity."[8] Accordingly, Spielberg's adaptation of *War of the Worlds* diverges from the Wellesian approach in its focus on spectacle over suspense, partly due to the medium in which it is expressed, film rather than radio. While Spielberg's *War of the Worlds,* like Welles's, wisely and profitably places itself within an updated historical context—in this case a post-9/11 spectacle of terror—it fails to engage the audience with the sense of "reality" that Welles's radio adaptation was able to imbue, never challenging the realm of fantasy. Focused on the spectacle of violence rather than the terror of invasion, Spielberg's *War of the Worlds* fails to authentically engage the audience.

The latter half of this chapter examines a countertradition to directorial branding that nonetheless emanates from the Wellesian brand. The concept of "truthiness" reflects the erosion of truth in mass media and the instability of individual notions of agency and truth. "Truthiness" thus implicitly problematizes the type of artistic unity that cinematic theories like auteurism celebrate. Instead, the exploration of "truthiness" focuses on community sense making and emphasizes comic satire over epic tragedy. The popularity of contemporary fake news shows like *The Daily Show* and *The Colbert Report* suggests that, while Welles provoked mass awareness of the potential of "truthiness" in his 1938 *War of the Worlds* broadcast, the logical (or illogical) conclusion of his career-long exploration of the line between fact and fiction has been the reduction of panic to laughter. The once provocative use of a news format for the purpose of fiction has become so familiar that it is now a joke. In fact, these fake news shows have more in common structurally with Welles's *War of the Worlds* broadcast than does Spielberg's direct adaptation of the original text. Ultimately, the Wellesian brand spawned as many progeny in political satire as in cinema.

Christ on Film in American Culture

At the heart of the rise and decline of *The Passion of the Christ* as a defining project for Mel Gibson as a director are two competing claims. The first assertion should sound familiar to disciples of Welles: Gibson staked his reputation as a star director on the assertion that his film was authentic in its attention to details of suffering and emotional resonance. Second, Gibson attempted to minimize the post-Shoah repercussions of any project focused on the crucifixion of Christ by aligning himself with the suffering protagonist and denying the potential for anti-Semitic interpretations of the film. The second assertion ultimately proved fatal to his emerging reputation as a star director (at least temporarily—as Welles would be the first to point out, there is always a chance for self-reinvention in Hollywood). Due to both the critical aftermath of *The Passion of the Christ* and Gibson's eventual self-destructive anti-Semitic outburst and arrest, he became an iconic image of how to be a negative spokesperson for a directorial brand.

Attitudes toward the commercial representation of Christ shifted during the forty years between Welles's Christ proposal and Gibson's project, but some aspects of religious controversy were retained. Certainly there is much to be studied in terms of the commodification of Christianity—and of religion in general—in twenty-first-century American society.[9] But central to Gibson's Christ story, and to many other directorial interpretations of Christ as well, is the spectacle of suffering. The Christ project engages star directors for the same reason that the Holocaust film proves an alluring field on which to establish directorial credibility: it affords both prestige and controversy. The controversy in Welles's time as in Gibson's tended to focus on the desire for "authenticity," although the definitions of this term relative to Christianity have changed over time. As discussed in the first chapter, the potential debate over the Wellesian *Life of Christ* centered primarily on a Christian perception of gospel-based accuracy—would Welles present Jesus as divine, and would he be willing to depict the Jews as responsible for his crucifixion? In Gibson's millennial era, concern with Hollywood's representation of the divine appears minimal, and negative comments regarding *The Passion*'s representation of Jesus arose mainly in terms of the extreme violence performed on his body, which was celebrated as "authentic" by some viewers and was criticized as emotionally exploitative by others. Although Welles ran into solid resistance from clergy in terms of trusting Hollywood to interpret the Bible, twenty-first-century clergy had few such hesitations, instead seeing it as a good public relations opportunity for Christianity. Post-Holocaust, however, the anti-Semitic potential of Christian propaganda became a greater concern than theological or historical accuracy for many critics and viewers.

The sheer number and status of modern directors who have chosen to take on a Christ project testifies to its relevance as a directorial "test." Christ projects include D. W. Griffith's *Intolerance* (1916), Cecil B. DeMille's *The King of Kings* (1927) and Nicholas Ray's subsequent remake (1961), Franco Zeffirelli's mini-series *Jesus of Nazareth* (1977), and Martin Scorsese's *The Last Temptation of Christ* (1988). Mel Gibson's *Passion of the Christ,* however, stands apart in its entertainment draw for Christian audiences, many of whom seemed to accept its images as closer to Biblical "truth" than earlier dramatizations. Thus the theological debate surrounding this film took a backseat to cultural debates over its emotional impact, including potential anti-Semitism and violence that could be seen as either inspirational or offensive.

Gibson positioned his film as an authentic rendering of Christ's last hours through three major strategies: use of Aramaic, Hebrew, and Latin languages[10] to give a sense of historical context, invocation of key scenes from the Bible to establish textual accuracy, and stylized use of violence to establish emotional connections to Christ's suffering. These strategies were largely effective, although there were signs that the claim to authenticity would be problematic even in early viewings. For example, a widely reported endorsement of the project by the Pope dissipated under pressure[11]: in September 2003 and again in December, Vatican officials refuted the alleged papal assertion that the film accurately depicted Christ's death: "It is as it was."[12] Ultimately, the claim to authenticity would center on the film's ability to create an emotional viewing experience through graphically violent images of prolonged suffering—emotional rather than historical accuracy.

While some critics and scholars did attempt to examine *The Passion of the Christ* as an interpretive work of fiction within the Hollywood tradition of representing Christ's life via the gospels, even these critics returned to questions of violence and anti-Semitism in the film. For example, Adele Reinhartz surveys depictions of Christ on film throughout the twentieth and twenty-first centuries, looking specifically at which portions of the gospels appear in various adaptations. Echoing the comments of Welles's era, but from a Jewish perspective, Reinhartz is particularly concerned with the representation of Caiphas and the Jewish crowds as potentially anti-Semitic. Reinhartz points out that Gibson's *Passion* draws from all four gospels and primarily focuses on the spectacle of Jesus's suffering, even from its opening citation of the "suffering servant text from Isaiah 53: 3–5."[13] The film emphasizes in this initial epigraph that the crowd will be healed by Christ's wounds; therefore, the wounds themselves become the centerpiece of the film. The question of authenticity in Gibson's version of the Christ story shifted from the representation of history as based on the Gospels to the authenticity of emotion—and the power of the viewer's experience dictated what "truth" lay in the viewing experience.

Far from relying on the gospels as literal interpretation, Gibson uses the suffering servant quote, dating from 700 B.C.E., to provide "a rationale for the relentless violence to which the film subjects both Jesus and the viewer."[14] Bruce Zuckerman, examining Gibson's film for realism, finds instead a highly emotional and subjective interpretation. But this, he reminds readers, is an inherent challenge of any Christ project, since the gospels are examples of creative artistry and storytelling, and the true details of destruction and crucifixion—smoke and flies in Zuckerman's terminology—can distract viewers from the emotional experience of the film. Thus, Gibson immerses his film in emotional, rather than realistic, details of Christ's suffering.

The exaggerated and prolonged violence of the film divided audiences and was considered moving by many Christian viewers but as disturbing or even pornographic by others. Despite Caleb Deschanel's highly stylized cinematography and the film's heavy use of symbolism, musical score, special effects, flashback, and other techniques not usually associated with cinematic realism, the "realistic" nature of the film was frequently singled out for praise by viewers on online chat boards. Kelly Denton-Borhaug's analysis of viewer reactions on the Internet Movie Database (IMDb) indicates that such "sacrificial images" were "absorbed uncritically by a huge portion" of viewers."[15] She argues that the viewing of this violence was ritually cathartic for Christian viewers who saw it as part of the "calculus of salvation."[16] For these viewers, to suffer with Christ seemed to become more authentically Christian. They thus perceived *The Passion* as "not a theological movie nearly so much as it is a visceral contemplation of the agony of Jesus' willing sacrifice."[17]

This ability of *The Passion* to arouse viewing pleasure through violence can also be seen in secular terms, an example of the power of spectacle as an antidote to postmodern alienation. Stuart Robertson suggests *The Passion* aroused "deeper emotions than sports or patriotism" and thus filled a void in the postmodern viewer for whom strong, authentic emotion is a rarity.[18] This explains the appeal of the film for viewers who did not readily identify themselves as Christian but nonetheless found the film's prolonged contemplation of violence to Christ's body moving. "Realism" for these viewers emerged through their emotional relationship to images of suffering.

For critics of the film, the spectacle of suffering proved more problematic. Critical reactions tended to position the film as melodramatic or pornographic but not historically authentic. Several critics saw the violence as a direct reflection of Gibson's own imagination, following in the tradition of his earlier and equally violent (yet also profitable) historical fiction, *Braveheart*.[19] Although both of these films were controversial box-office hits, *Braveheart* was additionally celebrated by the film industry, in part because it was seen as an engaging historical epic, winning five Academy Awards, including Best Picture, and grossing more than $210 million worldwide.[20] *The Passion,* while nominated for three Academy Awards, in make-up, cinematography, and score, won none and was a greater box-office than award-show success.

The hyperemotional impact of *The Passion* led to its association with two traditionally disrespected cinematic modes: melodrama and pornography. Melodrama often connotes an excessive and maudlin emphasis on emotional suffering. Lester Friedman points out that protagonists in melodrama "suffer for our sins; their torment caused by the intolerance, rigidity, and repressive codes of conventional social order."[21] The experience of shared suffering through spectacle makes the protagonists "innocent victims worthy of our compassion and admiration. Thus melodramatic characters attain moral status chiefly through their suffering."[22] For many viewers, *The Passion* achieved this formula of identification through suffering and produced a powerful emotional experience, and it is precisely the level of violence that is often cited by viewers as moving and praiseworthy in their online reactions to the film. For many other viewers, however, the hyperbolic violence of Gibson's *The Passion* crossed into the realm of soliciting pleasure through violent voyeurism.[23] Denton-Borhaug, invoking the work of Linda Williams on the ecstasy of both the horror film and the melodrama, suggests that *The Passion* elicits the pleasure of *scopophilia* often found in the pornographic snuff film.[24] For Denton-Borhaug, the spectacle of violence in *The Passion* becomes "a form of divine domestic violence."[25] Similarly, James Moore finds *The Passion* "nearly pornographic in its violence."[26] By regarding *The Passion* as either melodramatic or pornographic, these critics position the film in genres known for exploitative images of feminine ecstasy and suffering—a gender inversion of the *Braveheart*–William Wallace association of violence with masculine adventure fantasies. In turn, the association with these low-brow film genres assured the film's lack of critical acceptance, even as it guaranteed box-office success. Thus Gibson was treated as a star director but not as a budding auteur.

One of the most interesting, yet underexamined, aspects of *The Passion* is its exploration of nontraditional gender imagery within a traditional genre.

Its cross-gender appeal also broadened its potential swath of consumers. Gibson's film represents perhaps the height of this populist genre of the life of Christ as melodramatic action-adventure film. The film's use of gender inversion makes sense, however, when one considers Friedman's assertion that the protagonists of melodrama are really much closer to protagonists of action-adventure than one might expect. Although the former is equated with a feminine form and the latter with a masculine, the suffering action hero is really just a melodramatic protagonist moved outside the confines of the middle-class, bourgeois domestic setting. Both are spectacles of suffering, but the melodramatic protagonist suffers the "whips and arrows imposed by representatives of a vast social network of values, while the action/adventure heroes endure suffering as a necessary prelude to glorious deeds of bravery and valor."[27] Gibson's suffering Christ straddles these two modes, suffering for social and cultural values but rising again in bravery and valor through crucifixion. As depicted by Gibson, Christ is a suffering icon who fulfills both masculine and feminine ideologies, individually triumphing while sacrificing for the community. This cross-gender representation also appears in the androgynous representation of Satan in *The Passion*, creating a sense of symmetrical gender ambiguity between protagonist and antagonist.

In a post-Holocaust context, however, the Christ-story genre has become increasingly problematic. In the pre–World War II context of Orson Welles's *Life of Christ*, before the horrors of the Holocaust were fully known to U.S. viewers, the potential impact of anti-Semitic interpretations of the Christ story were rarely publicly considered. Concerned for the potential impact of the project, Welles wrote to Christian, not Jewish, leaders. Furthermore, the reactions by clergy show concern for "authenticity" only in terms of their idea that the Jewish community be represented as directly responsible for Christ's death. American culture had yet to acknowledge the severity or the depth of potential anti-Semitic violence. While "authenticity" was a major concern in Gibson's post-Holocaust era, the question of perspective also become paramount—*whose* authenticity?

In a contemporary cultural context, the question of depicting the Jewish community as responsible for the death of Christ (or the even greater crime of deicide) invokes an array of concerns that demand consideration. Steven Leonard Jacobs reviews the multiple reactions to Gibson's film within the American Jewish community and argues that the discrepancy between Jewish and Christian viewing experiences lies in the perception by Christians that the film was a "*religio-theological* experience; for Jews the film was an *historical* experience."[28] For viewers of any denomination, the emotional power of the film was diminished if seen in the context of historically anti-

Semitic representations of Judaism and realities of Jewish suffering. The film's prolonged exploration of crucifixion at the expense of themes like resurrection and salvation increased the sense of pornography for viewers who did not experience an emotional connection with these images of violence. Specifically rejecting the hyperemotional focus on Christ's suffering, James Moore argues that contemporary contexts call for a move "away from theologies of sacrificial suffering toward theologies of respect for the other as the central redeeming act."[29] These calls for a post-Shoah reinterpretation of the violent spectacle of Christ's suffering are made all the more potent by Gibson's ensuing drunken anti-Semitic tirade, undermining his denial during the controversy surrounding *The Passion* that there were anti-Semitic images within his film. In a post-Shoah context, even Gibson had to acknowledge the existence of anti-Semitism, even if only to disavow it.

As a star director, Gibson enjoyed a meteoric rise in 2004, followed by a disastrous fall after his drunk-driving arrest and accompanying anti-Semitic outburst in July 2006. *The Passion of the Christ* had an overwhelmingly positive impact on Gibson's star director status: in 2003 Gibson didn't even appear on the *Forbes* list of top one hundred celebrity power rankings.[30] In 2004, he was at the top of the list, buoyed in part by his $210 million profit from *The Passion*.[31] Gibson used an innovative marketing strategy for *The Passion* that helped solidify a broad Christian market. The film's low-key promotional strategy has been described as "below-the-radar" in its ability to target sympathetic audiences at small venues.[32] For example, Gibson took the film to Colorado Springs for a screening at Ted Haggard's New Life Church, where it was praised as "historically and theologically accurate" by Don Hodel, president of Focus on the Family. To this audience, Gibson emphasized his film as an ecstatic vision of religious truth: "The Holy Ghost was working through me on this film, and I was just directing traffic[. . . .] I hope the film has the power to evangelize."[33]

In contrast to Welles's active solicitation of perspectives on his Christ project, Gibson deeply resisted incorporating criticism from audiences beyond his target niche. He responded to prerelease criticism from a nine-person panel composed of Catholic and Jewish leaders by threatening to sue them.[34] Gibson was also contacted with concerns regarding *The Passion* by a variety of Jewish organizations, including the Simon Wiesenthal Center, which articulated two overall worries about the film's potential impact: that it might provoke anti-Semitism, including Holocaust denial, and that it might negatively affect Jewish-Christian relations.[35] Jewish organizations situated the potentially anti-Semitic images within the film as the latest in a vast repository of Jewish caricatures in Western literature and culture. The

Anti-Defamation League's advisor on interfaith affairs accused "Gibson of re-creating images akin to Fagin [. . .] or Shylock."[36] Both of these canonical figures hail from classic literature that Welles adapted for mass consumption, but they read quite differently in a post-Shoah popular culture. Even authors with the status of Dickens and Shakespeare are not immune to cultural re-evaluation, and the prestige of classic literary adaptation can become a yoke that weighs down the potential auteur.

The nine-member group of Catholic and Jewish scholars that convened prior to the film's release articulated at length the most prevalent concern regarding *The Passion*. The panel, convened by the Anti-Defamation League (ADL), produced "an 18-page report warning that parts of the film would revive charges that Jews collectively were Christ killers."[37] The assertion, initially dismissed by many viewers, that *The Passion* shows that "Christians have taken to heart the grotesque images of the Crusades, the medieval pogroms, and the Holocaust,"[38] holds more credibility in the context of its star director's later postproduction, off-set behavior.

Unlike Welles, Gibson remained deaf to even the most persistent and direct statements of unease regarding his film project. Gibson equated himself with his film project, playing both a "repentant sinner" who seeks redemption through the film and a suffering creator who fears persecution at the hands of an angry Jewish mob.[39] When Abraham Foxman, director of the ADL, wrote directly to Gibson on March 24, 2003, and again on January 23, 2004, asking him to soften any depiction of the Jews as responsible for Christ's death, Gibson at first refused to respond and then responded perfunctorily.[40] Asked in January 2003 if his film would upset Jewish viewers, Gibson said, "It may. It's not meant to. I think it's meant to just tell the truth. I want to be as truthful as possible."[41] By rejecting negative feedback and positioning his film as an authentic vision of the death of Christ, Gibson chose to market the film to a niche Christian market, and his marketing strategy wisely focused on this niche.

Gibson united two major segments of American Christian moviegoers—evangelical Christians and Catholics—by "combining a Baroque Catholic sensibility with Protestant blood-atonement theology" for a broad Christian appeal.[42] Describing the strength of the Christian market segment, Nicole Gull asserts, "They're organized, centralized, and easily motivated to rally around one man: Jesus Christ."[43] The distribution and marketing of the film catered to this audience: the distributor, Newmarket, specialized in locating niche audiences[44]; one of the companies hired to promote the film, InService America, "maintained a database of roughly 10 million Christian consumers" and "contacted nearly 100,000 pastors to ask them to mention the movie in their weekly congregation newsletters" prior to the film's release.[45] In addition, the Web site encourages readers to "spread the word" about the film, provides support materials for churches who want to host group viewings, and links to a merchandise page that sells film-related materials. This innovative grassroots approach to marketing proved highly effective, turning out Gibson's target demographic at comparatively low cost. Positive responses from these Christian viewers were also used to assert the film's emotional authenticity and refute allegations of its anti-Semitism, thus increasing its financial success. Gibson was effectively positioned as a spokesperson for a brand of Christian authenticity, as well as for the film itself.

The strategy to conflate Gibson and his work backfired, however, when his drunk-driving arrest in July 2006 threatened the market viability of his overall brand name. The ADL's Foxman recalled the controversy surrounding *The Passion* and used the incident to revive criticism of the film. He suggested that Gibson's drunken anti-Semitic outburst revealed "his true self and shows that his protestations during the debate over his film [. . .] were a sham."[46] Gibson publicly denounced his behavior, pronouncing himself "wrong" and "ashamed."[47] Gibson's budding directorial brand suffered, and his reputation was damaged. Fellow producers such as Jerry Weintraub expressed personal disappointment, and Disney dropped Gibson's planned Holocaust miniseries.[48] His few defenders tended to tie their defense to authenticity in *The Passion*. For example, James Dobson of Focus on the Family reasserted his opinion that *The Passion* was not anti-Semitic and stood by Gibson.[49] Dobson may have been responding in part to a sense among some Christian groups that Foxman and the ADL had launched a "defamatory campaign against Mel Gibson's film [. . .] that treated Christianity as innately anti-Semitic."[50] Thus the defense of Gibson was seen as a defense of Christianity itself.

The Passion was an attempt by Gibson to solidify his budding reputation as a powerhouse director and to complete his shift from actor-as-star to star-as-director. This was a shift that Welles, like other directors, had wanted to accomplish in part via a life-of-Christ project. Gibson partially succeeded, since as Anthony Burke Smith points out he does fit the "popular image of the rebel auteur" who goes outside the Hollywood establishment to get his artistic vision screened. However, the controversy that accompanies any Christ film risks long-term brand appeal. Welles wisely recognized that while his *Life of Christ* would bring both prestige and controversy, two hallmarks of his budding film brand, the circulation of the image of Christ in contemporary popular culture is very difficult to contain. In a post-Holocaust context, the Christ narrative is even more culturally complex, particularly when coupled with the spectacle of iconic suffering and deicide. The Christ project as a genre, while commercially viable, appears difficult to integrate into a body of work and to sustain as a complement to a film director's overall career because it risks alienating any one of a variety of Jewish and Christian communities for whom the narrative has great personal relevance. Therefore, while it can meet the needs of a niche market product, it seems an unlikely source to enhance an overall "blockbuster" cinematic brand.

Steven Spielberg's *War of the Worlds*

Another star-director vehicle, Spielberg's 2005 adaptation of *War of the Worlds*, offers a sharp contrast to Gibson's project in terms of aesthetics and marketing strategy. Spielberg, widely regarded as a blockbuster director, also adapted a former Wellesian project as part of his directorial brand. Although Gibson, Spielberg, and Welles could all be seen as pursuing the ideal of star director, each has a very different approach to the balance between creative authorship and salesmanship. Spielberg attained the commercial success that eluded Welles but remains largely uncelebrated by film theorists.

Although Spielberg's *War of the Worlds* emphasizes spectacle in ways that Welles's radio play could not, there are some similarities between his adaptation technique and that of Welles a half-century earlier. In particular, both directors accentuate the use of a limited-view, first-person narrator as envisioned by the original author, H. G. Wells. Both the earlier novel and its radio adaptation produced narratives that coalesced with fears of their audience—namely the fear of invasion by another technologically superior sovereign nation. Friedman suggests that the appeal of *War of the Worlds* for both the original H. G. Wells audience and the later Welles audience was that it "encapsulat[ed] first England's and then America's worst communal nightmare: invasion followed by annihilation[. . . .] It was easy to envision the Germans or the Russians attacking England or America, to substitute their frightening war machines for the rampaging Martians."[51] In both cases, this fear of invasion was specifically conveyed through a first-person narrator, engaging the audience directly in the process of interpreting events as they unfold. In this way, Wells as author and Welles as adaptor invoke the same first-person-singular technique to establish panic in their audiences.

Spielberg shared with Welles the goal of directly embedding his audience in the action of *War of the Worlds*, and the press kit for Spielberg's film describes a camera technique that reminds one of Welles's attempts to engage the audience in a first-person sensory experience in his first RKO project, *Heart of Darkness*. The press kit describes Spielberg's use of "previsualization," a technique that strings animated storyboards into three-dimensional digital sequences with the goal of putting "the audience inside the events of the film."[52] Spielberg also tried to capture H. G. Wells's original sense of first-person perspective by using "restricted narration, in which we share Ray's lack of knowledge of the aliens' activity."[53] This restricted narration also recalls Orson Welles's use of the reporter Carl Phillips to position the audience as first-hand observers to the events unfolding during the 1938 invasion. In each case, the audience is invited into the process of sense making, creating a participatory experience for the reader, listener, or viewer.

Another connection between the Welles and Spielberg adaptations is their use of a "common man" protagonist with whom the audience identifies. Welles accomplished this by using Carl Phillips to report "man on the street" reactions to the invasion, while Spielberg chose to use the blue-collar everyman Ray for his protagonist. This tendency to filter large sociopolitical events through the eyes of an individual is a recurrent Spielberg technique, which Friedman argues helps to create a sense of "common people swept up in events beyond their control," thus narrowing "the gap between viewer and protagonist."[54] Spielberg supported this narrative technique with a correlating visual style, using sympathetic motion of the camera to help convey "the first person perspective that is so crucial to Wells's novel."[55] This restricted camera motion mimics Welles's use of the microphone in the 1938 radio broadcast, which similarly limited the listener's experience by making some noises almost inaudible to force the listener closer to the radio, using cross talk to create the sense of listening to a crowd, or incorporating silence to give the sudden sense of being cut off from the broadcast itself. These audio techniques create an effect similar to that of sympathetic camera motion, helping "to create the film's relentless, terrifying mood."[56]

Welles used Phillips's on-site interviews with witnesses to the alien landing in rural New Jersey as a highly effective method for narrowing the distance between the listener and the characters within his fiction, creating the sense of a roving "eye" for the listener. Phillips's microphone allowed the audience to "see" the fictional events unfold but also dictated their experience of events, just as camera movement in film manipulates the viewer's perspective. Welles's technique, in part because of its use in a live-broadcast, in-home format, proved so effective at creating audience identification that it created real panic from a fake event. This audio technique was a direct precursor to his "I = eye" camera use as articulated for *Heart of Darkness.* The ocular equation reappears in Spielberg's *War of the Worlds* in his use of handheld camera shots, which "simulate an individual's point of view" and cram "*War of the Worlds* with visual images and verbal references to eyes and seeing, not surprising in a post-9/11 America[. . . .]"[57] Friedman equates these images with a post-9/11 preoccupation with surveillance, a postmodern condition of living within the confines of technology, but a gesture toward this condition, if not its full realization, appears quite clearly in Welles's early work as well.

Spielberg is sometimes juxtaposed against Welles in a low-brow/high-brow dichotomy[58] that stresses Welles's association with unmarketable yet sophisticated cinema and downplays his huckster-magician entertainment moments, which are particularly evident on television variety shows and commercials. In contrast, Spielberg is often thought of "as little more than modern P. T. Barnum, a technically gifted and intellectually shallow showman who substitutes spectacle for substance and emotion for depth."[59] His films are consistently commercial successes, offering a prime example of a directorial brand with significant audience pull over multiple decades, films that can be advertised as the "new Spielberg film" rather than sold via the starring actors. He is widely acknowledged as a savvy businessman with undeniable commercial success. DreamWorks was sold to Viacom for $1.6 billion in 2005, making him "the most financially successful director in Hollywood history."[60] A clear example of the star director, Spielberg averages around $150 million domestic gross per film; his first project to gross over $200 million was *Jaws* (1975), and his most recent film to gross over $200 million was *War of the Worlds* (2005).[61] For more than a generation, Spielberg has consistently produced blockbuster films. He has also, however, directed a variety of critically respected, award-winning films, including *Munich* (2005), *Saving Private Ryan* (1998), *Schindler's List* (1993), and *The Color Purple* (1985).

Spielberg sharply contrasts Gibson in his sensitivity to cultural context and his ability to tap into cultural impulses not at a single moment or in a niche market but over a wide range of time for vast audiences. Spielberg's functional equivalent of the Christ project would be *Schindler's List*, which although controversial in its marketing of the Holocaust, struck a critically and commercially successful tone in its depiction of history and religious suffering. Aimed not at a niche audience but rather at the broadest possible segment of viewers, the film combined high-quality aesthetic choices in its use of cinematography, narrative, and actors with a Holocaust storyline that could appeal to both Christian and Jewish audiences. It was awarded seven Academy Awards, including those for best picture and best director. Unlike Gibson, Spielberg avoided alienating portions of his audience and paid close attention to the cultural context of his work.

These elements of success in Spielberg's work as a star director might suggest that *War of the Worlds* would be a cultural event with impact similar to that of Welles's 1938 radio broadcast. The cultural context for Spielberg's

War of the Worlds seemed ripe for a film about the spectacle of terror in an American city, and just as Gibson's Christ project cannot be read without taking into account a post-Shoah context, Steven Spielberg's *War of the Worlds* demands a post-9/11 interpretation. Referring to Spielberg's use of "the iconography of the World Trade Center attacks" and the "panic and terror of such a violent experience," Buckland calls *War of the Worlds* Spielberg's "9/11 movie."[62] Friedman sees the images of "urban apocalypse" in the film as evoking media coverage of both Vietnam and 9/11.[63] Both these interpretations emphasize a spectacle of violence that Hayden White describes as a "modernist event" in which the magnitude of violence represented would have been unimaginable prior to the twentieth-century.[64] Spectacle is central to the Spielberg brand, which is widely known for using strong visual images to create blockbusters.

Despite his attempts to engage the audience with techniques from the earlier novel and radio adaptation, however, there seemed to be a fundamental lack of immediacy in Spielberg's film. At the time of its release, Spielberg's adaptation—unlike Welles's—appeared not to speak to the underlying cultural fear of American viewers who live in an era in which they are more likely to invade than to be invaded, and who thus fear random acts of violence over organized invasion. Unlike Welles's *War of the Worlds*, Spielberg's version reflects a spectacle of terror rather than invoking terror itself. (Spielberg does not make the theater go dark, giving the audience the sense that they are under attack, for example.) This could help explain its minimal impact on the viewing audience, which appeared entertained but certainly not panicked by its images.

Although there are many explanations for the film's ultimate lack of power, Friedman offers a compelling explanation based on the film's function as cultural critique rather than cultural mirror:

> Spielberg propels American viewers into a position of fear and trembling, of feeling what it must be like to have our country invaded, and of facing a technologically superior foe intent on destroying our country. [. . .] By doing so, he raises uncomfortable questions about America's role in the world as the remaining superpower, questions about both its past actions and its future endeavors."[65]

Thus, Spielberg's *War of the Worlds* opens itself to a counterinterpretation as representative of the Iraqi civilian experience during American occupation.[66] While this implication would seem to be lost on most viewers, it would explain the general lack of impact experienced by audiences. Whether one attributes the film's failure to connect viscerally with audiences to its overemphasis on spectacle at the expense of first-person experience or its poor thematic match to its cultural context, it appears that the audience was not tempted to confuse its fiction with fact. In contrast, the power of Welles's radio adaptation came from his ability to create the perception of invasion as reality rather than entertainment. This perception was fed by the medium of radio, since it beamed performance into domestic space. Much of Wellesian performance seeks this conjunction between public and private performance, and in many ways this theme is better suited to television and the Internet as performance media than it is to film. These media also lend themselves to the exploration of the fine line between fact and fiction, a theme that may well be the greatest legacy of the Wellesian brand.

Tricks and Treats: Welles's *War of the Worlds* and *F for Fake*

Welles is often positioned as a trickster figure in part because of his systematic exploration of "truthiness." While one can read *War of the Worlds* as a timely meditation on the threat of invasion or as a critique of the dangerous assumption that radio was a trustworthy medium, it can also be read (and was in fact presented by Welles himself) as a mere Halloween "trick" played on an unsuspecting audience.[67] Radio in 1938 occupied a rhetorical space similar to that of television today in the American imagination. Radio then, like television today, served as a media source that Americans turned to for reliable, real-time information about the world outside their homes, but in Welles's hands it was an equal source of tricks and treats for the American public. The audience trust in technology has shifted over the past forty years, and in the twenty-first century, misleading the American public by media manipulation has become a common political and entertainment strategy, although it was regarded as dangerous and subversive in Welles's era. In addition, the advent of the Internet has added yet another media venue to the American home, one that explicitly flirts with lines of public/private and true/false.

Wellesian performance fits new media venues beautifully because it so often challenges these very lines of public/private and fact/fiction. Welles's cinematic experimentation with the line between fact and fiction originated in radio broadcast and reflects a postmodern interest in eroding the concept of the "real." In an era of seemingly unbelievable political events ranging from Germany's pre–World War II invasions of Europe[68] to the advent of nuclear warfare, Welles became adept at representing the confusion of modern consciousness as it evolved toward postmodern disorientation. His characters often demonstrate an inability to construct a single "truth" when it comes to personal or public history,[69] and we can see their legacy in contemporary broadcast formats that emphasize the concept of "truthiness."

Robert Spadoni describes how Welles duped the audience into accepting fiction as truth in *War of the Worlds*, saying its fictitious news announcer led "already wildly imagining listeners toward still wilder visions[. . . .]"[70] Welles would later often use constructed figures of authority like the news announcer to mediate his tales: journalists, policemen, lawyers, and other traditional arbiters of "truth" in society often appear as his narrators—most famously the reporter Thompson in *Citizen Kane*. *War of the Worlds* parodied the trend of radio as a live news source by using radio as trickster rather than truth teller. At the same time Welles revealed the potential power of broadcast entertainment to forge a mass experience—based on anger and fear in this case.

This shared American experience was, in fact, a stylized technique for simulating a feeling of "real" experience from performance. Welles established a set of performance codes in *War of the Worlds* that helped create fact from fiction in the minds of the audience. Harry Geduld locates five specific techniques that Welles used to increase the believability of his broadcast: familiar-sounding political voices (FDR mimics), sound techniques such as interruption and fade (music interrupted by "urgent" news), direct allusions to the microphone itself (requests to move it closer for better sound), references to real places (Princeton, New Jersey), and fragmented narrative that increased a sense of spontaneity (cuts to and away from broadcast locations, simulated intercepted military transmissions).[71] The conjunction of the news broadcast format, ordinarily associated with truth, and a fictitious content created powerful confusion in his audience. Anchored in the pre–World War II political climate, the strength of this confusion increased to the point of panic. The panic Welles created with *War of the Worlds* not only helped solidify his career but also spurred an interest that would continue to preoccupy him throughout his career in radio, film, and television—an interest in exploring the line between fact and fiction in performance.

Catherine Benamou reads *War of the Worlds* "as a carnivalesque exercise in poking fun at publicly revered sources of institutional authority—academia, the government, the news media[. . . .]"[72] Interpreting the broadcast as an instructive lesson for the audience in how to evaluate credible information via technology, Benamou asserts that the broadcast taught "listeners not to take for granted their access to, and reliance upon, radio communication during an historical period when radio provided the most significant source of news for the majority of the U. S. population."[73] But the broadcast was also instructive in brand loyalty and listening habits—listeners who misinterpreted the broadcast tended to have tuned into the broadcast after it had begun, since it had been framed by Ernest Chappell and Welles's traditional opening to

Mercury Theatre on the Air and would clearly have been an entertainment broadcast to those who listened from start to finish.[74]

Welles's Halloween "trick" had technical and thematic hallmarks that became indicative of his brand of entertainment, and of later genres of "truthiness" as well. Benamou sees the combination of "realism, fabrication, and narrative discontinuity" as tying together *War of the Worlds, Citizen Kane,* and *F for Fake.*[75] As we have seen in earlier chapters, the exploration of truthiness appears perhaps most intensely in Welles's unfinished projects and in fact may have interfered with their marketability. These works seem, in many ways, ahead of their time. We can wonder with Benamou what would have happened if Welles had lived long enough to engage the moment when the "cybernetic revolution reached the average middle-class household in the United States[. . . .]"[76]

Given Welles's innovative use of radio, one suspects he could have had great fun with an interactive medium like the Internet. More important than wishful nostalgia for technological evolutions of the Wellesian brand, however, is the analysis of how the brand is being impacted even now by the cybernetic revolution. Welles's unfinished works, once relegated to studio film vaults and Walter Benjamin's "trash of history,"[77] now have the potential to be recovered, interacted with, either viewed in traditional theatrical settings[78] or manipulated at home by viewers, readers, and listeners on all types of media devices. Although significant obstacles remain in terms of copyright, access, and preservation, technology now offers unprecedented options for interactively engaging with Wellesian performance works.

In part because of his fascination with the line between fact and fiction, as well as new interest in his unfinished works, Welles has developed into a cult media figure. Stagings of both Welles's more obscure or unfinished works and new dramas based on his life remain popular. In the past year Washington, D.C., metropolitan-area theatres featured Welles as a character in his own *Moby Dick—Rehearsed,* Marcus Wolland's *Lost Eden: The Magnificent Welles,* and Austin Pendleton's *Orson's Shadow.* Each of these performances explores the line between the factual and fictional Welles; each creatively interprets dramatic moments from Welles's own life in theater, and each depends on the audience experiencing pleasure from these presentations' theatrical versions of truth.

F for Fake offers us perhaps the best insight into what would or could have become of Wellesian truthiness in the postmodern era. *F for Fake* makes explicit Welles's preoccupation with both the first-person singular and truthiness, as he acts as the audience's guide through a world of fakes and forgeries in which he is himself implicated. Welles opens the film with a sequence depicting himself as a magician and then positions this magic—and his other performance moments—as fakes or forgeries akin to those of Clifford Irving and François Reichenbach. Welles calls himself a fake, a charlatan, extensively citing his own *War of the Worlds* broadcast and his use of the *News on the March* sequence in *Citizen Kane* as artistic trickery.[79] Recalling the reception of *War of the Worlds* as truth by some audience members, Welles positions their reaction as ridiculous by adding absurd visuals of flying saucers attacking national icons as he describes the panic surrounding his broadcast. This strange dissonance between his narration of the panic and visuals undermining the realism of his broadcast have the effect of creating a fake documentary regarding his own work, mocking his earlier fake news techniques while critically commenting on the original work. Benamou additionally describes Welles's use of newsreel footage of Howard Hughes in *F for Fake* "as a mockumentary," firmly positioning Welles as an early participant in the burgeoning fake documentary genre.[80] Whereas Benamou agrees with Scott Bukatman's position that *F for Fake* is a "profoundly modernist document on the postmodern moment," one could also argue that this film reveals Welles's postmodern process in a modernist product.[81] Either way, *F for Fake* is the closest example viewers have of what Welles's unfinished works might have looked like had they been "finished," that is to say, mass marketed in a palatable form to consumers of their era.

Faking It: News in the Aftermath of Truthiness

> [H]istory is untrue; true history is irretrievable;
> and fake histories can be real.
>
> —Alexandra Juhasz and Jesse Lerner, introduction to *F Is for Phony: Fake Documentary and Truth's Undoing*

> The truths of storytelling are not the truths of reportage. The truths of reportage finally depend upon their correspondence to an externally verifiable reality[. . . .] The truths of storytelling may incorporate the so-called "real event," but they don't depend for their effect on the fact that a researcher can corroborate the event occurred. They have to come alive in the imagination of the viewer. And for that to occur the necessary precondition is that they come alive in the imagination of the storyteller.
>
> —David Milch, interview by Keith Carradine

Studying Spielberg, Gibson, and Welles offers insight into divergent approaches to becoming a star director, each of which struggles to establish artistic authenticity or "truth." Whereas directors like Gibson and Spielberg strive to create a sense of emotional truth for their audience that often correlates with fantasy or spectacle, Welles played with the possibility of unraveling objective truth. As David Milch describes above, the truths of storytelling are not those of reportage, and when the signifiers of these two forms of entertainment mix—as they did in various Wellesian productions—new possibilities and confusions ensue. Blending storytelling and reportage was a career-long interest of Welles's, and the erosion of trust in mass media and the establishment of "truthiness" as mass entertainment may be his most lasting entertainment dowry. We can see Hayden White's notion of a modern sensibility to trauma shift toward postmodern absurdity when looking at a distant media progeny of Welles's *War of the Worlds*: the "fake news" entertainment format. The fake news format demonstrates that what used to instigate panic now provokes laughter in postmodern audiences.

"Truthiness," voted "word of the year" by Merriam-Webster in 2006, acknowledges media manipulations of truth, accompanied by personal rejection of the notion of a fixed truth. While the word itself is not new,[82] it has been redefined as it moves into the mainstream vocabulary. Stephen Colbert defined "truthiness" on *The Colbert Report* in October 2005 as "truth that comes from the gut, not books," and "[n]ot long afterward, the American Dialect Society named 'truthiness' its 2005 Word of the Year."[83] The following year, the public voted the term word of the year in an online survey by Merriam-Webster, reflecting mainstream preoccupation with the concept of personal truths at odds with public truths. In the Merriam-Webster survey, "truthiness" beat out "google" for word of the year by a "five-to-one margin."[84] The proliferation of technology and its role in truth making is integral to the concept of "truthiness," and it is not coincidental that both top contenders for word of the year relate to new technologies of knowledge.[85]

Welles dabbled in truthiness throughout his career, but the proliferation and multitextual availability of current fake news marks a millennial shift from the skepticism and self-referentiality of the modern to the endlessly repeating, constantly shifting, seemingly ubiquitous availability of the postmodern. Thus one can see shows like *The Daily Show* multiple times a day, view excerpts on YouTube, and download and transport broadcasts to an iPod or iPhone, even as Jon Stewart crosses from Comedy Central to CNN's *Crossfire* to be interviewed as a news figure. These media co-brands are interdependent, and Stewart's show needs CNN to generate its comedy, just as CNN in turn needs Stewart's comedy to generate news. The endless circularity of this self-sustaining loop between news and "fake" news creates what Aaron McKain refers to as a "tail-eating snake" and marks the blurry boundary between the modern and the postmodern.[86]

Contemporary fake news shows like *The Daily Show* and *The Colbert Report* suggest that truthiness is a product of technological proliferation and conglomeration, which encourage the blending of entertainment genres and products. Truthiness flourishes through a process that Steve Gennaro calls "convergence," the merger of corporations and technologies to sell products more widely and the resulting consolidation of the "culture industries."[87] Gennaro notes, "At the turn of the millennium, the power of the culture industries lay in the hands of five multi-national media companies: Disney, NewsCorp, Viacom, Vivendi Universal, and AOL Time Warner."[88] These culture-making industries financially merge news and entertainment modes, producing news entertainment formats in which CNN becomes narrowly distinguishable from its AOL Time Warner co-brand, *The Daily Show.* These complementary brands extend the audience demographic, appealing to a broad cross-section of consumers. As Tad Friend remarks, "AOL is using the show to extend the reach of its infotainment programming to a younger market segment."[89]

A precursor to the concept of "truthiness" might be "newsiness"—news that incorporates aspects of the real but is subjectively altered for purposes of entertainment. There is, however, no clear line between "newsiness" and news (a theme Welles raised in *Citizen Kane*). On the contrary, with the advent of increasingly intrusive and manipulative technologies, media concepts of "news" began to shift. By 1996 the word "objectivity" had been removed from the Journalistic Code of Ethics, replaced with "truth, accuracy, and comprehensiveness."[90] The journalist's problem has become how to establish truth without the concept of objectivity, whereas the entertainer's challenge increasingly focuses on exploring the play between multiple subjective truths, often revealed through "newsiness."

Welles experimented early and often with "newsiness." As scholars have pointed out, his use of the *News on the March* sequence in *Citizen Kane* juxtaposes truth and entertainment, news and propaganda, public and private selves. In fact, this segment represents a pioneering moment of an entertainment genre that Alexandra Juhasz and Jesse Lerner study at length in their anthology, *F Is for Phony: Fake Documentary and Truth's Undoing.* Fake documentary depends on the audience interpreting the codes of fact and fiction and placing fraudulent news within the rubric of entertaining fiction. Pointing to Welles as an early pioneer of the "fake doc" genre, Juhasz and Lerner suggest the *News on the March* sequence elevates "the fake documentary's critical gaze from small-time office to big-time politics."[91]

The fake doc emphasizes its skeptical role in relation to truth-telling genres: while documentary attempts to claim "an unmediated, objective and truthful transcription of the real," fake documentary undoes "documentary form and its traditional tropes of truth telling."[92] In this way, "Documentary lends itself to a nostalgia of authenticity, while fake documentary acts to inoculate against such easy revival and reclamation of what are, always, only images."[93] For example, Welles's *News on the March* scene in *Citizen Kane* "looks authentic—because Welles expertly mimics the realist style of his time[. . . . I]t uses this form to tell the story of a recognizably fake but almost true person. It is this *known lie* that brings what would otherwise be transparent form into focus."[94] The "known lie" allows the audience to identify the simulation of truth without confusing it with truth itself. Welles's use of the fake newsreel within fiction highlights the potential fraud of newsreel as a genre of information, and makes questioning this fraud an integral part of audience pleasure. Thus fake docs revel in "newsiness" rather than news. Fake documentaries critique the very possibility of objective documentation, pointing out that "many documentaries lie to tell the truth, and that all documentaries are 'fakes' in that they are *not* the world they so faithfully record."[95]

The difference between Welles's use of the fake-news sequence in *Citizen Kane* and that in his *War of the Worlds* broadcast, then, is simply the proportion of the audience who had knowledge of "the lie," who were in on the joke. The concept of the "known lie" is critical to understanding the line between panic and laughter when employing "truthiness" in entertainment. No audience, however, uniformly interprets the codes of the "known lie" accurately. Hence, there are always a number of people who seek "real" news from sources like *The Daily Show*,[96] who panic during the *War of the Worlds*, and who confuse Charles Foster Kane with William Randolph Hearst. In other words, fake documentary is never uniformly "fake." There resides in it a gut instinct level of "truthiness" that is not confined by authorial intentionality. Audience members are ultimately invited to construct their own levels of truth within truthiness, and a repeated image can signify differently over time. As Juhasz and Lerner assert, "Fake docs can blend the strict binary lines that usually serve to comfort, stabilize, and segregate."[97]

The Legacy of Fake News: *The Daily Show* and *The Colbert Report*

During the early 1970s—the same era as *F for Fake*—the fake news show entered the scene of American television entertainment in *Saturday Night Live*'s "Weekend Update" segment, which debuted in 1975. The popularity of this segment spawned spin-offs that evolved toward today's half-hour fake news format for *The Daily Show. The Daily Show* (*TDS*) and its own spin-off, *Colbert Report*, occupy a privileged position in television entertainment in that they spoof "real" news while also participating in its creation. With the diminishing possibility of objective truth, the question remains how (or whether) it is possible to negotiate an accurate and comprehensive truth.

The importance of this question and the evolution of this form of entertainment took on increased national resonance post-9/11. To make sense of the terror as it unfolded, people turned to a combination of news media and personal communication devices. Even those most directly involved in 9/11, the victims themselves, used cell phones to contact outsiders who could help them make sense of the events happening to them by relaying information from a combination of Internet and television sources. On this single day American audiences relied intensely on technology to translate an unthinkably horrifying reality into meaning, in the process revealing the dangers of unreliable technology (and thus unreliable meaning). The events of 9/11 sharply focused American culture on the anxieties of technological breakdown and the potential for panic. *War of the Worlds* suddenly became relevant again in terms of the spectacle of violence and panic broadcast at a national level. What had seemed impossible—images from the realm of entertainment—suddenly and disturbingly became real.[98]

The Daily Show and *The Colbert Report* share several traits in both form and content, and both recall Welles's *War of the Worlds* form in terms of using a central journalistic personality to deliver newslike messages that are nevertheless framed as entertainment rather than information. Yet unlike Welles's *War of the Worlds* broadcast (although much like his later broadcasts in series like *Hello Americans*), both shows also offer information in the form of interviews with political figures—newsworthy information, as well as comic spoofs of news. As many critics have pointed out, the news content of Stewart's *Daily Show* markedly increased post-9/11, when comedy about the news seemed to demand some journalistic interpretation as well.

The humor of these shows, like the fake doc, depends on the audience being able to recognize the "known lie." To be able to read satirical codes, it helps to have a single personality through which the satire is filtered. Like Welles's *War of the Worlds*, both shows rely on a central "anchor" personality, a first-person singular, to establish the tone of "truthiness." Because of the essential need for the audience to read the codes of satire, the anchor personality becomes more than a spokesperson for the show; he becomes a brand name. Although Jon Stewart inherited *The Daily Show* from his predecessor, Craig Kilborn, the show has now widely become associated with Stewart personally through public awards, interviews, and the establishment of spin-off brands like *The Colbert Report* and products like *The Daily Show with Jon Stewart Presents America (the book): A Guide to Democracy Inaction*.[99] Based on the success of Colbert's performances on *The Daily Show*, *The Colbert Report* was created with just such a first-person filter in mind. The show is designed as a vehicle for Colbert, and the title of the show reflects the correlation between host personality and his truthiness brand, making clear he cannot be replaced. The title also spoofs its own self-centeredness through reflexive comedy—to match the egocentrism of the host, the "t" at the end of "Report" is not pronounced, matching the pronunciation of "Colbert."

Post-9/11, *The Daily Show* faced a problem shared with every comedy show: how to make an audience laugh in the face of the unspeakable. But *TDS* faced an additional obstacle in that its brand of humor depended on political satire, and political events in the immediate aftermath of 9/11 were very difficult to satirize. Comedians like Bill Maher were publicly chastened for attempts to satirize conventional political wisdom, and most political comedians had to find new comedic ground, at least temporarily. Stewart addressed this problem both by articulating his personal distress over 9/11 on *TDS* (a move he later derided as unmanly in an interview with Howard Stern)[100] and by inviting political and academic guests on the show to talk directly about the war. Tad Friend argues this twin strategy creates a centrist, mediating persona for Stewart, a centrism situated "not between the right and the left but between the top (our leaders) and the bottom (crappy TV)."[101] By combining the sentimentality of the lowbrow, man-on-the-street reaction to 9/11 with high-power policy-oriented guests who could discuss the political context for these events, Stewart solidified his position as mediator between the mass audience and credible authorities. As Friend remarks, "One sure sign that our country is returning to normal is that 'The Daily Show' is back, and is being watched with pleasure by even more Americans who once again, could care less."[102] The reaction to spectacular terror in postmodern life seems to be a diminishment of sensitivity, a distancing that allows daily existence to continue despite knowledge of the potential for horror. In contrast to the heightened emotional realm of *The Passion*, which was pitched as realism but is more akin to melodrama, the entertainment challenge of fake news shows after 9/11 was to address a heightened emotional sense of tragedy at odds with the goal of comedy—reality was impeding "entertainment." Stewart's ability to lead the American audience back into a comfortably distanced state, then, was an act of public service, allowing the panic to subside into comedy.

Stewart's mediating position led to the rise of *TDS* as a source of "real" news rather than just comic satire. Increasingly, *TDS* holds a complicated and symbiotic relationship to its co-brand "real" news channel, CNN. *The Daily Show* has been called the "most trusted source for political news on television."[103] As Gennaro remarks, "The fact that *The Daily Show* calls itself fake news but is perceived by the audience as being real, allows it to say things that other news programs could not[. . . .]"[104] Its ability to walk the line between news and comedy gives it latitude to critique current political events rather than to report them. This also makes the show dependent on "real" news from other channels for its material. As McKain observes, *TDS* has a "necessarily parasitic" relationship with "real" news shows, and its appropriation of news stories for satire serves to "instill faith in the host [organism], reifying conventional News."[105] Since *The Daily Show* depends on "real" news broadcasts to produce the material it then turns into comedy, it "is formally dependent on the News's gatekeeping function *even when* it is critiquing it."[106] In other words, the "real" news still decides what is "newsworthy," since *TDS* uses the news broadcasts as a springboard for its own program content and accepts as newsworthy topics being covered by the "real" news channels.

To differentiate his reedited, fake "comic" news from the "real" news broadcasts that it raids for material, Stewart, like Welles, evokes a variety of codes of authenticity but does so for the purpose of defamiliarizing these codes for the audience. Many of these tropes are familiar from the 1938 *War of the Worlds* broadcast: the live, on-location broadcast, the interview with the man-on-the-street, the deference to experts in interviews, all "the performative and formal qualities or 'strategies' of the conventional broadcast, all the things that convince an audience that News is News."[107] But Stewart's broadcast also heightens or intensifies these codes of authenticity to make them visible to the audience and thus to make their manipulative power visible as well. For example, the use of self-consciously nonlive "live" reports in which the reporter, ostensibly on location, is in fact standing in front of a blue screen only a few feet from the anchor desk, reveals that such gestures of authenticity are silly and that illusions of time and space are easily manipulated with technological tricks.[108] The pleasure in this type of comedy lies precisely in the access to the "known lie." The audience feels like sophisticated, jaded insiders, capable of deconstructing the codes of authenticity and laughing at their absurdity. But in return, the expectations for these codes are reinforced: "the more capable the parody, the more it legitimizes current gatekeeping configurations."[109] Thus the parody of news codes reinforces the codes themselves, and the humor is less revolutionary than cathartic.

Comedy produced by the news can also become the news, in a reversal of the process discussed above. Since *The Daily Show* does feature political interviews and commentary by Stewart himself, clips of it can also be cannibalized by "real" news shows. McKain discusses the most obvious examples of this, including the weekly "The Funnies" segment on George Stephanopoulos's ABC *This Week*. In this segment, Stephanopoulos runs segments of late-night political comedy that comment on politics of the day.

By reabsorbing the comic within the authentic, *This Week* appropriates the perspective of these shows without having to give up the obligations of a "real" news show "to index views and maintain an appearance of impartiality."[110] It uses late-night comedians to articulate viewpoints that would violate its own codes of authenticity. Thus fake news moves into the realm of the "real." As McKain aptly summarizes, "[T]he more *TDS* appears in the News as a source of news, the more its ethos as an expert source is emboldened and the more easily it slides in as a source."[111]

Following the logical trajectory of the erosion of the line between truth and entertainment in the news, McKain locates two future outcomes as most likely: first, that "the News takes its cue from *TDS* and incorporates more comedy and more entertainment into its broadcasts[. . . .]"[112] Katie Couric's move from *The Today Show* on NBC to the *CBS Nightly News*, offers a clear example of this. Bringing in a morning show host to the evening news was an attempt to increase ratings and entertainment value, making evening news resemble "the lighter fare of morning news."[113] Couric was recruited to compete for younger news viewers from the Internet and other alternative new sources, and her news format includes an accompanying live Webcast and the blog "Couric & Company."[114] Couric joins the genre of personality-driven, niche news brands that target specific viewer demographics and "have easy-to-understand names, such as 'Anderson Cooper' and 'Keith Olbermann.' And rather than appeal to the taste buds, these brands are engineered to please the *opinion buds* of specific kinds of people."[115] Other traditional political commentary shows like *Crossfire* and *Larry King Live* blend codes from entertainment talk shows and nightly news shows to create an infotainment hybrid. So, it seems that this potential outcome is already coming to fruition. As Gennaro says, "*The Daily Show*, traditionally only of comedic value, is used as a source of news, while traditional hard news is becoming entertainment."[116] So, it would seem that McKain's first likely outcome has already occurred as even network news blends entertainment into its delivery format.

McKain's second likely outcome would be for the News to embrace the very aspects that Stewart critiques: to accept that "The News is fake, a pseudo-event."[117] Of course the difference between the first and second option is largely a matter of accent, since either outcome produces a hybrid mix of entertainment and information—a move already acknowledged in the word "infotainment," which we can add to the roster of vocabulary reflecting the increasing instability of meaning along with "google" and "truthiness."

As Welles's own work from *War of the Worlds* to *F for Fake* demonstrates, unstable meanings also open opportunities for alternative understanding, offering an antidote to fascist truths imposed on the public by tightly regimented and controlled media images. Welles was an early innovator in terms of the use of silence in broadcast, and one of the most revolutionary tools of fake news shows might well be their use of restrained editing to keep or create long periods of silence in interviews with pundits. Traditional news formats reject silence and use editing and staged questions to give quick and facile answers from "experts." By refusing to edit out moments in which these media "experts" are "shown not to have the answers or to be silently contemplating them or to be flat-out dumbstruck," *The Daily Show* acknowledges fissures in authoritative knowledge.[118] While this gives the sense that *The Daily Show*'s use of less heavily edited footage is more authentic, it really "is just as edited as conventional News, except that it is edited in such a way as to call attention to how the [. . .] broadcast was edited[. . . .]"[119] Similarly, Colbert's unorthodox questioning of guests often creates moments of awkward or flummoxed silence, resulting in his audience's laughter. The joke is that there are no experts anymore, that the trappings of authority are fake. This cycle of reflexivity and self-critique echoes Welles's earlier methods of cultural interrogation, making *The Daily Show* and the *Colbert Report* inheritors of a key tradition of the Wellesian brand. In fact, these shows derive more directly from Wellesian entertainment than do superficially related projects like Gibson's *The Passion* and Spielberg's *War of the Worlds*. The reality television movement echoes the fundamental issues and interests of the Wellesian brand in a way that adaptations of specific texts do not.

The primary legacy of the Wellesian brand is to create models for constructing alternative truths. With his *War of the Worlds* broadcast, Welles opened up the possibility for listeners to construct their own meanings and to pose hypothetical "what ifs" that were both disturbing and revolutionary. Welles's response to the restrictive Hollywood studio system was to turn again to innovative forms of deconstruction, using projects like *Heart of Darkness* and *It's All True* to push the boundaries of what cinema could represent and how it could convey political meaning. The result was a series of innovative, challenging, yet unmarketed and distributed projects that resonate with American culture today as much as when they were first created. His unfinished RKO projects are powerful reminders that unfinished works can hold as much meaning—in fact can more easily embrace plural meanings—than can finished works, and therefore can support a range of possible interpretations. New media forms offer a potential for regenerating these important parts of the Wellesian brand in their unfinished, multifaceted states. In contrast to a linear script or a finished narrative film, perhaps the more appropriate medium for examining these unfinished projects would be their interactive presentation as a series of fragmentary texts, audio files, correspondence, photographs, interviews, blogs, storyboards, and media ephemera that invite a new generation of individual readers into the construction of meaning. Intertextuality and irresolution are central to Wellesian technique, and at last possibilities for enjoying these aspects of his work exist. A generation after his death, media capabilities are finally catching up with Wellesian innovation.

Notes
Bibliography
Index

Notes

Introduction: A Postmodern Auteur? Approaches to the Unfinished Wellesian Works

1. Krin Gabbard, "Cinema and Media Studies: Snapshot of an 'Emerging' Discipline," *Chronicle of Higher Education,* February 17, 2006, B14.

2. Ibid.

3. James Naremore suggests these characters "use language as a hoax, attempting to become colonizers of consciousness." "Between Works and Texts: Notes from the Welles Archive," *Persistence of Vision: Special Issue on Orson Welles* 7 (1989), 14.

4. Catherine Benamou draws an analogy between Thompson's quest for meaning and that of the cinematic scholar in search of Welles's vision for his unfinished film *It's All True. It's All True: Orson Welles's Pan American Odyssey* (Berkeley: U of California P, 2007).

5. Dudley Andrew, "Echoes of Art: The Distant Sounds of Orson Welles," in *Perspectives on Orson Welles,* ed. Morris Beja (New York: G. K. Hall, 1995), 174.

6. The griot/auteur paradigm captures the tension between capitalist and communal traditions of storytelling. Whereas the West African griot figure reflects an oral tradition of communal history, the director embodies the concept of individual creativity, key to capitalism.

7. "Negotiates RKO Contract," *New York Times,* June 25, 1941, sec. 17: 2. This contrasts truly "griot" filmmakers like West African Sembéne Ousmane, who attempt to reject aspects of the auteurist tradition, even while being self-consciously influenced by it. See Jonathan Peters, "Sembéne Ousmane as Griot: *The Money-Order* with *White Genesis,*" in *African Literature Today* 12 (1982): 88–103.

8. Orson Welles Manuscripts. Material from the collection is reproduced courtesy of the Lilly Library, Indiana University, Bloomington, Indiana. All references to the Orson Welles Manuscripts will be given hereafter simply as "Welles Mss." accompanied by the date, if available, of the manuscript or typescript cited.

9. See Miriam Bratu Hansen, "The Mass Production of the Senses: Classical Cinema as Vernacular Modernism," *Modernism/Modernity* 6, no. 2 (1999): 59–77, for an interesting discussion of the hallmarks of "classic" cinema and its relationship with popular, or vernacular, modernism.

10. The story of Paramount tossing much of the footage for *It's All True* into the Pacific Ocean appears in several sources but is best positioned in context of the surviving footage by Catherine L. Benamou in *It's All True: Orson Welles's Pan-American Odyssey,* 278.

11. Catherine L. Benamou, "*It's All True* as Document/Event: Notes towards an Historiographical and Textual Analysis," *Persistence of Vision* 7 (1989): 130.

12. For example, he revived his stage adaptation of Shakespeare's *Julius Caesar,* charged with references to modern fascism, for his radio show.

13. *The Magnificent Ambersons*, his unfinished *Heart of Darkness*, and the unproduced *Pickwick Papers* all derived from performances during a single year of radio production, 1938. Even the grand first-person singular of *Citizen Kane* resonates in the title of the 1938 radio series, *First Person Singular*. Welles's radio plays had a profound effect on his process of narrative construction in cinema.

1. Origins of the First-Person Singular: Mercurial Theatre on the Air

1. Simon Anholt and Jeremy Hildreth, *Brand America: The Mother of All Brands* (London: Cyan, 2004), 70.

2. Similarly, Michael Anderegg situates Welles's work as part of a budding mass-market culture in America focused on selling the intellectual as a commodity, a movement marked by the creation of the Book-of-the-Month Club in 1921, Great Books seminars, and the use of radio as a "movement to popularize culture." *Orson Welles, Shakespeare, and Popular Culture* (New York: Columbia UP, 1999), 11.

3. Martin Lindstrom, *Brand Sense: Build Powerful Brands through Touch, Taste, Smell, Sight, and Sound* (New York: Free Press, 2005), 135.

4. Ibid.

5. Patrick Hanlon, *Primal Branding: Create Zealots for Your Brand, Your Company, and Your Future.* (New York: Free Press, 2006), 26.

6. A later script by Norman Rosten for the 1942 show, at that point named "Ceiling Unlimited," reinforced the classical artistry association by having Leonardo da Vinci visit the Lockheed Vega airfield in California because he decided to "see what the century is up to in aviation" (Welles Mss.).

7. Unless stated otherwise, all personal correspondence, press releases and draft scripts are taken from the Welles Mss., Lilly Library, Bloomington, Indiana. This letter, dated October 18, 1942, is also quoted in Simon Callow, *Orson Welles Volume 2: Hello Americans* (New York: Viking, 2006), 157.

8. Dudley Andrew, "Echoes of Art: The Distant Sounds of Orson Welles," in *Perspectives on Orson Welles*, ed. Morris Beja (New York: G. K. Hall, 1995), 180.

9. Michael Denning, "Towards a People's Theater: The Cultured Politics of the Mercury Theater," *Persistence of Vision: Special Issue on Orson Welles* 7 (1989): 29. Slavoj Žižek refers to these characters as "larger-than-life" in his "Four Discourses, Four Subjects," in *Cogito and the Unconscious* (Durham, NC: Duke UP, 1998), 91–101.

10. James Naremore assesses this pattern in Welles's work overall: "the audience is invited to sympathize with characters who are also treated critically." "The Death and Rebirth of Rhetoric," *Society for Cinema Studies Conference,* March 11, 2000, rpt. in *Senses of Cinema* 5 (April 2000), http://www.sensesofcinema.com.

11. Robert Spadoni, "The Seeing Ear: The Presence of Radio in Orson Welles's *Heart of Darkness*," in *Conrad on Film*, ed. Gene M. Moore (Cambridge: Cambridge UP, 1997), 85.

12. Welles Mss. CBS Press Release, June 15, 1938.

13. Titus Ensink, "Collective Misunderstandings Due to Misframing: The Cases of Orson Welles (1938) and Philipp Jenninger (1988)." In *Semiotics around the World: Synthesis in Diversity*, vol. 2, ed. Irmergard Rauch and Gerald Carr (New York: Mouton de Gruyter, 1997), 1132. Tim Crook explicitly ties Welles's broadcast to Herbert Morrison's live description of the Hindenberg disaster. *International Radio*

Journalism: History, Theory, and Practice (London: Routledge, 1998), 95–96. For a further discussion of the techniques Welles used to confuse fact and fiction in this broadcast, see chapter 5.

14. Ibid., 1134.

15. Paul Arthur, "Reviving Orson: or Rosebud, Dead or Alive," *Cineaste* 25 (2000): 10–14.

16. Andrew, "Echoes of Art" 181.

17. Slavoj Žižek, ed., "Four Discourses, Four Subjects," in *Cogito and the Unconscious* (Durham, NC: Duke UP, 1998), 93.

18. Frank Tomasulo, "Narrate and Describe? Point of View and Narrative Voice in *Citizen Kane*'s Thatcher Sequence." *Wide Angle: A Film Quarterly of Theory, Criticism, and Practice* 8 (1986): 48.

19. Naremore links Welles's visual rhetoric in cinema to the fundamental tenets of modernism: a preference for showing over telling, invisible narration, pastiche of convention, and an at least purported lack of concern with audience" ("The Death and Rebirth of Rhetoric").

20. André Bazin, *Orson Welles: A Critical View.* Foreword by Francois Truffaut; profile by Jean Cocteau; trans. Jonathan Rosenbaum (New York: Harper and Row, 1978), 135.

21. Welles Mss., *Radio Annual*, n.d.

22. Ronald Gottesman, ed., *Focus on Orson Welles* (Englewood Cliffs, NJ: Prentice-Hall, 1976), 16–17.

23. Naremore, "The Death and Rebirth of Rhetoric." This quotation originally appears in "A Trip to Quixoteland: Conversations with Orson Welles," by Juan Cobos, Miguel Rubio, and J. A. Pruneda, trans. Rose Kaplin, in *Cahiers du Cinéma* 5 (1966): 37–47. Rpt. in Gottesman, *Focus*, 7–24.

24. Dudley Andrew points out, "The issue of authenticity and certitude has always been at the center of his films." "Echoes of Art," 173.

25. Naremore, "The Death and Rebirth of Rhetoric."

26. Critics create various labels for the instability of narrative voice and suspicion of speech within *Citizen Kane*. Stephanie Dennison and Lisa Shaw see it as a problem of populism and propaganda (*Popular Cinema in Brazil, 1930–2001* [New York: Manchester UP, 2004]); Tomasulo calls it an "unstable economy of discourses" ("Narrate and Describe?," 51); in contrast, James Morrison asserts that despite the rhetorical instability of the film, it is "precisely a world in which truths can be discovered." "From *Citizen Kane* to *Mr. Arkadin*: The Evolution of Orson Welles's Aesthetics of Space" *New Orleans Review* 16 (fall 1989): 17.

27. Žižek suggests that this questioning of the "Real, the impossible kernel, the antagonistic tension, is the very heart of modern subjectivity." "Four Discourses," 96. He regards this interest in the "truth of the fake" as a "Nietzscheanism." "Four Discourses," 94.

28. Dennison and Shaw call this style "a contestation and rearticulation of the rhetorical strategies of mass broadcasts and propagandists." *Popular Cinema in Brazil*, 33.

29. As Paul Arthur remarks, "Negotiating the skittery line between fictional and non-fiction discourses is a hallmark of Welles's overall career." "Reviving Orson."

30. Arthur, "Reviving Orson."

31. Naremore captures the positive role of the Mercury Theatre in influencing the Wellesian brand, asserting, "The entire apparatus of representation in the Mercury Theatre was keyed to his ideolect, allowing his manner to become so recognizable and impressive that later in his career it could occasionally assert itself in movies directed by other people." "Between Works and Texts," 16.

32. To quote Rosenbaum, "claiming that *any* version could have conformed to his 'intentions' necessarily entails a certain amount of distortion as well as wishful thinking." *The Complete Mr. Arkadin A.K.A. Confidential Report* (Criterion, 2006). Similarly Naremore acknowledges, "Even if we could recover every frame of film he shot, we would not be able to restore his career to an imagined fullness" ("Between Works and Texts," 22). This nostalgia for an imagined wholeness also recalls Stuart Ewen's reinterpretation of Barthes' "dream of identity" in which an elusive whole self can be assembled via commodities. *All Consuming Images* (New York: Basic Books, 1982), 79.

33. Quoted in Naremore, "Between Works and Texts," 16.

34. Linda Ruth Williams, *Critical Desire: Psychoanalysis and the Literary Subject* (London: Edward Arnold, 1995), 1.

35. For example, Tomasulo argues that in *First Person Singular* "the players became mere functionaries of that 'singular' narrational agency and *magister ludi*, Orson Welles" ("Narrate and Describe?" 45). Slávoj Žižek similarly contends that "the allegorical character of Welles's obsession with such larger-than-life characters" reflects the fact that their failure is "clearly a stand-in [for] Welles himself, of the hubris of his own artistic procedure and its ultimate failure ("Four Discourses, Four Subjects," 92).

36. Michael Roemer argues, "If we need to believe absolutely that our will is free and that our actions lead to predictable results, we had best not tell or hear stories." *Telling Stories: Postmodernism and the Invalidation of Traditional Narrative* (London: Rowman and Littlefield, 1995), 35.

37. Andrew, "Echoes of Art," 172.

38. Tomasulo, "Narrate and Describe?" 50.

39. As Linda Ruth Williams asserts, "Upon fantasy the subject is built[. . . .] The subject is a creation *of* the story." *Critical Desire: Psychoanalysis and the Literary Subject*, 17.

40. Citing the Brechtian notion of the "provisional" nature of the performance text, Naremore notes that these texts emerge "from the interaction of performance and audience on a specific occasion. Once the occasion passes, the performance survives only in memory or in fragmentary records." "Between Works and Texts," 13. The Wellesian performance text results neither in a neatly finished commodity nor in "radicalized, collective, or corporate discourse" but rather in "an unorthodox way of speaking." Naremore, "Between Works and Texts," 17.

41. Lindstrom, *Brand Sense*, 131.

42. Welles partnered on radio with at least two brands that remain iconic today: Campbell Soup and Lockheed aeronautics. Anholt and Hildreth cite both companies as examples of leading American brands (*Brand America*, 18–19). Lindstrom, Hanlon, and Anholt all cite Campbell Soup as a long-term brand that has held sway since the late nineteenth century.

43. Welles Mss, box 1.

44. Welles Mss.

45. Hanlon, *Primal Branding*, 6.

46. Ibid., 78.

47. Anholt and Hildreth, *Brand America: The Mother of All Brands*, 36.

48. For more on his Brazilian creation story, see chapter 4. Based on an article in *A Noite*, February 9, 1942, and Tom Pettey's correspondence on April 2, 1942 (Welles Mss.).

49. Welles Mss.

50. Hanlon, *Primal Branding*, 19.

51. Welles Mss.

52. "First Person Singular: Welles Innovator on Stage, Experiments on the Air," *Newsweek*, July 11, 1938, 25.

53. James Naremore, *The Magic World of Orson Welles* (Dallas: Southern Methodist UP, 1989), 13.

54. Welles Mss.

55. Ibid.

56. Hanlon, *Primal Branding*, 54.

57. Ibid., 72, 73.

58. Žižek interprets Welles's use of deep focus as a visual rhetoric that conveys his thematic preoccupation with the larger-than-life individual, a manifestation of the first-person singular, and his "trademark formal procedure." "Four Discourses," 92.

59. Anholt and Hildreth, *Brand America*, 78.

60. Arthur, "Reviving Orson."

61. William Simon, "Orson Welles: An Introduction," *Persistence of Vision: Special Issue on Orson Welles* 7 (1989), 10.

62. In "Reviving Orson," Arthur uses the example of the film *Casanova's Big Night*, which turns its extravagant ending into a joke played out by "Bob 'Orson Welles' Hope." The ensemble musical comedy format of Hope's movies strongly contrasts the sensibility of the Wellesian brand as outlined here. Welles seems to have been aware of the disparity between his own work and that of Hope. A script of *It's All True* in box 16 of the Welles Mss contains the following scene:

> Med. Shot Passengers looking at Welles.
> ENGINEER: "Isn't that Bob Hope?"
> ARMY OFFICER: "I don't know—who's Bob Hope?"

63. Dennison and Shaw, *Popular Cinema in Brazil*, 36.

64. Denning, "Towards a People's Theater," 27.

65. Ibid., 34.

66. Arthur, "Reviving Orson."

67. Lorna Fitzsimmons, "*The Magnificent Ambersons*: Unmasking the Code," *Literature Film Quarterly* 28, no. 4 (2000). For recent examples of the nostalgic auteurist approach, see David Kamp's article "Magnificent Obsession," which searches for the authentic Wellesian version of *The Magnificent Ambersons* (*Vanity Fair*, January 2002, 122–37), and the similar-themed dramatic interpretation by Marcus Wolland, "Lost Eden: The Magnificent Welles" (PBS DVD, 2004).

68. Welles Mss.

69. Ibid., 2.

70. Ibid.

71. November 30, 1939, Welles Mss.

72. This project's use of another Wellesian rhetorical mode, primitivist expressionism, is discussed at length in chapter 3.

73. Spadoni, "The Seeing Ear," 84.

74. For further discussion of Welles and Dickens, see chapter 2.

75. *Heart of Darkness,* "Revised Estimating Script," Welles Mss., November 30, 1939, 2.

76. Naremore, *The Magic World of Orson Welles,* 21.

77. As Naremore points out, this I/eye approach is invoked as well in the script for "Mexican Melodrama" or "The Way to Santiago," in which the lead character has no name; thus the script instructs he will be "referred to in the first person" (*Magic World of Orson Welles,* 23).

78. Spadoni, "Seeing Ear," 80.

79. Guerric DeBona, "Into Africa: Orson Welles and *Heart of Darkness,*" *Cinema Journal* 33, no. 1 (1994): 20.

80. Tomasulo, "Narrate and Describe?" 52.

81. Ibid., 49.

82. Ibid., 51.

83. William Simon, "Orson Welles: An Introduction," 10.

84. The national theme was emphasized in the project's original title, "American."

85. James Morrison disagrees that Kane is unknowable, since he reads the film as revealing "truths" and "essences" ("From *Citizen Kane* to *Mr. Arkadin,*" 7). This interpretation would not challenge the assumption of this study, however, which is merely that the process of Truth making is being questioned.

86. Dennison and Shaw, *Popular Cinema in Brazil,* 33. The tension between nation building and the deconstruction of subjectivity arises even more markedly in Welles's RKO project *It's All True,* which adopts a news feature format for the purposes of Pan-American public diplomacy and is fully discussed in chapter 4.

87. Naremore, *The Magic World of Orson Welles,* 17.

88. Richard B. O'Brien, "Unmasking a Hobgoblin in the Air," *New York Times,* October 29, 1939, sec. 9: 12.

89. Michael Anderegg, *Orson Welles, Shakespeare, and Popular Culture,* 15.

90. Welles Mss., December 13, 1940.

91. Welles Mss.

92. Naremore, *The Magic World of Orson Welles,* 18.

93. "First Person Singular," 25.

94. "The Talk Shows," *New York Times,* August 14, 1938, sec. 9: 10.

95. "Radio Notes," *Newsweek,* July 11, 1938, 26.

96. "Marvelous Boy," *Time,* May 9, 1938, 30.

97. For detailed discussions of the evolution of the script of *Citizen Kane,* see *The Making of "Citizen Kane"* by Robert Carringer (Berkeley: U California P, 1985), as well as Pauline Kael's 1969 "Raising Kane" essay in the *New Yorker,* rpt. in *The Citizen Kane Book* (Boston: Little, Brown, 1971), and Peter Bogdanovich's response to Kael—rumored to be coauthored by Welles—"The *Kane* Mutiny" in *Esquire,* October 1972, 95–105, 180–90. Joseph McBride offers a synopsis of these articles as well in *What Ever Happened to Orson Welles?* (Lexington: UP of Kentucky, 2006), 37–38; Clinton Heylin reviews various changes to the scripts in his chapter "The Wellesian Mosaic," in *Despite the System* (Chicago: Chicago Review Press, 2005), 39–74.

98. Wilson-Welles Archives, University of Michigan, Ann Arbor, box 18.

99. Most of the correspondence for these years is contained in box 1 of the Welles Mss.

100. For more on Welles's FBI file and *Native Son*, see McBride, *What Ever Happened to Orson Welles?* 52.

101. Welles Mss., December 9, 1940. In contrast to the fractious debate over authorship at RKO, Welles continued to collaborate on stage and radio. A February 14, 1941, memo indicates a partnership for *Native Son*, in which stock was divided among Welles, Houseman, and Mankiewicz. Mankiewicz received 5 percent of profits. Welles and Houseman got 15 percent total: "5% stock interest plus 10% for their services" (Welles Mss., box 6). *Native Son* continued to offer Welles income through May 1942, when it went into stock production.

102. Welles Mss., January 18, 1941.

103. Welles Mss., January 22, 1941.

104. Wilson-Welles Archives, box 18.

105. Welles Mss.

106. "Hearst vs. Orson Welles," *Newsweek*, January 20, 1941, 62.

107. Schaefer left the studio in 1942, a departure that helped ensure the incompletion of Welles's Brazilian project, *It's All True*. *It's All True* is discussed further in chapter 5 and at length in Catherine Benamou's study, *It's All True: Orson Welles's Pan-American Odyssey* (Berkeley, CA: U of California P, 2007).

108. This letter appears in both the Welles Mss. and the Wilson-Welles Collection.

109. Tomasulo, "Narrate and Describe?" 49.

110. See *This Is Orson Welles* for a brief description of the potential project concept as described by Welles to Peter Bogdanovich. Jonathan Rosenbaum, ed. (New York: HarperCollins, 1992), 361.

111. Andrew, "Echoes of Art," 180.

112. The romanticism of domestic violence was deemed uncontroversial at this point in time, with no outcry against a radio play in which the protagonist admits to beating his wife and that features a loud audio slap as Liliom hits his daughter. The play ends with a troubling exchange between mother and daughter:

> LOUISE: Is it possible for someone to hit you, mother . . . hard like that . . . real loud and hard, and not hurt you at all?
>
> JULIE: It is possible, dear . . . that someone may beat you and beat you and beat you and never hurt you at all . . . (MUSIC UP).
>
> (*Liliom*, Radio Script, Welles Mss., Sunday, October 22, 1939, 114)

113. Most correspondence regarding *Liliom* took place between Diana Bourbon of the Wheelock Agency and various Mercury employees (including Houseman and Welles) in August 1939. Welles Mss.

114. *Liliom*, a.

115. Ibid., b.

116. Ibid., c.

117. Ibid., c.

118. These letters from clergy are contained in Correspondence, box 1, of the Welles Mss.

119. An exception to this would be the blunt reply from the president of the Northern Baptist Convention: "The production of such a picture [. . .] would require

a delicacy of taste, and a depth of understanding, which are not ordinarily associated with the motion picture industry and its actors[. . . .] Your suggestion, therefore, is distinctly unwelcome to me and I should be very happy if the idea were allowed to die before it is full born" (September 3, 1940).

120. September 3, 1940.

121. September 3, 1940.

122. September 3, 1940.

123. September 9, 1940.

124. September 3, 1940.

125. September 9, 1940.

126. September 9, 1940.

127. In a detail revealing the intimate connections between Hollywood and religious organizations, he suggests that he can "be reached at the home of Irene Dunne about the 11th" (September 9, 1940).

128. Welles Mss, box 1, 1–2.

129. Ibid., 2.

130. Ibid.

131. Ibid.

132. Ibid., 2–3.

133. Christ would have presented an interesting challenge to Žižek's reading of the larger-than-life character's "essential 'immoral' goodness [which] is cosubstantial with what their environs perceive as their threatening, 'evil,' 'monstrous' dimension" ("Four Discourses," 94). The question remains how Welles would have shown the moral struggles of Jesus Christ, and if his character would have incorporated the dark complexity of Falstaff, Quinlan, and Harry Lime.

134. Welles Mss.

135. Anderegg, *Orson Welles*, 14.

136. By his last RKO project, the growing discomfort with Welles as a romantic lead is clear. In a script for the Rio project, his weight gain is referenced as an obstacle to playing the role of romantic lead. The script girl character, Shifra (based on Welles's real-life assistant Shifra Haran), refers to Welles as "a fat wreck" (Welles Mss., box 16, folder 19, 33). In several drafts of this script, Welles is positioned as losing out to a local man in a battle for a love interest—whether losing Shifra in Brazil or Marguerita in Mexico. In a revised, more romantic version of the Rio script based on Brazilian musical "*saudades*," Welles tries to reposition himself as the love interest, writing, "Jack is the hero of the story. (That's me. And, if you don't think I can play it, wait 'til I take off another 40 pounds. The fact that Jack is Swiss or French, or something, shouldn't lead you to suppose *for a minute* [handwritten addition] that the part is suitable for Mr. Boyer)" (Welles Mss, box 16, folder 23, 4).

137. Welles was a leader in the trend toward using stardom as collateral to move into the field of directing. The power and legacy of this trend is discussed fully in the afterword.

2. Classics for the Masses: Dickens and Welles

1. Robert Carringer stated in a 1979 interview that Welles "started out wanting to be an American Charles Dickens." Qtd. in Joseph McBride, *What Ever Happened to Orson Welles? A Portrait of an Independent Career* (Lexington: UP of Kentucky, 2006), 87.

2. Grahame Smith, *Dickens and the Dream of Cinema* (New York: Manchester UP, 2003), 195.

3. Smith says, "In short, these two great artists are vulgar, they are of the people, and this vulgarity is a felt presence in their work[. . . .]" *Dickens and the Dream*, 184. To which Welles offers this interesting counter quotation: "Working for posterity is vulgar." Qtd. in Benamou, "*It's All True* as Document/Event: Notes towards an Historiographical and Textual Analysis" *Persistence of Vision* 7 (1989), 121. In this sense, Welles rejects the notions of "classic" cinema for which his work is later celebrated.

4. A. Johnston and F. Smith describe Welles's adaptation of Archibald MacLeish's social commentary play about the 1933 banking crisis, *Panic*, for *March of Time*. "How to Raise a Child," *Saturday Evening Post* (February 3, 1940), 40. Welles had first been cast by and worked with Houseman in *Panic*, so both their collaboration and Welles's interest in radio adaptations had emerged by 1935.

5. Brett Wood, *Orson Welles: A Bio-Bibliography* (New York: Greenwood P, 1990), 92–97.

6. Michael Anderegg, *Orson Welles, Shakespeare, and Popular Culture* (New York: Columbia UP, 1999). Anderegg's study of Welles regards bricolage as "characteristic of . . . Welles's activities over the years" (40).

7. Orson Welles Mss., Lilly Library, Indiana University, Bloomington. Unless stated otherwise, all personal correspondence, press releases, and draft scripts are taken from the Welles Mss. For further discussion of this publicity release, including quoted excerpt, see chapter 1.

8. Qtd. in Smith, *Dickens and the Dream*, 7.

9. Welles Mss.

10. Anderegg, *Orson Welles, Shakespeare, and Popular Culture*, 13.

11. Leonard Manheim, "A Tale of Two Characters: A Study in Multiple Projection," in *Critical Essays on Dickens's "A Tale of Two Cities,"* ed. Michael Cotsell (New York: G. K. Hall, 1998), 65.

12. "First Person Singular: Welles Innovator on Stage, Experiments on the Air," *Newsweek*, July 11, 1938, 25; James Naremore, *The Magic World of Orson Welles* (Dallas: Southern Methodist UP, 1989), 13.

13. Grahame Smith ties this impulse to develop a fan base to Dickens as well, suggesting that Welles desired "a public, a public of the kind seemingly effortlessly commanded by Dickens in his lifetime" (*Dickens and the Dream*, 182).

14. Catherine Gallagher, "The Duplicity of Doubling," in *Charles Dickens's A Tale of Two Cities*, ed. Harold Bloom (New York: Chelsea House, 1987), 76.

15. "Metalevel" here derives from Robert Scholes's term "metanovel," meaning the foregrounding of the role of author and reader in a process of co-invention of fiction, a particularly important theory for performance and the study of metatheater, which was a topic of persistent interest to Welles.

16. Manheim, "Tale of Two Characters," 65.

17. Harold Bloom, *Charles Dickens's "A Tale of Two Cities"* (New York: Chelesa House, 1987), 5.

18. Sergei Eisenstein, "From *Dickens, Griffith, and the Film Today*," in *Twentieth Century Interpretations of A Tale of Two Cities*, ed. Charles Beckwith (Englewood Cliffs, NJ: Prentice, 1972), 100.

19. Eisenstein, "From *Dickens, Griffith, and the Film Today*," 102.

20. At the same time, however, Madame Defarge alienates the metalevel reading public forever, paving the way for the reader's pleasure in her own dramatic death at the hand of Miss Pross.

21. Charles Dickens, *A Tale of Two Cities* (New York: Modern Library, 1996), 357.

22. Bloom, *Charles Dickens's "A Tale of Two Cities,"* 7.

23. His later radio version of *The Pickwick Papers* also focused on a courtroom setting through the case of Bardell vs. Pickwick, according to discussions of the performance in a 1939 meeting (Welles Mss.).

24. Several times in the bound radio script, Oliver's lines are mistakenly attributed to Brownlow, requiring handwritten corrections. "Oliver Twist," bound radio script, October 2, 1938. Welles Mss.

25. Ibid.

26. Ibid.

27. Ibid.

28. Ibid.

29. In his detailed chronology of Welles's career, Jonathan Rosenbaum also lists Welles as playing Oliver Twist in this broadcast, but this would have represented a last-minute casting change. This seems unlikely, since Welles also performed in an episode of *The Shadow* the same night. *This Is Orson Welles: Orson Welles and Peter Bogdanovich* (New York: HarperCollins, 1992), 346.

30. Guerric DeBona, "Dickens, the Depression, and MGM's *David Copperfield,*" in *Film Adaptation,* ed. James Naremore (Piscataway, NJ: Rutgers UP, 2000), 109.

31. Martin Norden, *John Barrymore: A Bio-Bibliography* (Westport, CT: Greenwood P, 1995), 143.

32. Welles Mss.

33. Anderegg discusses this performance in his study *Orson Welles, Shakespeare, and Popular Culture* as an example of a "wedding of entertainment and scholarship" (11). The show itself is available at the Library of Congress.

34. "Marvelous Boy," *Time,* May 9, 1938, 34.

35. Welles Mss.

36. "Marvelous Boy," 34.

37. Houseman reiterates this goal in a letter on October 13, 1937 (Welles Mss.).

38. Qtd. in Barbara Leaming, *Orson Welles: A Biography* (New York: Penguin, 1985), 152–53.

39. "Welles Laments Wane of Theatre," *New York Times,* June 29, 1938, 12.

40. Ibid., 12.

41. By 1940 his interests would swing back toward theater. In an article proposed to *Collier's* and later transformed into a lecture on what was wrong with Hollywood, he predicted "within three years there will be a flourishing theatre in Hollywood, a theatre devoted [. . .] to the presentation of a program almost identical with that of the Mercury Theatre" (Welles Mss.).

42. "Marvelous Boy," 32.

43. Naremore, *Magic World,* 17.

44. Welles Mss., May 19, 1937.

45. Howard addresses the letter to "Housman" and writes that he wants "to express my enthusiasm for what you and Orsen [*sic*] Welles have done between you" (Welles Mss.).

46. Welles Mss., February 9, 1937.

47. Naremore calls RKO "chiefly a designer's studio." *Magic World,* 17.

48. B. R. Crisler, "The Movies Come of Age Again, Etc.," *New York Times,* August 20, 1939, 3.

49. Naremore, *Magic World,* 13.

50. DeBona, "Dickens, the Depression, and MGM's *David Copperfield,*" 110.

51. Welles Mss., October 24, 1940.

52. Welles's draft number was 2525, and Weissberger considered it a "good omen that your age should be duplicated in your draft number" (Welles Mss., October 30, 1940). As with so many biographical details of Welles's life, there are multiple versions of why he never served in the military: flat feet, bone problems, and asthma have all been cited. For a summary of these stories, see McBride, *What Ever Happened,* 66–67.

53. Welles Mss. November 13, 1940.

54. Ibid.

55. Welles Mss., November 25, 1940.

56. Welles Mss., November 28, 1940.

57. Welles Mss., November 13, 1940.

58. Welles Mss.

59. Naremore, *Magic World,* 85.

60. Johnston and Smith, "How to Raise a Child," 40.

61. See chapter 1 for further discussion of the controversies surrounding *Citizen Kane.*

62. Naremore, *Magic World,* 18.

63. Welles Mss., December 7, 1939

64. Welles Mss.

65. B. R. Crisler, "A Week of Orson Welles," *New York Times,* January 28, 1940, 5.

66. They sought to keep their affair private because of her marriage during the initial stages, but it emerged in the media, and they began appearing publicly as a couple in 1941.

67. The Wilson-Welles archive holds sixteen-millimeter footage for this project (University of Michigan, Ann Arbor). Draft scripts for all of the Latin American RKO proposals can be found in the Welles Mss.

68. Welles Mss.

3. Exploiters in Surroundings Not Healthy for a White Man: Primitivism and the Identity Detour

1. *Heart of Darkness* "Plot Treatment." Welles Mss., Lilly Library, Indiana University, Bloomington (September 15, 1939), 1. Unless stated otherwise, all personal correspondence, press releases, and draft scripts are taken from the Welles Mss. at the Lilly Library.

2. Guerric DeBona, "Into Africa: Orson Welles and Heart of Darkness," *Cinema Journal* 33, no. 3 (spring 1994): 16–34.

3. By the late 1930s, *Amos 'n' Andy,* like Welles's *Mercury Theatre on the Air,* was sponsored by Campbell Soup on CBS. *Amos 'n' Andy*'s popularity was well established in the 1930s, although its audience dropped from 29 million to 19.5 million over the course of the decade, according to Elizabeth McLeod ("'Amos 'n' Andy'—by the

Numbers: Analyzing Audience Statistics for Radio's All Time Favorites," http://www.midcoast.com/~lizmcl/aa.html). Producer Ward Wheelock worked with CBS and Campbell Soup on both shows.

4. Qtd. in Tim Crook, *Radio Drama: Theory and Practice* (London: Routledge, 1999), 14.

5. Qtd. in Marianna Torgovnick, *Gone Primitive* (Chicago: Chicago UP, 1990), 8.

6. DeBona, "Into Africa," 17. The self-critical aspect of populist modernism, a precursor to postmodern narrative, is often criticized for limiting artistic function. For example, Dudley Andrew finds that Welles's films "exemplify a cloying cleverness that cheapens the artistry." "Echoes of Art: The Distant Sounds of Orson Welles." In Beja, *Perspectives on Orson Welles* (New York: G. K. Hall, 1995), 173.

7. Werner Sollors, *Amiri Baraka/LeRoi Jones: The Quest for a "Populust Modernism"* (New York: Columbia UP, 1978), 8. Sollors applies this term to the work of Amiri Baraka a generation after that of Welles, but it is interesting how well this term captures the work of both artists. Sollors describes this impulse in Baraka as desire, despite his radicalism, for "unity of life and art, literature and society through all his periods and changes" (8).

8. Kobena Mercer, *Welcome to the Jungle* (New York: Routledge, 1994), 245. DeBona mistakes populist modernism for a substantive critique of "the Hollywood culture industry" and fascism ("Into Africa," 17). This essay agrees with Mercer that the critique is ultimately superficial, not embedded in the structure of the text and its production.

9. Welles denied that the Haitian Macbeth was his idea and credited it to his wife at the time, Virginia. Qtd. in Barbara Leaming, *Orson Welles, a Biography* (New York: Viking Penguin, 1985), 10.

10. Ibid., 240.

11. Welles Mss., translated by Tom Pettey from "I've Come to Brazil to Learn," *A Noite*, February 9, 1942, 5.

12. George Crandall, "Misrepresentation and Miscegenation: Reading the Racialized Discourse of Tennessee Williams's *A Streetcar Named Desire*," *Modern Drama* 40 (1997), 342.

13. Torgovnick, *Gone Primitive*, 8.

14. Some plays, like Angelina Weld Grimké's *Rachel* (1916) sought to use this nostalgia and romanticism to further African American political goals and to target a white female audience, but such sentimentalism was often seen more as light entertainment than heavy-hitting politics.

15. Torgovnick, *Gone Primitive*, 9.

16. Miriam Bratu Hansen prefers the term *vernacular modernism* to *popular modernism* because it emphasizes the quotidian, "with connotations of discourse, idiom, and dialect, with circulation, promiscuity, and translatability." "The Mass Production of the Senses: Classical Cinema as Vernacular Modernism," *Modernism/Modernity* 6, no. 2 (1999), 60. I would argue that vernacular modernism is a linguistically focused subset of populist modernism

17. The portion of the Negro Theatre Unit devoted to African American written, directed, and acted work was handed over to Countee Cullen and Zora Neale Hurston, among others. Simon Callow, "Voodoo *Macbeth*," in *Rhapsodies in Black: Art of the Harlem Renaissance* (Los Angeles: U of California P, 1997), 36.

18. Richard France suggests that Welles's Macbeth may have been influenced by W. W. Harvey's *Sketches of Hayti* (1827). Richard France, "The 'Voodoo' *Macbeth* of Orson Welles," *Yale/Theatre* 5, no. 3 (1974), 69.

19. Leaming, *Orson Welles, a Biography*, 104.

20. Ray Browne, "Shakespeare in American Vaudeville and Negro Minstrelsy," *American Quarterly* 12 (fall 1990), 384.

21. *Amos 'n' Andy*'s longevity is stunning: it began in 1926 as "Sam 'n' Henry" with Freeman Gosden and Charles Correll and ended with *Amos 'n' Andy Music Hall* in 1960. It also devoted two episodes to live-audience minstrel shows in December 1937, roughly contemporary to the Welles performances discussed in this chapter (McLeod, "*Amos 'n' Andy*—by the Numbers")

22. "Voodoo" *Macbeth*'s Harlem association also tapped into desire for the "urban primitive," a term Peter Stanfield defines as offering a "lowbrow populist rebuke to the dehumanizing subjugation of modernity" by evoking the agrarian roots of black American culture against the modern cityscape. "An Excursion into the Lower Depths: Hollywood, Urban Primitivism, and *St. Louis Blues*, 1929–1937," *Cinema Journal* 41, no. 2 (2002), 90. This would explain the longing of many New York critics for African American vernacular to replace Shakespeare's language, thus completing the fantasy of urban primitivism by removing overt evidence of white elitism from the production.

23. James Naremore, *The Magic World of Orson Welles* (Dallas: Southern Methodist UP, 1989), 8. In this play, three men in a fishing cabin are driven to madness and murder by the sound of Native American burial drums (5–7).

24. Burroughs's son, Norris, has produced a graphic novel recounting his father's experience in this production. Norris Burroughs, "Voodoo Macbeth" (Engine Comics), 68 pp. http://www.forbiddenplanet.co.uk/.

25. Orson Welles, *Macbeth*, Draft Script (Welles Mss., box 5), 1.1. Since the draft script contains page numbers rather than scene numbers, all references refer to act and page numbers. Additionally, the Welles Mss. draft script contains only two act divisions rather than the three acts of the final production, but the draft script is cited here to include handwritten comments. Draft and final copies progress identically until act 2, scene 3 in draft becomes act 3, scene 1 in the performance copy. A copy of the April 14, 1936, script is reprinted in Richard France, *Orson Welles on Shakespeare: The W. P. A. and Mercury Theatre Playscripts* (New York: Routledge, 2001), and the production notebook and supplementary materials are also available in the Library of Congress American Memory project at http://memory.loc.gov/ammem/fedtp/ftmb1.html.

26. This despite the fact that the "Haitian" drummers were from Sierra Leone, according to Wendy Smith, "The Play That Electrified Harlem," *Civilization* (January-February 1996), rpt. Library of Congress American Memory Project, http://memory.loc.gov/ammem/fedtp/ftsmth00.html (accessed July 22, 2003).

27. Simon Callow, *Orson Welles*, vol. 1, *The Road to Xanadu* (London: Jonathan Cape, 1995), 242.

28. France, "The 'Voodoo' Macbeth of Orson Welles," 68.

29. John Houseman, *Unfinished Business: A Memoir* (London: Chatto and Windus, 1986), 97.

30. Currently there is a four-minute clip of the performance available on YouTube (www.youtube.com; accessed October 25, 2008).

31. The Haitian drumbeat spread outside the performance itself. Fascination with the drummers' witchcraft underlay the popular story that their curse caused the death of Percy Hammond after he wrote a bad review of the play. Simon Callow implies that Welles was taking great risks by referring to the silent and imposing lead drummer, "a genuine witchdoctor," as "Jazbo" (*Orson Welles*, 234). Houseman recalled that that the drummers would not sing spells to summon evil spirits for fear that the spells would work, and that they requested live goats to make into drum skins. He described the lead drummer, Abdul, as knowing "no language at all except magic." Tellingly, however, he also remembers Abdul approaching him with Hammond's review and asking if it was the work of a "bad man" in his version of the Percy Hammond curse (*Unfinished Business*, 97). It seems the pre-lingual primitive had been reading his own reviews with a critical eye.

32. Qtd. in France, "'Voodoo' Macbeth of Orson Welles," 68.

33. Callow, *Orson Welles*, vol. 1, *The Road to Xanadu*, 240.

34. Qtd. in Ibid., 240.

35. The *Indianapolis Star* devotes a three-paragraph story to the trio of child actors playing Fleance and Macduff's children ("The Stage," August 27, 1936, 10). The children's book *Tree of Hope* also dramatizes the importance of this production in terms of offering black actors work at this time. Amy Littlesugar and Floyd Cooper, *Tree of Hope* (New York: Puffin, 1999).

36. Qtd. in Leaming, *Orson Welles, a Biography*, 101, 102, 100, 101, 100.

37. Ibid., 101, 105.

38. Welles was not a solo player in this power game, since reportedly Houseman sought revenge on Welles for excluding him from rehearsals by carrying on long conversations with Virgil Thomson in French "so that Orson couldn't understand what they were saying" (Leaming, *Orson Welles*, 105).

39. This story is sometimes repeated with Welles replacing Carter in the touring role, but at this point Ellis had replaced Carter (see, for example, Simon Callow, *Orson Welles*, vol. 2, *Hello Americans*, 384).

40. Leaming, *Orson Welles*, 109.

41. Ibid., 109. This description does not match that of the local newspapers, which speak of Welles primarily as "former leading man for Katharine Cornell" and "authoritative Shakespearean student" ("Harlem 'Macbeth' on Stage Tonight at Keith Theater," *Indianapolis Star*, August 25, 1936, 8). The *Indianapolis Star* gives Ellis a tepid opening night review, and it remains unclear in which of the several performances Welles may have replaced Ellis.

42. Ibid., 102.

43. This interpretation of Lady Macbeth epitomizes Audre Lorde's widely anthologized statement at the Personal and the Political Panel of the Second Sex Conference, in New York, on September 29, 1979: "Only within a patriarchal structure is maternity the only social power open to women." *Macbeth*, with its focus on primogeniture and power, replicates this structure, which is emphasized in Welles's directorial approach.

44. Callow, *Orson Welles*, vol. 1, *The Road to Xanadu*, 237.

45. Qtd. in ibid., 237–38.

46. Robert G. Tucker, "New 'Macbeth' Presented at Keith's: Harlem Version of Bard's Drama Proves Unusual," *Indianapolis Star*, August 26, 1936, 11.

47. France, "'Voodoo' Macbeth of Orson Welles," 68. Original emphasis.

48. bell hooks's chapter "Eating the Other" in *Black Looks: Race and Representation* explores the erotics of racial identity politics. hooks describes the "assumption that sexual agency expressed within the context of racialized sexual encounter is a conversion experience that alters one's place and participation in contemporary cultural politics" (Boston: South End Press, 1992, 22).

49. This difference correlates with what Alexandra Juhasz and Jesse Lerner call the "known lie" of fake documentary forms, which is discussed further in the afterword. *F for Phony: Fake Documentary and Truth's Undoing* (Minneapolis: U of Minnesota P, 2006).

50. Titus Ensink, "Collective Misunderstanding Due to Misframing: The Cases of Orson Welles (1938) and Philipp Jenninger (1988)," in *Semiotics around the World: Synthesis in Diversity*, ed. Irmengard Rauch and Gerald Carr (New York: Mouton de Gruyter, 1997), 1132.

51. The supernatural suspense of phantasmagoria, which mixed scientific "tricks" with gothic spectacle as discussed by Tom Gunning, for example, in his address to the 2004 Literature on Film conference in Tallahassee, Florida.

52. For further discussion of this publicity release, including quoted excerpt, see chapter 1.

53. Houseman, *Unfinished Business*, 215.

54. Houseman wired Welles, "Our obligation to do new book first Sunday each month is arbitrary date existing only in our own minds" (Welles Mss., September 19, 1939). Bourbon responded, "Ward [Wheelock] adamant we do book first week October or discard new book idea" (Welles Mss., September 21, 1939).

55. Welles Mss., September 26, 1939.

56. "Algiers," Bound Radio Script, Welles Mss., 1. Notes on "Algiers" are taken from two related but slightly different sources: a recording of the broadcast itself (available from Old Time Radio at http://www.otrcat.com/campbellsplayhouse.htm or from the Museum of Television and Radio in New York City at http://www.mtr.org) and the bound radio script in the Welles Mss. Quotations followed by page citations are taken from the bound radio script; those without citations are performance variations during the broadcast itself.

57. Ibid., 1.

58. Welles Mss., 6.

59. All these adaptations were based on the novel by Rogers D'Ashelbe. *Algiers* starred Charles Boyer and Hedy Lamarr, and won Boyer an Academy Award nomination for best actor. In this sense it inverts the adaptation strategy Welles used for *Heart of Darkness*. If, as Robert Spadoni argues, *Heart of Darkness* attempted "to weave the fabric of the radio medium into the visual field of a film narrative," "Algiers" attempted the opposite: to bring a visual medium into an audio field. Robert Spadoni, "The Seeing Ear: The Presence of Radio in Orson Welles's *Heart of Darkness*," in *Conrad on Film*, ed. Gene M. Moore (Cambridge: Cambridge UP, 1997), 90.

60. Bosley Crowther, Review of "Pépé Le Moko," *New York Times*, March 4, 1941, www.filmforum.com/archivedfilms/pepenytimes.html (August 1, 2007).

61. Torgovnick, *Gone Primitive*, 203.

62. As Torgovnick notes, "public events made Freud increasingly willing to entertain the disturbing thought that civilization was not a stable category and

that civilized man could always, under pressures like war, become with impunity a murderer who shows less remorse than primitive man" (*Gone Primitive*, 197).

63. Torgovnick, *Gone Primitive*, 207.

64. Diana Bourbon, "Letter to Ernest Chappell," Welles Mss., October 9, 1939.

65. The follow-script evokes the upper-class white woman's body as a marker of civilization again. The scripted conclusion to the show was a conversation between Welles and Goddard in which he asserts, "when there are no more greatly beautiful ladies in the theatre profession, we'd better climb right back up into the trees because on that dark day the pleasant graces of our civilization will be no more, and the West will have declined, indeed. But be of good cheer, listeners, barbarism is not yet upon us. We are living in the age of Paulette Goddard" (Welles Mss., no page).

66. "Algiers," 10, 9.

67. Ibid., 70.

68. Stanfield, "An Excursion into the Lower Depths," 103.

69. Ibid., 103.

70. "Algiers," 10, 12, 23.

71. This continuing impulse toward "authenticity" would get Welles in trouble again in his unfinished film *It's All True*. See the next chapter for further discussion of expense and failure in his quest for the "authentic" in an ethnographic incarnation.

72. "Algiers," 69.

73. Gaby fits in a category of cinematic characters that I have labeled in other articles as "chatoyant," meaning racially ambiguous female bodies that appear variously light or dark according to context. See "Exhuming Dorothy Dandridge" and "Commodity, Tragedy, Desire" for a further discussion of chatoyant bodies.

74. Here desire for Gaby and rejection of Ines embody Torgovnick's assertion in *Gone Primitive* that oceanic oneness with the Other must be rejected for the concept of civilization to hold.

75. "Algiers," 1.

76. "Algiers," 69, 71, 33.

77. Welles Mss. October 9, 1939.

78. Welles Mss., October 12, 1939, 6.

79. "Algiers," 7B.

80. Ibid., 31, 72A.

81. Houseman, *Unfinished Business*, 215.

82. Welles Mss.

83. *Heart of Darkness*, "Plot Treatment," Welles Mss., September 15, 1939, 1.

84. This impulse toward universality of a psychological, moral struggle in *Heart of Darkness* distracts from political context and is often used to counteract the argument that the implicit racism of the text undermines its value. For a skillful synopsis and response to this debate, see the epilogue of Patrick Brantlinger's *Rule of Darkness: British Literature and Imperialism, 1830–1914* (Cornell UP: London, 1988).

85. Houseman, *Unfinished Business*, 215.

86. Patrick Brantlinger, *Rule of Darkness*, 268.

87. Michael A. Anderegg, *Orson Welles, Shakespeare, and Popular Culture* (New York: Columbia UP, 199), 12.

88. DeBona, "Into Africa," 18. Welles may have had Sidney Howard to thank for the idea for his modern Caesar. Howard wrote to Houseman on February 9, 1937, praising

the production of *Doctor Faustus* and suggesting "that you and Well[e]s would turn your attention to *Julius Caesar* in modern dress (I have such fine ideas on that if you want them)[. . . .] I have always believed that the best way to stimulate the writing of good modern plays is to keep the classics a part of what goes on" (Welles Mss.).

89. See Jonathan Rosenbaum's *This Is Orson Welles: Orson Welles and Peter Bogdanovich* (New York: HarperCollins, 1992), and James Naremore's *The Magic World of Orson Welles* for discussions of the connection between the fascistic radio broadcaster in *Mexican Melodrama* and other fascist figures, and Robert Spadoni to address the fascism in the *Heart of Darkness* film script and both radio broadcasts ("The Seeing Ear," 89). Richard France describes Welles's use of the audience's paranoia about the rise of fascism and the pending war in his study of the "Voodoo" *Macbeth* ("'Voodoo' *Macbeth* of Orson Welles," 67).

90. This is a similar approach to that of Coppola in his later adaptation of *Heart of Darkness*, which transformed the text into an interrogation of American imperialism in *Apocalypse Now*, but as Michael Roemer points out, Coppola's adaptation turns Marlow "into an active figure, whose encounter with Kurtz has him emerge a better man—the moral of many a Positivist tale." *Telling Stories: Postmodernism and the Invalidation of the Traditional Narrative* (London: Rowman and Littlefield, 1995), 277.

91. The other half of the show consisted of a performance of *Life with Father*, quite a contrast of themes: ordered bourgeois family life versus disordered psychological and imperial decay.

92. Brantlinger, *Rule of Darkness*, 265, and Jameson qtd. in the same work, same page.

93. DeBona, "Into Africa," 28.

94. Welles requested material from five reels of *Sanders*, including footage of a village dance, several uses of masks, animals, and drums, and the "Sound of medicine man." These requests represent literally stock visions of primitivism—cheaply had and widely culturally accepted at the time.

95. Brantlinger, *Rule of Darkness*, 271.

96. All notes on budget, salaries, and production detail of *Heart of Darkness* are taken from the Welles Mss. materials on this film unless otherwise noted.

97. Welles Mss, September 1939.

98. The naming of native characters is inconsistent among various draft scripts and budget estimates. Eventually, the effort to give names to such characters as "flogged native," "Native woman," and "Head of the Cannibal Crew" resulted in a list of "Names of Native Half-Breeds" generated by researchers, which contained names like "Popol, Kalmol, Weepal, Wroo, Mabol," etc.

99. Similarly, "Ladies Wardrobe" was budgeted at $450, but Native Woman received a separate wardrobe budget for $7.50. Since there was only one other major female character in the cast, it seems strange to stipulate a plural "Ladies" wardrobe that then specifically excludes Native Woman.

100. As the film drifted into deeper financial woes, Welles's solution was never to reduce his own remuneration but rather to keep his cash flowing through other projects. RKO spent most of its money on Welles himself or on the cost of creating the exotic locales, looks, and sounds of *Heart of Darkness*. Virtually none of the RKO budget went to the actors who played the native parts. One plan to get Welles more

money was to film *Smiler with a Knife*, a straightforward patriotic thriller, quickly, while waiting to get started on *Heart of Darkness*. According to a prebudget estimate for *Smiler* in January 1940, Welles was to receive no fee for acting, but "Welles and Mercury Productions" would get fifty thousand dollars for "Services." A handwritten note explains, "$55,000 has been paid to date for the services of Orson Welles and Mercury Productions. $50,000 of this has been included above. The other $5,000 and the $4,000 still to be paid are tentatively charged to *Heart of Darkness*. Including only the $5000 so far paid, the total accumulated cost on *Heart of Darkness* is $103,500 as of 1-13-40 exclusive of any overhead." That is a staggering amount to have spent in preproduction. In contrast, the total production budget for *Smiler with a Knife* was estimated at $373,490.

101. In the "Revised Estimating Script" this character is named Carbs de Arriaga.

102. Brantlinger, *Rule of Darkness*, 274.

103. DeBona, "Into Africa," 23.

104. Joseph Conrad, *Heart of Darkness* (London: Blackwood, 1902; New York: Penguin, 1999), 92.

105. *Heart of Darkness*, "Plot Treatment," Welles Mss. September 15, 1939, 2, 6.

106. *Heart of Darkness*, "Character List," no date, 10–11.

107. Brantlinger, *Rule of Darkness*, 266.

108. The September 15, 1939, plot treatment suggests, "In 'Heart of Darkness' the camera has to function not only as a mechanical recording device but as a character. The actors have to play the camera (which is Marlowe) [*sic*] just as if it were a human being and not a collection of lenses, cogs and film" (1).

109. Spadoni, "Seeing Ear," 89.

110. Guerric DeBona discusses the split of Marlow's experience between camera and voice-over ("Into Africa" 23), and Robert Spadoni attributes this strategy directly to Welles's experience with radio, remarking that Marlow's narration creates a sense of "radio with visual accompaniment" ("Seeing Ear," 85).

111. The September plot treatment even suggests that Welles's physical presence, if properly enhanced in terms of darkness and masculinity, will leave the audience satisfied in a way that more superficial romance narratives cannot: "Mr. Welles is a handsome young man as you know, and we feel that it is important in advertising that he be a broad, muscular, tanned and handsome leading man[. . . . W]e feel that once we get the audience in the theatre it will go away completely thrilled and satisfied by the film even though the picture is not exactly in the boy-meets-girl tradition" (*Heart of Darkness*, Plot Treatment, 2).

112. "Revised Estimating Script," 8–9. All quotes for Welles's script version of *Heart of Darkness* are taken from the November 30, 1939, "Revised Estimating Script," unless otherwise noted.

113. *Heart of Darkness*, "Revised Estimated Script," 2.

114. Spadoni, "Seeing Ear," 87.

115. This visual collage style of storytelling matches Welles's own creative process, as described in an unsigned letter to Leonard Lyons responding to his article in the *New York Post* on September 26, 1939. Probably authored by publicist Herb Drake, it outlines Welles's development of a script for *Heart of Darkness*: "Welles started work on "Heart of Darkness" by pasting up the book in a large portfolio and going through it page by page, editing it and making suggestions to himself.

After several weeks of this he began to dictate a breakdown on the story. This, as now bound, consists of 254 pages" (Welles Mss.). Welles's personal papers support this process description, since several of his scripts contain similar pasteups of the original sources for adaptation. Box 5, folder 32 in the Welles Mss. contains similar markups for *Julius Caesar.* His creative process is literally one of cutting and pasting of others' ideas into a type of conceptual pastiche. Heresy in the capitalist culture of copyright, this process and similar collaborations with Houseman and Mankiewicz would increasingly be hidden rather than celebrated in the Welles mythology (see chapter 1 for further discussion).

116. *Heart of Darkness,* "Revised Estimated Script," 5, 9, 10.

117. Ibid., 21.

118. As Spadoni remarks, "Welles was prepared to elevate the pun on the word 'see' to a structuring principle" by taking advantage of film's "opportunity to conflate optical and narrative point of view" ("Seeing Ear," 86).

119. This process is very similar to Conrad's "impressionism" in which, Brantlinger describes, "the narrative frame filters everything that is said not just through Marlow but also through the anonymous primary narrator" (*Rule of Darkness,* 257).

120. *Heart of Darkness,* "Revised Estimating Script," 42.

121. *Heart of Darkness,* "Revised Estimating Script," prologue, 1–10.

122. *Heart of Darkness,* "Revised Estimating Script," 50, 60, 61.

123. Ibid., 76.

124. Ibid., 108.

125. Ibid., 100, 99, 50, 106.

126. Ibid., 111, 112.

127. Ibid., 123.

128. Ibid., 131.

129. Ibid., 131.

130. Ibid., 132.

131. Ibid., 133, 144.

132. The September plot treatment of *Heart of Darkness* suggests, "Welles's study of Kurtz is a politically moral but psychologically sympathetic portrait of a dictator" (*Heart of Darkness* Plot Treatment, 3). But the root of this portrait in the tradition of romanticism is also specified: a handwritten note on a draft script asserts, "Kurtz is the Byron of a totalitarian state. What Byron would be if he had become president of Greece" (Welles Mss.).

133. *Heart of Darkness,* "Revised Estimating Script," 161–62.

134. Ibid., 147, 156.

135. Ibid., no pagination.

136. Spadoni refers to this configuration of sight and sound as creating "an impossible sense organ: a seeing ear" ("Seeing Ear," 86).

137. *Heart of Darkness,* "Revised Estimating Script," 167.

138. Ibid., 167.

139. Ibid., 168.

140. Ibid., 168, 170.

141. Ibid., 173.

142. Brantlinger, *Rule of Darkness,* 271.

143. *Heart of Darkness,* "Revised Estimating Script," 174.

144. *Heart of Darkness*, "Plot Treatment," 2.

145. DeBona, "Into Africa," 18.

146. Welles Mss., December 12, 1939. The Breen Commission also warned that Kurtz being insane might create a problem with the British Censor Board, who might refuse "to license pictures containing insane characters," as they would burials at sea, which were regularly deleted by the British (Welles Mss., December 15, 1939).

147. December 5, 1939, RKO Pre-Budget Estimate, Welles Mss.

148. Welles asked for comparable production budgets at this time. An undated, unsigned note to Welles offers figures for *Memory of Love*, with a cast cost of $239,000 and a total above-the-line budget of $420,636 for a 44-day shooting schedule, whereas *Fifth Avenue Girl* had a cast cost of $160,000, plus direction, story cost, and talent of $376,445 and a 47-day shooting schedule (Welles Mss.).

149. Welles Mss., November 27, 1939.

150. Brantlinger, *Rule of Darkness*, 268, 270.

4. *R* Is for *Real*: Documentary Fiction in *It's All True*

1. Catherine Benamou, "*It's All True* as Document/Event: Notes towards an Historiographical and Textual Analysis," *Persistence of Vision* 7 (1989). Benamou locates the film project "at the center of a hegemonic struggle between the United States [. . .] and the Axis Powers (primarily Nazi Germany) in Latin America" (126).

2. Benamou's comprehensive study of this project, *It's All True: Orson Welles's Pan-American Odyssey* (Berkeley: U of California P, 2007), takes a different approach and thus comes to a somewhat different conclusion, emphasizing the politically progressive potential of his work with the *jangadeiros*, Brazilian fishermen known for their use of single-sail rafts called *jangadas*. Because of this study's focus on the intertextuality of the project as it exists in an incomplete but thoroughly documented state in radio, film, and correspondence, I emphasize existing relationships within the Wellesian brand more than the artistic potential of actual recorded film images.

3. The story of Paramount tossing footage for *It's All True* into the Pacific Ocean appears in several sources but is best positioned in context of the surviving footage by Catherine Benamou in *It's All True: Orson Welles's Pan-American Odyssey*, 278.

4. Benamou, "*It's All True* as Document/Event," 130.

5. "Carnaval: Treatment for the Film Itself" (Welles Mss., Lilly Library, Indiana University, Bloomington, box 17, folder 6), 1. Unless stated otherwise, all personal correspondence, press releases, and draft scripts are taken from the Welles Mss.

6. Through the time of his proposed *Heart of Darkness*, Welles's articulation of the Mercury Theatre adaptation process stressed working with classic literary material, making it fresh and new for the audience. In contrast, *It's All True* embarked on a journalistic, yet fictional, exploration of contemporary life that extrapolated on the 1930s radio practice of "documentary expression," which William Simon describes as "a central practice" in "politics, the social sciences, and the arts" of the 1930s. "Orson Welles: An Introduction," *Persistence of Vision: Special Issue on Orson Welles* (1989), 7.

7. See Simon's "Orson Welles: An Introduction"; Harry M. Geduld's "Welles or Wells?—A Matter of Adaptation" in *Perspectives on Orson Welles*, ed. Morris Beja (New York: G. K. Hall, 1995); and Tim Crook's *International Radio Journalism: History, Theory, and Practice* (London: Routledge, 1998), for thorough discussions of the impact of radio journalism and documentary fiction on Welles in the 1930s.

8. Jeff Wilson, "'A New Kind of Radio Program,' Orson Welles (Lady Esther)." *Wellesnet: Radio,* http://www.wellesnet.com (August 1, 2005), 4.

9. In this way, Welles himself was uncomfortable with the "romantic notion of the author as a 'genius' at odds with the laws of the marketplace" in his construction of *It's All True,* even as the studio and handlers like Herb Drake and Tom Pettey promoted him through this paradigm (Benamou, "*It's All True* as Document/Event," 122).

10. Douglas Gomery offers a useful analysis of Welles's relationship with Hollywood in his article "Orson Welles and the Hollywood Industry," *Persistence of Vision* 7 (1989), 39–43, which also rejects the notion that Welles was passively victimized by RKO in favor the view that they shared a mutually tumultuous and yet beneficial relationship.

11. Robert Spadoni, in "The Seeing Ear: The Presence of Radio in Orson Welles's *Heart of Darkness,*" in *Conrad on Film,* ed. Gene M. Moore (Cambridge: Cambridge UP, 1997), describes the process of duping the audience into accepting fiction as truth in *War of the Worlds,* saying it used "a fictive agency disguised as a news announcer" to lead "already wildly imagining listeners toward still wilder visions" (86). Welles often invoked constructed figures of authority like the news announcer to mediate his tales: journalists, policemen, lawyers, and other traditional arbiters of "truth" in society often function as his narrators. For more on this, see chapters 1 and 5.

12. Geduld locates five specific techniques that Welles used to increase the believability of his broadcast: familiar-sounding voices, sound techniques like interruption and fade, direct allusions to the microphone, mixing references to real and imagined places, and fragmenting narrative to increase a sense of spontaneity ("Wells or Welles?—A Matter of Adaptation," 269). Welles's use of these truth markers to "trick" his audience is discussed further in the afterword.

13. See chapter 3 for further elaboration on Welles's use of expressionist referents to evoke "authentic" primitivism.

14. Stephanie Dennison and Lisa Shaw, *Popular Cinema in Brazil, 1930–2001* (Manchester: Manchester UP, 2004), 16.

15. Benamou points out that the funeral scene in "Four Men and a Raft," which was filmed about a month after Jacaré's disappearance, "must have provided a much-needed catharsis for a community in mourning" (*It's All True: Orson Welles's Pan-American Odyssey,* 94). Her research also indicates, however, that most of the reimbursement funds for his death never reached his children, and that although his family never blamed Welles for Jacaré's death, they never accepted it as being accidental (*It's All True: Orson Welles's Pan-American Odyssey,* 306–9).

16. "Rick's American Bar," Filmscript, Welles Mss., box 17, folder 1.

17. "Rick's American Bar," 20.

18. The only clue to authorship on this script is a handwritten note from "Les," dated 1/14. James Naremore suggests that a likely source for this note would be Les White, who collaborated with Welles in 1944 on a script titled "Don't Catch Me." Benamou sees the script as RKO's attempt to "appropriate and salvage" some of the Rio footage (*It's All True: Orson Welles's Pan-American Odyssey,* 282), but the number of revisions and dates on the script indicate he may have worked with this idea at an earlier stage of the project, discarded it, and then returned to it in a salvage effort. Whether Welles began working with this script idea in early 1942 or later, it represents the more traditional studio expectations for melodrama mixed with mystery, even if its themes of racism and fascism "would have proved too risky for

RKO management at this juncture" (Benamou, *It's All True: Orson Welles's Pan-American Odyssey*, 283).

19. Plot Treatment, Rio project, No Title, Welles Mss., box 17, folder 4, 1.

20. Ibid., 9.

21. Ibid., 37.

22. Benamou, *It's All True: Orson Welles's Pan-American Odyssey*, 69.

23. As Benamou has noted, there is a genre exploration in the stories as well, with "My Friend Bonito," the Mexican segment, correlating with tragedy; the Brazilian *jangadeiros* tale reflecting an epic form (*Time* magazine referred to their voyage as "Homeric"), while the Carnaval sequence could be seen as a blend of "straight" reportage and "romance" ("*It's All True* as Document/Event," 139).

24. In its early stages, the project also had an African American biographical component, exploring jazz through the story of Duke Ellington. Charles Higham describes this segment as "inspired by Welles' love of Negro life" ("It's All True," *Sight and Sound*, 1970, 93). As late as February 1942, RKO was preparing a contract between Mercury Productions and Ellington (Welles Mss.) Benamou points out that Ellington was still under RKO contract in July 1942, indicating Welles may have still been considering "The Jazz Story" (*It's All True: Orson Welles's Pan-American Odyssey*, 58).

25. In this way, Welles tried (and failed) to represent what Gloria Anzaldúa would later term the "mestiza consciousness," a borderlands sense of self that extends the boundaries of identity to incorporate multiple geographical, cultural, racial, and sexual perspectives and that derives its energy from "breaking down the unitary aspect of each new paradigm." *Borderlands/La Frontera*, 2nd ed. (San Francisco: Aunt Lute Books, 1999), 102. Brazilian Carnival offered a temporary, cathartic setting for this boundarylessness, since according to Robert Stam, during Carnival, "all that is marginalized and excluded [. . .] takes over the center in a liberating explosion of otherness" (qtd. in Dennison and Shaw, *Popular Cinema in Brazil*, 17).

26. Peter Stanfield, "An Excursion into the Lower Depth: Hollywood, Urban Primitivism, and *St. Louis Blues*, 1929–1937," *Cinema Journal* 41, no. 2 (2002), 93.

27. An initial news release dated January 1942 suggests, "The Brazilian section of the film was proposed by the Brazilian government to Joseph I. Breen and Rockefeller" in order to promote "better hemisphere understanding" (Welles Mss.). This would seem to support Welles's understanding that the motivation for the Rio project was as much political as aesthetic, an understanding that he invoked often when tensions with RKO increased in the late spring of 1942.

28. Welles Mss. Tom Pettey, Rio project journals, February 4, 1942.

29. Herb Drake's advice to Tom Pettey: "O.W. has certain unpleasant habits such as reading your mail [. . .] Don't mind him any if he is rude, he regards it as a time saving expedient [. . .] he trusts always genius or charm to get him out of any situation. Sometimes the irresistible force meets the immovable object. At such times, go into bomb shelter" (February 4, 1942).

30. Welles, qtd. in Benamou, "*It's All True* as Document/Event," 136.

31. Welles Mss. Tom Pettey, Rio project journals, May 5, 1942, 1.

32. In a shocking reminder of Hollywood's comfort with racism at the time, Pettey wrote to Drake, "Now we are doing the Voodoo or macambo stuff which is dynamite in Rio. We have a closed set, a studio full of jigiboos and a little set depicting a hut in the hills. I'll write you a feature about it" (May 5, 1942).

33. Unless otherwise specified, the translations of Brazilian media articles are contained in the Welles Mss., box 18, translated April 28, 1942.

34. Ibid., 1.

35. Ibid, translated May 20, 1942. Robert Stam also cites this article as evidence of Welles's impact on Cinema Novo in the 1960s. *Tropical Multiculturalism: A Comparative History of Race in Brazilian Cinema and Culture* (Durham, NC: Duke UP, 1997), 129–30.

36. Benamou, "*It's All True* as Document/Event," 136.

37. Of course not all Brazilians resisted the filming of the country's racial and class diversity. An article in *A Manhã* argues, "Our negro is an excellent value, or great expression. There is no reason to hide it[. . . .] We should show ourselves as we are, as we were made. Because if something good should come out of Brazil, it will come from this consciousness of our impurity and our provincialism" (April 20, 1942).

38. For an extensive analysis of the political implications of Welles's filming of the *jangadeiros* and the racial diversity of Brazilian Carnival, see Benamou, "*It's All True* as Document/Event" (136–37). She identifies the "representation of racial diversity" as "anathema to . . . the Brazilian power structure and RKO" (137).

39. Benamou persuasively argues that Welles's attempt to document the social realities of Brazilian life "was politically daring, prescient, and technically groundbreaking" (*It's All True: Orson Welles's Pan-American Odyssey*, 226). However, despite good intentions and high skills, he was unable to overcome the limitations of his cultural and economic privilege.

40. Benamou, *It's All True: Orson Welles's Pan-American Odyssey*, 93–94.

41. Contrast Jacaré's reflections on poverty to Tom Pettey's remarks to Herb Drake that the Brazilians "appreciate money, but have no love for it. They get along just about as well without it" (Rio project journals, Welles Mss. March 31, 1942).

42. Untitled, undated scripts for *It's All True* are in box 17 of the Welles Mss. Photographs and other supporting materials from this film project are also held in the Wilson-Welles collection of the University of Michigan, Ann Arbor.

43. Welles Mss., box 17, folder 12. March 8, 1942: 7.

44. Ibid. March 9, 1942.

45. Ibid. no date.

46. Most sources date his death as May 19 (Benamou, *It's All True: Orson Welles's Pan-American Odyssey*; Rosenbaum, *This Is Orson Welles*), but Tom Pettey dates the event in his journals as May 18, and an Operations Report for RKO also dates his death on May 18. Welles Mss., box 18, folder 12; box 17, folder 13. American variations of the story often add dramatic detail. For example, Charles Higham relates a colorful version in which a shark and a squid burst out of the water and upset the raft, then the shark eats Jacaré ("It's All True," 95). A variant of this story appears in a *Time* magazine article on June 8, 1942, which describes Jacaré's death "During the filming of a shark-octopus battle" ("Brazil: End of a Hero," 41). While Higham's version has been widely rebuffed, the drama and suspicion surrounding Jacaré's death remains in his family, who variously appear to think he was assassinated, was kidnapped, or planned his own disappearance (Benamou, *It's All True: Orson Welles's Pan-American Odyssey*, 306–7).

47. Welles Mss. May 20, 1942. Most clippings from the Rio project, and their translations, are in Welles Mss., box 18.

48. Welles Mss. May 21, 1942.

49. Welles Mss. May 23, 1942. Even these accounts blame the movie industry rather than Welles himself. Other responses aggressively defended Welles. The *Jornal dos Sports,* for example, published a piece signed by "Petronius" and titled "Orson Welles Cannot Be Blamed for 'Jacaré's' death." It asserts, "[I]f Jacaré had stayed in Fortaleza, living the unpretentious life of the carnauba-straw huts, he would later have suffered the death of all his working companions. Jacaré died as he should." Welles Mss. May 21, 1942. Benamou points out that perspectives on the event were politically and personally inflected: "none of those close to Jacaré ever blamed Orson Welles directly, and this disposition prevailed in the liberal Brazilian press at the time." *It's All True: Orson Welles's Pan-American Odyssey,* 53–54.

50. Sergio Augusto, "Quatro Homens, uma Jangada e um Cineasta," September 15, 2001, http://jangadanantes.free.fr/4homjang_br.htm.

51. Benamou, *It's All True: Orson Welles's Pan-American Odyssey,* 226.

52. Benamou, "*It's All True* as Document/Event," 132.

53. Miriam Bratu Hansen, "The Mass Production of the Senses: Classical Cinema as Vernacular Modernism," *Modernism/Modernity* 6, no. 2 (1999), 70.

54. Ibid., 63.

55. Ibid., 68.

56. Ibid., 68.

57. Barbara Leaming, *Orson Welles, a Biography* (New York: Viking Penguin, 1985), 114.

58. Qtd. in Higham, "It's All True," 94.

59. "Carnaval: Treatment for the Film Itself," 14.

60. Ibid., 2.

61. "Adeus, Praça Onze" was recorded by Welles in Cinédia Studios; "Saudades da Amélia" was recorded live for the Carnaval section of *It's All True* (Benamou, *It's All True: Orson Welles's Pan-American Odyssey,* 314).

62. "Ai Que Saudades Da Amélia (aka: Amelia)" by Ataulpho Alves and Mario Lago. Published and controlled Irmaos Vitale. Administered by Peer International Corporation. International Copyright secured. Used by permission. All rights reserved. In a draft script for the broadcast, "Linda" (probably intended to be Linda Batista, who was cast in the Carnaval section of *It's All True*) in the script deftly translates the lyrics for Welles, explaining, "He's singing to one girl and thinking about another" (Welles Mss. March 6, 1942).

63. Welles Mss., box 17, folder 6, 27.

64. For an elaboration on the role of Praça Onze in the cultural life and music of Rio, see Daniella Thompson's Web site, featuring articles republished from the online magazine *Daniella Thompson on Brazil.* http://daniellathompson.com/Texts/Praca_Onze/praca_onze.pt.2.htm

65. Lyrics translated and reprinted in Welles Mss., box 19, folder 38. Original lyrics by Herivelto Martins and Grande Otelo.

66. Dudley Andrew, "Echoes of Art: The Distant Sounds of Orson Welles," in *Perspectives on Orson Welles,* ed. Morris Beja (New York: G. K. Hall, 1995), 176.

67. Benamou, "*It's All True* as Document/Event: Notes towards an Historiographical and Textual Analysis," 138.

68. Grande Othelo developed a career representing Brazilian Carnival, and in

the 1957 *A Cut above the Rest* he again represents "true racial and social democracy" during Carnival (Dennison and Shaw, *Popular Cinema in Brazil*, 17).

69. "Carnaval: Treatment for the Film Itself," 9.

70. Plot Treatment, Rio project, 22.

71. Tom Pettey, Rio project journals, Welles Mss., box 17, folder 20, March 4, 1942.

72. Ibid., March 26, 1942.

73. Benamou, *It's All True: Orson Welles's Pan-American Odyssey*, 140.

74. Pettey, Rio project journals, March 20, 1942.

75. Many of the scenes described in this plot treatment exist in the posthumous compilation coordinated by Bill Krohn and Richard Wilson. The footage was released in 1993 under the title *It's All True*, but not necessarily in the sequence described here and without the Wellesian soundtrack.

76. Benamou, "*It's All True* as Document/Event," 135.

77. Phyllis Goldfarb, "Orson Welles's Use of Sound," in *Perspectives on Orson Welles*, ed. Morris Beja (New York: G. K. Hall, 1995), 111.

78. "Carnaval: Treatment of the Film Itself," 5.

79. Ibid., 7–8.

80. Dolores Del Rio could have been central to Welles's project, and according to Higham, Welles had originally promised that Norman Foster, the director of both *Journey into Fear* and the "Bonito" section of *It's All True*, "would direct Dolores Del Rio in a previously abandoned Mexican melodrama" ("It's All True," 93). A Mercury Productions press release from Herb Drake on February 3, 1942, confirms the idea for a "fictional adventure story against a Mexican background [that] will star Dolores Del Rio," but by April several columnists and Pettey were reporting the fracture of Welles's personal and professional relationship with Del Rio (Welles Mss.).

81. "Carnaval: Treatment of the Film Itself," 15.

82. Ibid., 3.

83. Benamou, "*It's All True* as Document/Event," 134.

84. "Carnaval: Treatment of the Film Itself," 4.

85. Ibid., 4.

86. Ibid., 5, emphasis his.

87. *Hello Americans*, "Brazil," Draft radio script, Welles Mss., box 10, 1942, 4.

88. "Carnaval: Treatment of the Film Itself," 6.

89. Robert Carringer, "*Citizen Kane, The Great Gatsby,* and some Conventions of American Narrative," in *Perspectives on Orson Welles*, ed. Morris Beja (New York: G. K. Hall, 1995), 120.

90. Ibid., 120. Carringer further identifies certain American traits in narrative that explain Welles's literary appeal, such as the ability of fatherless characters to reinvent themselves, the feeling of a special destiny, ambition, and the belief that with "pragmatic genius and innocent faith that all things will turn out well" ("*Citizen Kane*," 127).

91. Qtd. in Hansen, "Mass Production of the Senses," 65.

92. Qtd. in Ibid., 65.

93. Pettey, Rio project journals, March 20, 1942.

94. Benamou makes a similar point using Barthes's description of the difference between "work" and "text." In the text, which this study equates with the project

rather than the film, "we are invited to return to the work of the filmmaker and the crew while on location, an experience that is usually lost in the editing process as select images come to eclipse the range of viewpoints and creative possibilities found in the rushes" (*It's All True: Orson Welles's Pan-American Odyssey,* 62).

95. See Benamou for a further discussion of these visual and aural juxtapositions ("*It's All True* as Document/Event," 133).

96. Benamou, "*It's All True* as Document/Event," 134.

97. Ibid., 126.

98. Ibid., 128.

99. Welles's correspondence with Nelson Rockefeller at the Office of the Coordinator of Inter-American Affairs in D.C. captures the political and artistic tensions in this project. Welles's October 10, 1942, letter asks for Rockefeller's support in salvaging *It's All True* as both an artistic work and a political project and stresses the political success of his radio broadcasts; Rockefeller's distanced November 11, 1942, response praises the radio work as well but suggests that Welles subordinate his artistic interests to national interests when it comes to *It's All True* (Wilson-Welles Collection).

100. See Higham ("It's All True," 93) and Benamou ("*It's All True* as Document/Event,"123) for further discussion of this shift at the behest of Rockefeller.

101. This office existed from 1941 to 1945.

102. The CIAA memo is dated April 22, 1942 (Welles Mss., box 17, folder 19, 5).

103. On February 28, 1942, Schaefer reassured Gordon Youngman that he doubted the cost of the film would go over a million dollars, "but then, we never made the deal predicated on limiting the cost to any set figure. After all, we must have a good picture, and since the Government protects us up to 30% but not more than $300,000, there is every incentive for us to limit the cost to $1,000,000" (Wilson-Welles).

104. *Da Noite,* Welles Mss., box 18, February 9, 1942.

105. *Da Noite,* February 9, 1942, Welles Mss. In contrast, Welles's correspondence with his attorney Arnold Weissberger paints a very different picture of his attempts to avoid the draft by pleading his status as sole financial support for his ex-wife, Virginia, and daughter, Christopher.

106. Pettey, Rio project journals, April 2, 1942.

107. Benamou, "*It's All True* as Document/Event," 127.

108. Ibid., 137.

109. CIAA Memo, "Office of Coordinator of Inter-American Affairs Motion Picture Division," 22 April 1942 (Welles Mss., box 17, folder 19), 8.

110. Benamou, "*It's All True* as Document/Event," 133.

111. Correspondence between Lynn Shores, Walter Daniels, and Reginald Armour from March of 1942 indicates that the studio had lost enthusiasm for the project at this point and was discussing various ways of restricting Welles's supplies and financial resources (Wilson-Welles). See also Joseph McBride, *What Ever Happened to Orson Welles?* (Lexington: UP of Kentucky, 2006), 69–79. McBride includes a damning transcription of a phone conversation between Armour and Phil Reisman, RKO's foreign manager, that indicates the antagonistic nature of the relationship between the studio and Welles at this point.

112. Benamou, "*It's All True* as Document/Event," 129.

113. Ibid., 128.

114. Budget and salary statistics for *It's All True* are in box 17 of the Welles Mss. See appendix 2 in Benamou's *It's All True: Orson Welles's Pan-American Odyssey* for statistics regarding existing footage for *It's All True,* including type of film, location, and preservation status (310–17).

115. On a six-month contract for the child actor, his name appears as "Jesus Vasques" and he is promised a bonus in American dollars at the end of filming. Welles Mss., box 17, folder 13.

116. Pettey, Rio project journals, March 29, 1942.

117. Frederick Othman, United Press, Welles Mss., box 17, folder 21, April 28, 1942.

118. Pettey, Rio project journals.

119. Othman, Welles Mss., April 28, 1942.

120. Petty, Rio project journals.

121. Qtd. in Petty, Rio project journals, April 2, 1942.

122. *Cine Radio Journal,* May 20, 1942.

123. Benamou, *It's All True: Orson Welles's Pan-American Odyssey,* 286.

124. *Hello Americans,* "Brazil" Draft Radio Script, Welles Mss., box 10, 1942 (Music), 2.

125. Ibid., 2.

126. Ibid., March 6, 1942.

127. Ibid., Insert 1–2.

128. Ibid., 1–2

129. Ibid.

130. Ibid., 1–3.

131. Benamou still finds "a sense of plurivocality" in Welles's dialogue with Carmen Miranda, but the multiplicity of Brazilian voices from the earlier drafts is lost in the dialogue (*It's All True: Orson Welles's Pan-American Odyssey,* 286).

132. *Hello Americans,* "Brazil," 13.

133. Ibid., 14.

134. The parrot imagery recurs in each of the drafts, but the description of them as so close you can touch them while eating lunch at a restaurant is refuted by Pettey's assertion, "The subject of fifty percent of the jokes in Rio is either a monkey or a parrot but you could search the city for days and never find one" (Welles Mss., Rio Journals, March 31, 1942).

135. *Hello Americans,* "Brazil."

136. The image of the urban/pastoral binary once again connects to the exoticism of African American folk life, as Stanfield notes ("An Excursion into the Lower Depths," 94).

137. *Hello Americans,* "Brazil."

138. Ibid., 20.

139. This structure would appear again in the 1955 British television series *Around the World with Orson Welles.*

140. *Hello Americans,* "Brazil," 12.

141. Pettey, Rio project journals.

142. Ibid. April 2, 1942.

143. Ibid., May 5, 1942.

144. Ibid.

145. Enéas Viany, "They Think It Is but It Is Not," Welles Mss., box 18, folder 11, April 1942.

146. "Carnaval: Treatment of the Film Itself."

147. Welles Mss., box 15, folder 19, 38.

148. Ibid., 38.

149. Ibid., 42.

Afterword: Wellesian Legacies—What, If Anything, Do Mel Gibson, Stephen Colbert, and Steven Spielberg Have in Common?

1. The star director can be defined as a spokesperson for an overall cinematic brand who creates box-office successes through the mere association with his or her name. In extreme cases, star directors can sell products that they do not themselves direct but with which they are associated as producers.

2. The passion play is controversial enough to merit an official examination by the National Conference of Catholic Bishops, who produced the "Criteria for the Evaluation of Dramatizations of the Passion." This document gives guidelines for appropriate dramatization of the passion and specifically rejects interpretations that "explicitly or implicitly seek to shift responsibility from human sin onto this or that historical group, such as the Jews" since they "can only be said to obscure a core gospel truth" (Bishops' Committee for Ecumenical and Interreligious Affairs. National Conference of Catholic Bishops, 1988. U.S. Catholic Conference: www.nccbuscc.org).

3. Gibson's next film, *Apocalypto* (2006), had a domestic gross of only $15 million on its opening weekend, despite widespread release. This seems meager compared with *The Passion*'s opening weekend, which garnered more than $83 million. Perhaps more significantly, *Apocalypto* had a $40 million production budget but grossed only $50 million domestically, whereas *The Passion* grossed more than ten times its $30 million production budget in domestic sales alone (Box Office Mojo, www.boxofficemojo.com).

4. Warren Buckland, *Directed by Steven Spielberg: Poetics of the Contemporary Hollywood Blockbuster* (New York: Continuum, 2006), 23. Buckland ties effective branding to six emotions outlined by Rolf Jensen that are essential to advertising (adventure, love and friendship, care, self-identity, peace of mind, and beliefs and convictions), all of which he finds in Spielberg's films (23).

5. Ibid., 25.

6. Ibid., 26.

7. Ibid., 26.

8. Ibid., 224.

9. Even a directorial project as commercially and critically successful as Spielberg's *Schindler's List*, for example, was criticized for its "'Americanization' of the Holocaust and its commodification into [. . .] popular culture." Lester Friedman, *Citizen Spielberg* (Chicago: U of Illinois P, 2006), 318.

10. As scholars have noted, Gibson's use of these languages was not so much historically accurate as evocative of historical accuracy. The choice of Latin and the use of Biblical quotations familiar to viewers gave the sense of a documentary rather than interpretive version of the events represented. Brian Doyle, "Conversation about *The Passion of the Christ*" (paper presented at Marymount University, Arlington, VA,

April 2004.). In this sense, Gibson's film fits within the fake documentary category discussed later in this chapter.

11. Bruce Zuckerman gives a brief media genealogy of the controversy over the Pope's quote as reported on CNN.com, ABCnews.com, and the Catholic News Service in "Where Are the Flies? Where Is the Smoke? The Real and Super-Real in Mel Gibson's *The Passion*." *Shofar: An Interdisciplinary Journal of Jewish Studies* 23, no. 3 (2005), 130.

12. Steven Leonard Jacobs, "Jewish 'Officialdom' and *The Passion of the Christ:* Who Said What and What Did They Say?" *Shofar: An Interdisciplinary Journal of Jewish Studies* 23, no. 3 (2005), 116.

13. Adele Reinhartz, "Jesus of Hollywood from D. W. Griffith and Mel Gibson," *New Republic*, March 8, 2004, 29. The National Conference of Catholic Bishops specifically warns against this strategy of adapting the gospels in its 1988 document on dramatizing the passion, saying, "To attempt to utilize the four passion narratives literally by picking one passage from one gospel and the next from another gospel, and so forth, is to risk violating the integrity of the texts themselves" ("Criteria for the Evaluation").

14. Reinhartz, "Jesus of Hollywood," 29.

15. Kelly Denton-Borhaug, "A Bloodthirsty Salvation: Behind the Popular Polarized Reaction to Gibson's *The Passion*." *Journal of Religion and Film* 9, no. 1 (April 2005), 2. http://unomaha.edu/jrf.

16. Ibid., 4.

17. Stuart D. Robertson, "A View from the Pew on Gibson's *Passion*." *Shofar: An Interdisciplinary Journal of Jewish Studies* 23, no. 3 (2005), 109.

18. Ibid., 107.

19. Robertson cited the film as "evidence of the Gibsonian fascination with violence [in an attempt] to out-violate *Braveheart*" ("View from the Pew," 105). Reinhartz similarly argues that the violence was not gospel-based but rather "an expression of Gibson's own imagination" ("Jesus of Hollywood," 29). Robert Gehl laments, "Gibson's Jesus does no more than preach a doctrine of state power and humiliating punishment." "'Why Aren't We Seeing this Now?' Public Torture in *The Passion of the Christ* and *Fahrenheit 9/11*," *Nebula* 1, no. 2 (September 2004), 40. http://www.nobleworld.biz/journalhome.html.

20. Box Office Mojo. http://www.boxofficemojo.com (August 1, 2007).

21. Friedman, *Citizen Spielberg*, 64.

22. Ibid.

23. These two reactions to the violence are captured in the postings of "Michael R." and "bacgems" on IMDb. Michael R. praises Gibson's depiction of violence, stressing, "The movie is about the suffering/passion of Jesus, and turning the camera away would not have an impact on you. The movie shows what Jesus actually went through for all of mankind's sins (according to Christianity). Mel Gibson did not exagerate [*sic*] the violence or make it look like horror movie or Kill Bill violence." In contrast, bacgems found the violence to be grossly exaggerated, arguing that it made Christ seem like "a large man-shaped aquarium full of blood. He was not purported to have extraordinary powers of bleeding, was he? I thought I was seeing a movie about the Prince of Peace, and it was just some guy being tortured at close range" (IMDb, accessed August 1, 2007).

24. Denton-Borhaug, "A Bloodthirsty Salvation," 6–7.

25. Ibid., 8.

26. James Moore, "Mel Gibson's *The Passion of the Christ*: A Protestant Perspective," *Shofar: An Interdisciplinary Journal of Jewish Studies* 23, no. 3, (June 8, 2007) 102.

27. Friedman, *Citizen Spielberg*, 65.

28. Jacobs, "Jewish 'Officialdom' and the *Passion of the Christ*," 115.

29. Moore, "Mel Gibson's *The Passion of the Christ*: A Protestant Perspective," 104.

30. David Rooney, "'Passion' Play Lands Mel atop Power List," *Daily Variety Gotham* (June 18, 2004), 4. http://www.variety.com.

31. According to David Rooney, the *Forbes* ranking is "based on celebrity earnings over the past 12 months in addition to popularity, Internet profile, media attention, and magazine covers" ("'Passion' Play," 4). He cites the domestic box office for *The Passion* at $370 million ("'Passion' Play," 4), which when added to international gross produced $608.4 million in profits for the film. "Mel Sells," *Hollywood Reporter*, June 18–20, 2004, 6. http://www.hollywoodreporter.com.

32. Steven Zeitchick, "His Passion Is Showing," *Variety*, October 2–8, 2006, 6.

33. "Gibson's *Passion* Gets an Evangelical Blessing," *Christian Century*, July 26, 2003, 14.

34. Ibid., 14.

35. Jacobs, "Jewish 'Officialdom' and the *Passion of the Christ*," 119.

36. Ibid., 117.

37. "Gibson's *Passion* Gets an Evangelical Blessing," 15.

38. Robertson, "View from the Pew," 106.

39. Denton-Borhaug, "Bloodthirsty Salvation," 5.

40. Jacobs, "Jewish 'Officialdom' and the *Passion of the Christ*," 116.

41. "Gibson's *Passion* Gets an Evangelical Blessing," 15.

42. Anthony Burke Smith traces the major influences of Catholicism as being images from "the Stations of the Cross, Marian devotionalism, Baroque painting, and the mysticism of [. . .] Anne Catherine Emmerich." Burke Smith additionally places Gibson as the most recent "in a long line of Catholic filmmakers (including John Ford, Frank Capra, and Martin Scorsese) who have influenced American culture." "He's an Auteur." Rev. *Commonweal* 132, no. 10 (May 20, 2005): 26 (2). For further details of theological traditions represented by Gibson's film, see the two books reviewed by Burke Smith: *Jesus and Mel Gibson's "The Passion of the Christ": The Films, the Gospels, and the Claims of History*, ed. Kathleen Corley and Robert Webb (New York: Continuum, 2004), and *Mel Gibson's Passion and Philosophy: The Cross, the Questions, the Controversy*, ed. Jorge J. E. Gracia (Peru, IL: Open Court, 2004).

43. Nicole Gull, "Onward, Christian Marketer," *Inc.* (July 11, 2004).

44. Zeitchick, "His Passion Is Showing," 6.

45. Gull, "Onward, Christian Marketer."

46. "Gibson's Anti-Semitic Outburst Shocks Jews," *Christian Century* (August 22, 2006), 11.

47. Ibid., 12.

48. Ibid., 12.

49. "Character Witness," *Christian Century*, September 5, 2006, 7.
50. "More Duplicity from ADL's Foxman," *New American*, August 9, 2004, 8.
51. Friedman, *Citizen Spielberg*, 158–59.
52. Qtd. in Friedman, *Citizen Spielberg*, 157.
53. Buckland, *Directed by Steven Spielberg*, 215.
54. Friedman, *Citizen Spielberg*, 155.
55. Buckland, *Directed by Steven Spielberg*, 216.
56. Ibid., 216.
57. Friedman, *Citizen Spielberg*, 157.
58. Friedman offers an anecdote of a colleague who proclaims himself "anti-Spielbergian," a description that Friedman observes he had never heard applied to high-status directors like Welles (*Citizen Spielberg*, 2).
59. Friedman, *Citizen Spielberg*, 2.
60. Ibid., 3.
61. Box Office Mojo.
62. Buckland, *Directed by Steven Spielberg*, 215.
63. Friedman, *Citizen* Spielberg, 158.
64. Qtd. in Buckland, *Directed by Steven Spielberg*, 215.
65. Ibid., 161.
66. Ibid., 159.
67. Welles is often portrayed as a magician performing tricks for his audience. Paul Salmon quotes Simon Callow as rejecting formal dramatic analysis of the trailer for *Citizen Kane*, saying it is neither Brechtian nor Pirandellian, but just "a trick." Qtd. in "'The People Will Think What I Tell Them to Think': Orson Welles and the Trailer for *Citizen Kane*." *Canadian Journal of Film Studies* 15, no. 2 (fall 2006), 110. Welles even opens *F for Fake* with this metaphor applied to himself as filmmaker.
68. Critics such as Edward Oxford have linked *War of the Worlds'* ability to panic the listeners to a culture of prewar fear, when unlikely invasions suddenly seemed possible. "Martians Invade the Airwaves in 1938," excerpted from "Night of the Martians," in *American History Illustrated* (October 1998), rpt. *The 1930s*, ed. Louise I. Gerdes (San Diego: Greenhaven P, 2000), 207–22.
69. *Touch of Evil*'s bloated Quinlan, floating downstream in garbage, condemned by the sound of his own recorded voice crying "guilty . . . guilty . . ." offers an example of this kind of failure to reconcile public and private selves, one that was important enough for Welles to defend in his memo to Ed Muhl, in which the director begged for this scene to remain, uncut, in the film (Wilson-Welles Collection, box 5).
70. Robert Spadoni, "The Seeing Ear: The Presence of Radio in Orson Welles's *Heart of Darkness*," in *Conrad on Film*, ed. Gene M. Moore (Cambridge: Cambridge University Press, 1997), 86.
71. Harry M. Geduld, "Welles or Wells?—A Matter of Adaptation," in *Perspectives on Orson Welles*, ed. Morris Beja (New York: G. K. Hall, 1995), 269.
72. Catherine L. Benamou, "The Artifice of Realism and the Lure of the 'Real' in Orson Welles's *F for Fake* and Other Treasures," eds. Alexandra Juhasz and Jesse Lerner, *F is for Phony: Fake Documentary and Truth's Undoing* (Minneapolis: University of Minnesota Press, 2006), 151.
73. Ibid., 152.

74. Edward Oxford attributes the midprogram radio switching to a musical spot on the popular *Chase and Sanborn Hour* that bored listeners into switching their radio dial to Welles's broadcast twelve minutes into the show ("Martians Invade the Airwaves," 211). Simon Callow attributes it to a break in the *Edgar Bergen and Charlie McCarthy Show. Orson Welles: The Road to Xanadu* (London: Jonathan Cape, 1995), 401.

75. Benamou, "The Artifice of Realism," 153.

76. Ibid., 168.

77. Benamou explores the theoretical implications of this phrase as it applies to *It's All True* fully in *It's All True: Orson Welles's Pan-American Odyssey* (Berkeley: U California P, 2007), 8–9.

78. Excerpts of Welles's *Don Quixote, Merchant of Venice,* and other unfinished projects were screened at the Transnational Welles conference at Yale in November 2006, for example.

79. Benamou, "Artifice of Realism," 147.

80. Ibid., 154.

81. Qtd. in Benamou, "Artifice of Realism," 160. Bukatman's words originally appear in *Persistence of Vision* 7 (summer 1989).

82. H. R. Stoneback points out that "truthiness" appears in the 1824 *Oxford English Dictionary,* at which point it simply meant truthfulness. "*Under Kilimanjaro*—Truthiness at Late Night: Or Would Oprah Kick Hemingway Out of Her Book Club," *Hemingway Review* 25, no. 2 (spring 2006), 126.

83. Sue Khodarahmi, "Words of the Year," *Communication World* (March-April 2007), 1. http://www.iabc.com/cw. The Dialect Society provides this online definition of the term: "preferring concepts or facts one wishes to be true, rather than concepts or facts known to be true" and cites Colbert's explanation of the concept: "I don't trust books. They're all fact, no heart." (American Dialect Society).

84. Khodarahmi, "Words of the Year," 12.

85. To "google" is one contemporary method of negotiating collective "truth" by searching for random public representations of the self, whether facts, opinions, or fictions. But to "google" also indicates that truth itself has become increasingly unstable and tenuous, subject to instantaneous negotiation and renegotiation, interpretation and reinterpretation, since googling depends on a constantly shifting set of cyber allusions and cross-references.

86. Aaron McKain, "Not Necessarily Not the News: Gatekeeping, Remediation, and *The Daily* Show," *Journal of American Culture* 28, no. 4 (Dec 2005), 426.

87. Steve Gennaro, "*The Daily Show:* The Face of American News in 2005," *Kritikos* 2 (April 2005): 6–7. http://www.gannet.acns.fsu.edu.

88. Ibid., 7.

89. Tad Friend, "Is It Funny Yet?" *New Yorker,* February 11, 2002.

90. McKain, "Not Necessarily Not the News," 417.

91. Juhasz and Lerner, "Introduction," 3.

92. Ibid., 28.

93. Ibid., 15.

94. Ibid., 5, emphasis added.

95. Ibid., 12.

96. The Pew Research Center for the People and the Press reported that "21 percent of viewers aged 18–29 learnt most of their 2004 presidential campaign news primarily from *The Daily Show* and *Saturday Night Live*" (qtd. in Gennaro, "Daily Show," 5). The conjunction between election reality and entertainment was highlighted in 2008 by the creation of special editions of *Saturday Night Live* after each national debate that both mirrored and mimicked the debates.

97. Juhasz and Lerner, "Introduction," 13.

98. Television commentators compared the visuals of 9/11 to a Jerry Bruckheimer movie, implying that the images unfolding before them came from the world of entertainment, spectacular horror, rather than from daily life. *The Onion*, a satirical print news source, featured the 9/11 headline, "American Life Turns into Bad Jerry Bruckheimer Movie" (qtd. in David S. Cohen, "Deeds, Not Words," *Variety* July 10, 2006, 3. Arts Module. ProQuest.

99. Stewart's career centers on an essential performance of himself. As explained by interviewer Tad Friend, "Stewart understands that he is not an actor but a performer—someone who can deliver a heightened version of himself" ("Is It Funny Yet?").

100. Stewart employs a masculinist comic style that made it difficult to incorporate his emotional reaction to 9/11. His phone call to Stern, whose show targets male listeners, depicted his distress as a moment of feminine weakness due to menses, thus allowing a cathartic purge and denial of what was positioned as an emotional anomaly.

101. Tad Friend, "Is It Funny Yet?"

102. Tad Friend, "Is It Funny Yet?" Mayor Bloomberg appears to agree, responding to a 2007 terrorism scare in which F.B.I. agents arrested a retired cargo handler with plans to blow up J.F.K. airport by saying, "There are a lot of threats to you in the world[. . . .] You can't sit there and worry about everything. Get a life" (Michael Powell, "New York: Yours, Mine and Theirs," *New York Times*, June 10, 2007, sec. 4, col. 1, 3. *Lexis-Nexis*).

103. Gennaro, "*Daily Show*," 1.

104. Ibid., 9.

105. McKain, "Not Necessarily Not the News," 416.

106. Ibid., 418, original emphasis.

107. Ibid., 425.

108. Ibid., 418.

109. Ibid., 419.

110. Ibid., 426.

111. Ibid., 427.

112. Ibid., 428.

113. David Vaina, "Moving Backwards: Network News Losing Battle of Gravitas," *St. Louis Journalism Review* (Dec. 2006/Jan. 2007), 21.

114. Michael Learmonth, "CBS Targets Youth: Net to Simulcast Couric News on Web," *Daily Variety Gotham*, 5. http://www.variety.com. As Deborah Potter remarks, "Couric's new bosses are counting on her to build a bigger audience that includes more women and younger viewers. The reason, simply put, is money." "Breaking the Mold: Katie Couric's Shift to Solo Network News Anchor Represents a Milestone for Women—and an Opportunity to Attract New Viewers." *American Journalism Review* 28, no. 3 (June-July 2006), 64.

115. William Powers, "Brand Aid," *National Journal* (March 17, 2007), 54.

116. Gennaro, "*The Daily Show*," 2. Stewart was even rumored to be competition for Couric as a possible successor to Dan Rather on CBS (Vaina, "Moving Backwards,"15).

117. McKain, "Not Necessarily Not the News," 428. McKain's analysis is based on his interpretation of Slavoj Žižek's *The Sublime Object of Ideology.*

118. Ibid., 420.

119. Ibid., 421.

Bibliography

All citations of the Welles Manuscripts refer to the collection at the Lilly Library, Indiana University, Bloomington.

"Algiers." Bound radio script. October 8, 1939. Welles Manuscripts.

American Dialect Society. http://www.americandialect.org (accessed August 2, 2007).

Anderegg, Michael A. *Orson Welles, Shakespeare, and Popular Culture*. New York: Columbia UP, 1999.

Andrew, Dudley. "Echoes of Art: The Distant Sounds of Orson Welles." In Beja, *Perspectives*, 171–85.

Anholt, Simon, and Jeremy Hildreth. *Brand America: The Mother of All Brands*. London: Cyan, 2004.

Anzaldúa, Gloria. *Borderlands/La Frontera*. 2nd ed. San Francisco: Aunt Lute Books, 1999.

Arthur, Paul. "Reviving Orson: or Rosebud, Dead or Alive." *Cineaste* 25 (2000): 10–14. Gale Group. http://galegroup.com (accessed August 29, 2003).

Augusto, Sergio. "Quatro Homens, uma Jangada e um Cineasta." September 15, 2001. http://jangadanantes.free.fr/4homjang_br.htm (accessed August 8, 2007).

Bazin, Andre. *Orson Welles: a Critical View*. Foreword by Francois Truffaut, profile by Jean Cocteau, translated by Jonathan Rosenbaum. New York: Harper and Row, 1978.

Beja, Morris, ed. *Perspectives on Orson Welles*. New York: G. K. Hall, 1995.

Benamou, Catherine L. *It's All True: Orson Welles's Pan-American Odyssey*. Berkeley: U of California P, 2007.

———. "*It's All True* as Document/Event: Notes towards an Historiographical and Textual Analysis." *Persistence of Vision: Special Issue on Orson Welles* 7 (1989): 121–52.

———. "The Artifice of Realism and the Lure of the 'Real' in Orson Welles's *F for Fake* and Other Treasures." In Juhasz and Lerner, 143–70.

Bloom, Harold, ed. *Charles Dickens's "A Tale of Two Cities."* New York: Chelsea House, 1987.

Bogdanovich, Peter. "The Kane Mutiny." *Esquire*, October 1972, 95–105, 180–90.

Bolton, H. Philip. *Dickens Dramatized*. London: Mansell Publishing, 1987.

Bourbon, Diana. "Letter to Ernest Chappell." October 9, 1939. Welles Manuscripts.

Box Office Mojo. http://www.boxofficemojo.com (accessed August 1, 2007).

Brantlinger, Patrick. *Rule of Darkness: British Literature and Imperialism, 1830–1914*. London: Cornell UP, 1988.

"Brazil: End of a Hero." *Time*, June 8, 1942, 41–42.

Browne, Ray. "Shakespeare in American Vaudeville and Negro Minstrelsy." *American Quarterly* 12 (Fall 1990): 374–91.

Buckland, Warren. *Directed by Steven Spielberg: Poetics of the Contemporary Hollywood Blockbuster.* New York: Continuum, 2006.

Burke Smith, Anthony. "He's an Auteur." Rev. *Commonweal* 132, no. 10 (May 20, 2005): 26 (2). Expanded Academic ASAP. http://find.galegroup.com (accessed July 23, 2007).

Burroughs, Norris. "Voodoo Macbeth." Engine Comics. http://www.forbiddenplanet.co.uk (accessed January 23, 2009).

Callow, Simon. *Orson Welles,* vol. 1: *The Road to Xanadu.* London: Jonathan Cape, 1995.

———. *Orson Welles,* vol. 2: *Hello Americans.* New York: Viking, 2006.

———. "Voodoo Macbeth." In *Rhapsodies in Black: Art of the Harlem Renaissance.* Los Angeles: U of California P, 1997. 34–43.

Carby, Hazel V. *Reconstructing Womanhood: The Emergence of the Afro-American Novelist.* New York: Oxford UP, 1987.

"Carnaval: Treatment for the Film Itself." Welles Manuscripts, box 17, folder 6.

Carringer, Robert. "*Citizen Kane, The Great Gatsby,* and some Conventions of American Narrative." In Beja, *Perspectives,* 116–34.

———. *The Making of "Citizen Kane."* Berkeley: U of California P, 1985.

"Character Witness." *Christian Century,* September 5, 2006, 7.

"A Christmas Carol." Bound radio script. December, 23 1938. Welles Manuscripts.

CIAA Memo. "Office of Coordinator of Inter-American Affairs Motion Picture Division." April 22, 1942. Welles Manuscripts, box 17, folder 19.

Cohen, David S. "Deeds, Not Words." *Variety,* July 10, 2006, 2–4, 63. Arts Module. ProQuest.

The Complete Mr. Arkadin/A.K.A. Confidential Report. DVD and booklet. Written and directed by Orson Welles (1955). Criterion, 2006.

Conrad, Joseph. *Heart of Darkness.* London: Blackwood, 1902. Reprint, New York: Penguin, 1999.

Crandall, George. "Misrepresentation and Miscegenation: Reading the Racialized Discourse of Tennessee Williams's *A Streetcar Named Desire.*" *Modern Drama* 40 (1997): 337–46.

Crisler, B. R. "The Movies Come of Age Again, Etc." *New York Times,* August 20, 1939, sec. 9, 3.

———. "A Week of Orson Welles." *New York Times,* January 28, 1940, sec. 9, 5.

"Criteria for the Evaluation of Dramatizations of the Passion." Bishops' Committee for Ecumenical and Interreligious Affairs. National Conference of Catholic Bishops, 1988. U.S. Catholic Conference. www.nccbuscc.org. Republished at http://www.bc.edu/bc_org/research/cjl/meta-elements/texts/cjrelations/resources/documents/catholic/Passion_Plays.htm (accessed January 23, 2009).

Crook, Tim. *International Radio Journalism: History, Theory, and Practice.* London: Routledge, 1998.

———. *Radio Drama: Theory and Practice.* London: Routledge, 1999.

Crowther, Bosley. Review of "Pépé Le Moko." *New York Times,* March 4, 1941. http://www.filmforum.com/archivedfilms/pepenytimes.html (accessed August 1, 2007).

DeBona, Guerric. "Dickens, the Depression, and MGM's *David Copperfield.*" In *Film Adaptation,* edited by James Naremore, 106–28. Piscataway, NJ: Rutgers UP, 2000.

———. "Into Africa: Orson Welles and Heart of Darkness" *Cinema Journal* 33 (spring 1994): 16–34.

Denning, Michael. "Towards a People's Theater: The Cultured Politics of the Mercury Theatre." *Persistence of Vision: Special Issue on Orson Welles* 7 (1989): 24–38.

Dennison, Stephanie, and Lisa Shaw. *Popular Cinema in Brazil, 1930–2001*. Manchester: Manchester UP, 2004.

Denton-Borhaug, Kelly. "A Bloodthirsty Salvation: Behind the Popular Polarized Reaction to Gibson's *The Passion*." *Journal of Religion and Film* 9, no. 1 (April 2005). http://www.unomaha.edu/jrf. (accessed June 12, 2007). 9 pp.

Dexter, Walter, and J. W. T. Ley. *The Origin of Pickwick: New Facts Now First Published in the Year of the Centenary*. London: Chapman and Hall, 1936.

Dickens, Charles. *A Tale of Two Cities*. Modern Library edition. New York: Random, 1996.

Doyle, Brian. "Conversation about *The Passion of the Christ*." Marymount University, Arlington, VA, April 2004.

Drake, Herbert. "Letter to Tom Pettey." February 4, 1942. Welles Manuscripts, box 2.

Eisenstein, Sergei. "From *Dickens, Griffith, and the Film Today*." In *Twentieth Century Interpretations of "A Tale of Two Cities,"* edited by Charles Beckwith, 100–104. Englewood Cliffs, NJ: Prentice, 1972. Reprinted from "Dickens, Griffith, and the Film Today." *Film Form*, edited and translated by Jay Leyda, 211–16. New York: Harcourt, Brace, 1949.

Ensink, Titus. "Collective Misunderstanding Due to Misframing: The Cases of Orson Welles (1938) and Philipp Jenninger (1988)." In *Semiotics around the World: Synthesis in Diversity*, edited by Irmengard Rauch and Gerald Carr, 1131–34. New York: Mouton de Gruyter, 1997.

Ewen, Stuart. *All Consuming Images*. New York: Basic Books, 1982.

"First Person Singular: Welles Innovator on Stage, Experiments on the Air." *Newsweek*, July 11, 1938, 25.

Fitzsimmons, Lorna. "*The Magnificent Ambersons*: Unmasking the Code." *Literature Film Quarterly* 28, no. 4 (2000), 10 pp. Academic Search Elite (accessed 2003).

"Four Men on a Raft." *Time*, December 8, 1941, 30.

France, Richard. *Orson Welles on Shakespeare: The W. P. A. and Mercury Theatre Playscripts*. New York: Routledge, 2001.

———. "The 'Voodoo' Macbeth of Orson Welles." *Yale/Theatre* 5, no. 3 (1974): 66–78.

Frederickson, George. *The Black Image in the White Mind: The Debate on Afro-American Character and Destiny, 1817–1914*. New York: Harper and Row, 1971.

Friedman, Lester D. *Citizen Spielberg*. Chicago: U of Illinois P, 2006.

Friend, Tad. "Is It Funny Yet?" *New Yorker*, February 11, 2002, 28+. ProQuest (accessed June 12, 2007), 9 pp.

Gabbard, Krin. "Cinema and Media Studies: Snapshot of an 'Emerging' Discipline." *Chronicle of Higher Education*, February 17, 2006, B14. ProQuest (accessed June 13, 2007).

Gallagher, Catherine. "The Duplicity of Doubling." In Bloom, 73–94.

Geduld, Harry M. "Welles or Wells?—A Matter of Adaptation." In Beja, *Perspectives*, 260–72.

Gehl, Robert. "'Why Aren't We Seeing This Now?' Public Torture in *The Passion of the Christ* and *Fahrenheit 9/11*." *Nebula* 1, no. 2 (September 2004): 37–47. http://www.nobleworld.biz/journalhome.html (accessed June 12, 2007).

Gennaro, Steve. "*The Daily Show*: The Face of American News in 2005." *Kritikos* 2 (April 2005), 13 pp. http://gannet.acns.fsu.edu (accessed June 12, 2007).

"Gibson's Anti-Semitic Outburst Shocks Jews." *Christian Century*, August 22, 2006, 11–12.

"Gibson's *Passion* Gets an Evangelical Blessing." *Christian Century*, July 26, 2003, 14–15.

Goldfarb, Phyllis. "Orson Welles's Use of Sound." In Beja, *Perspectives*, 107–15.

Gomery, Douglas. "Orson Welles and the Hollywood Industry." *Persistence of Vision: Special Issue on Orson Welles* 7 (1989): 39–43.

Gottesman, Ronald, ed. *Focus on Orson Welles*. Englewood Cliffs, NJ: Prentice-Hall, 1976.

Gull, Nicole. "Onward, Christian Marketer." *Inc.*, July 1, 2004. Proquest.

Hanlon, Patrick. *Primal Branding: Create Zealots for Your Brand, Your Company, and Your Future*. New York: Free Press, 2006.

Hansen, Miriam Bratu. "The Mass Production of the Senses: Classical Cinema as Vernacular Modernism." *Modernism/Modernity* 6, no. 2 (1999): 59–77. Project Muse (accessed July 9, 2004).

"Harlem 'Macbeth' on Stage Tonight at Keith Theater." *Indianapolis Star*, August 25, 1936, 8.

"Hearst vs. Orson Welles." *Newsweek*, January 20, 1941, 62–63.

Heart of Darkness. "Revised Estimating Script." November 30, 1939. Welles Manuscripts.

Heart of Darkness. Plot treatment. September 15, 1939. Welles Manuscripts.

Heart of Darkness. Character list. No date. Welles Manuscripts.

"Heart of Darkness." *This Is My Best*. Radio series. March 13, 1945. Audio recordings. Welles Manuscripts.

"Heart of Darkness; Life with Father." *Mercury Theatre on the Air*. Radio series. November 6, 1938. Audio recordings. Welles Manuscripts.

Hello Americans. "Brazil." Draft radio scripts. 1942. Welles Manuscripts, box 10.

Heylin, Clinton. *Despite the System: Orson Welles versus the Hollywood Studios*. Chicago: Chicago Review Press, 2005.

Higham, Charles. "It's All True." *Sight and Sound* (1970), 92–98.

hooks, bell. "Eating the Other." In *Black Looks: Race and Representation*. Boston: South End Press, 1992, 21–40.

Houseman, John. *Unfinished Business: A Memoir*. London: Chatto and Windus, 1986.

Internet Movie Database (IMDb). http://www.imdb.com (accessed August 1, 2007).

Jacobs, Steven Leonard. "Jewish 'Officialdom' and *The Passion of the Christ:* Who Said What and What Did They Say?" *Shofar: An Interdisciplinary Journal of Jewish Studies* 23, no. 3 (2005): 114–23.

Jensen, Rolf. *The Dream Society: How the Coming Transformation from Information to Imagination Will Transform Business*. New York: McGraw-Hill, 1999.

Johnston, A., and F. Smith. "How to Raise a Child." *Saturday Evening Post,* February 3, 1940, 27+.

Juhasz, Alexandra, and Jesse Lerner. "Introduction." In *F Is for Phony: Fake Documentary and Truth's Undoing,* edited by Juhasz and Lerner, 1–35. Minneapolis: U of Minnesota P, 2006.

Kael, Pauline. "Raising Kane." *New Yorker* (February 20, 27, 1971). Reprinted in *The Citizen Kane Book.* Boston: Little, Brown, 1971.

Kamp, David. "Magnificent Obsession." *Vanity Fair,* January 2002, 122–37.

Kastrup, Mathilde. "Diary." March 3–11, 1942. Welles Manuscripts, box 17, folder 12.

Khodarahmi, Sue. "Words of the Year." *Communication World* (March-April 2007), 11–12. http://www.iabc.com/cw (accessed June 14, 2007).

Leaming, Barbara. *Orson Welles, a Biography.* New York: Viking Penguin, 1985.

Learmonth, Michael. "CBS Targets Youth: Net to Simulcast Couric News on Web." *Daily Variety Gotham,* 5, 17. http://www.variety.com (accessed August 18, 2006).

Liliom. Radio script. October 22, 1939. Welles Manuscripts.

Lindstrom, Martin. *Brand Sense: Build Powerful Brands through Touch, Taste, Smell, Sight and Sound.* New York: Free Press, 2005.

Littlesugar, Amy, and Floyd Cooper. *Tree of Hope.* New York: Puffin, 1999.

Lorde, Audre. "The Master's Tools Will Never Dismantle the Master's House." Comments at "The Personal and the Political" panel of the Second Sex Conference, New York, September 29, 1979.

Macbeth. Draft script. Welles Manuscripts, box 5.

Macbeth. Production notebook. April 14, 1936. Library of Congress American Memory Project. http://memory.loc.gov/ammem/fedtp/ftmb1.html (accessed July 23, 2003).

Manheim, Leonard. "A Tale of Two Characters: A Study in Multiple Projection." *Critical Essays on Dickens's "A Tale of Two Cities,"* edited by Michael Cotsell, 61–73. New York: G. K. Hall, 1998.

"Marvelous Boy." *Time,* May 9, 1938, 27–34.

McBride, Joseph. *What Ever Happened to Orson Welles? A Portrait of an Independent Career.* Lexington: UP of Kentucky, 2006.

McKain, Aaron. "Not Necessarily Not the News: Gatekeeping, Remediation, and *The Daily Show.*" *Journal of American Culture* 28, no. 4 (December 2005), 415–30.

McLeod, Elizabeth. "Amos 'n' Andy—by the Numbers: Analyzing Audience Statistics for Radio's All Time Favorites." http://www.midcoast.com/~lizmcl/aa.html (accessed June 6, 2006).

"Mel Sells." *Hollywood Reporter,* June 18–20, 2004, 6. www.hollywoodreporter.com

Mercer, Kobena. *Welcome to the Jungle.* New York: Routledge, 1994.

Milch, David. Interview by Keith Carradine. "An Imaginative Reality." *Deadwood: The Complete First Season.* HBO Video DVD, 2004.

Moore, James. "Mel Gibson's *The Passion of the Christ*: A Protestant Perspective." *Shofar: An Interdisciplinary Journal of Jewish Studies* 23, no. 3 (2005), 101–4. Project Muse.

"More Duplicity from ADL's Foxman." *New American,* August 9, 2004, 8.

Morrison, James. "From *Citizen Kane* to *Mr. Arkadin*: The Evolution of Orson Welles's Aesthetics of Space." *New Orleans Review* 16 (fall 1989): 5–13.

Naremore, James. "Between Works and Texts: Notes from the Welles Archive." *Persistence of Vision: Special Issue on Orson Welles* 7 (1989): 12–23.

———. "The Death and Rebirth of Rhetoric." *Society for Cinema Studies Conference,* March 11, 2000. Republished in *Senses of Cinema* 5 (April 2000). http://www.sensesofcinema.com.

———. *The Magic World of Orson Welles.* Dallas: Southern Methodist UP, 1989.

"Negotiates RKO Contract." *New York Times,* June 25, 1941, sec. 17: 2.

Norden, Martin. *John Barrymore: A Bio-Bibliography.* Westport, CT: Greenwood P, 1995.

O'Brien, Richard B. "Unmasking a Hobgoblin of the Air." *New York Times,* October 29, 1939, sec. 9: 12.

"Oliver Twist." Bound radio script. October 2, 1938. Welles Manuscripts.

Othman, Frederick. United Press. April 28, 1942. Welles Manuscripts, box 17, folder 21.

Oxford, Edward. "Martians Invade the Airwaves in 1938." Excerpt from "Night of the Martians." In *American History Illustrated* (October 1998). Reprinted in *The 1930s,* edited by Louise I. Gerdes, 107–22. San Diego: Greenhaven P, 2000.

The Passion of the Christ. Directed by Mel Gibson. Newmarket, 2004.

Pensky, Max. "The Trash of History." In *Melancholy Dialectics: Walter Benjamin and the Play of Mourning.* 211–239. Amherst: U Mass P, 2001.

Peters, Jonathan. "Sembéne Ousmane as Griot: *The Money-Order* with *White Genesis." African Literature Today* 12 (1982): 88–103.

Pettey, Tom. Rio project journals. Welles Manuscripts, box 17, folder 20.

Plot treatment, Rio project. No title. Welles Manuscripts, box 17, folder 4.

Potter, Deborah. "Breaking the Mold: Katie Couric's Shift to Solo Network News Anchor Represents a Milestone for Women—and an Opportunity to Attract New Viewers." *American Journalism Review* 28, no. 3 (June-July 2006): 64.

Powell, Michael. "New York: Yours, Mine, and Theirs." *New York Times,* June 10, 2007, sec. 4, col. 1, 3. *Lexis-Nexis.*

Powers, William. "Brand Aid." *National Journal,* March 17, 2007, 54.

"Radio Notes." *Newsweek,* July 11, 1938, 26.

Reinhartz, Adele. "Jesus of Hollywood from D. W. Griffith to Mel Gibson." *New Republic,* March 8, 2004, 26–29.

"Rick's American Bar." Filmscript. Welles Manuscripts, box 17, folder 1.

Rippy, Marguerite H. "Commodity, Tragedy, Desire: Female Sexuality and Blackness in the Iconography of Dorothy Dandridge." In *Classic Hollywood, Classic Whiteness,* edited by Daniel Bernardi, 178–209. Minneapolis: U of Minnesota P, 2001.

———. "Exhuming Dorothy Dandridge: The Black Sex Goddess and Classic Hollywood Cinema." *CineAction* 44 (fall 1997): 20–31.

Robertson, Stuart D. "A View from the Pew on Gibson's *Passion." Shofar: An Interdisciplinary Journal of Jewish Studies* 23, no. 3 (2005): 105–9.

Roemer, Michael. *Telling Stories: Postmodernism and the Invalidation of the Traditional Narrative.* London: Rowman and Littlefield, 1995.

Rooney, David. "'Passion' Play Lands Mel atop Power List." *Daily Variety Gotham*, June 18, 2004, 4. www.variety.com.

Rosenbaum, Jonathan, ed. *This Is Orson Welles: Orson Welles and Peter Bogdanovich.* New York: HarperCollins, 1992.

Salmon, Paul. "'The People Will Think What I Tell Them to Think': Orson Welles and the Trailer for *Citizen Kane*." *Canadian Journal of Film Studies* 15, no. 2 (fall 2006): 96–113.

"The Shadow Talks." *New York Times*, August 14, 1938, sec. 9: 10.

Simon, William. "Orson Welles: An Introduction." *Persistence of Vision: Special Issue on Orson Welles* 7 (1989): 5–11.

Smith, Grahame. *Dickens and the Dream of Cinema*. New York: Manchester UP, 2003.

Smith, Wendy. "The Play That Electrified Harlem." *Civilization* (January-February 1996). Rpt. Library of Congress American Memory Project. http://memory.loc.gov/ammem/fedtp/ftsmthoo.html (accessed July 22, 2003).

Sollors, Werner. *Amiri Baraka/ LeRoi Jones: The Quest for a "Populist Modernism."* New York: Columbia UP, 1978.

Spadoni, Robert. "The Seeing Ear: The Presence of Radio in Orson Welles's *Heart of Darkness*." In *Conrad on Film*, edited by Gene M. Moore, 78–92. Cambridge: Cambridge UP, 1997.

"Stage, The." *Indianapolis Star*, August 27, 1936, 10.

Stam, Robert. *Tropical Multiculturalism: A Comparative History of Race in Brazilian Cinema and Culture.* Durham, NC: Duke UP, 1997.

Stanfield, Peter. "An Excursion into the Lower Depths: Hollywood, Urban Primitivism, and *St. Louis Blues*, 1929–1937." *Cinema Journal* 41, no. 2 (2002): 84–108.

Stoneback, H. R. "*Under Kilimanjaro*—Truthiness at Late Night: Or Would Oprah Kick Hemingway Out of Her Book Club." *Hemingway Review* 25, no. 2 (spring 2006): 123–27.

"Tale of Two Cities." Bound radio script. July 25, 1938. Welles Manuscripts.

"The Talk Shows." *New York Times*, August 14, 1938, sec. 9: 10.

Thompson, Daniella. *Daniella Thompson on Brazil*. http://daniellathompson.com (accessed January 23, 2009).

Tomasulo, Frank. "Narrate and Describe? Point of View and Narrative Voice in *Citizen Kane*'s Thatcher Sequence." *Wide Angle: A Film Quarterly of Theory, Criticism, and Practice* 8 (1986): 45–52.

Torgovnick, Marianna. *Gone Primitive*. Chicago: U of Chicago P, 1990.

Tucker, Robert G. "New 'Macbeth' Presented at Keith's: Harlem Version of Bard's Drama Proves Unusual." *Indianapolis Star*, August 26, 1936, 11.

Vaina, David. "Moving Backwards: Network News Losing Battle of Gravitas." *St. Louis Journalism Review* (December 2006–January 2007), 14–15, 21.

Viany, Enéas. "They Think It Is but It Is Not." April 1942. Welles Manuscripts, box 18, folder 11.

War of the Worlds. Directed by Steven Spielberg. Paramount, 2005.

Welles Manuscript Collection. Lilly Library, Indiana University, Bloomington.

Welles, Orson. "Letter to Diana Bourbon." October 10, 1939. Welles Manuscripts.

———. Correspondence. Welles Manuscripts, boxes 1–4.

———. "A Tale of Two Cities" on *Theatre of the Imagination* [sound recording]. Santa Monica, CA: Voyager Company, 1988.

Welles, Orson, and John Houseman. "The Summing Up: The Directors of the Mercury Theatre Look Over Their First Year." *New York Times*, June 12, 1938, sec. 10: 1–2.

"Welles Laments Wane of Theatre." *New York Times*, June 29, 1938, 12.

Williams, Linda Ruth. *Critical Desire: Psychoanalysis and the Literary Subject.* London: Edward Arnold, 1995.

Wilson, Jeff. "'A New Kind of Radio Program.' Orson Welles (Lady Esther)." Wellesnet: Radio, 8 pages. http://www.wellesnet.com (accessed August 1, 2005).

Wilson-Welles Collection. University of Michigan Special Collections, Ann Arbor.

Wolland, Marcus. "Lost Eden: The Magnificent Welles." PBS DVD, 2004.

Wood, Brett. *Orson Welles: A Bio-Bibliography.* New York: Greenwood P, 1990.

Zeitchik, Steven. "His Passion Is Showing." *Variety*, October 2–8, 2006, 6, 139.

Žižek, Slavoj. "Four Discourses, Four Subjects." In *Cogito and the Unconscious*, ed. Žižek, 74–113. Durham, NC: Duke UP, 1998.

Zuckerman, Bruce. "Where Are the Flies? Where Is the Smoke? The Real and Super-Real in Mel Gibson's *The Passion*." *Shofar: An Interdisciplinary Journal of Jewish Studies* 23, no. 3 (2005): 129–35.

Index

Marguerite H. Rippy is an associate professor of literature at Marymount University in Arlington, Virginia, where she teaches twentieth-century literature with a focus on multicultural literature and performance studies. She has published articles on film and drama, addressing topics ranging from the representation of race and sexuality in cinema to adaptations of Shakespeare on film and television. Her film reviews have appeared in the *Chronicle of Higher Education.*